ALWAYS
PACK A
CANDLE

MARION McKINNON CROOK

ALWAYS PACK A CANDLE

A NURSE IN THE CARIBOO-CHILCOTIN

Heritage House Publishing Company Ltd.
heritagehouse.ca

Cataloguing information available from Library and Archives Canada
978-1-77203-362-5 (paperback)
978-1-77203-363-2 (ebook)

Edited by Paula Marchese
Interior design by Setareh Ashrafologholai
Cover design by Jacqui Thomas
Cover images: KN2018 / Shutterstock.com (Chilcotin background),
Anton Sokolov / creativemarket.com (Chevy),
IakovKalinin / iStockphoto.com (road)
Map by Eric Leinberger

The interior of this book was produced on 100% post-consumer recycled
paper, processed chlorine free, and printed with vegetable-based inks.

Heritage House gratefully acknowledges that the land on which
we live and work is within the traditional territories of the Lkwungen
(Esquimalt and Songhees), Malahat, Pacheedaht, Scia'new, T'Sou-ke,
and W̱SÁNEĆ (Pauquachin, Tsartlip, Tsawout, Tseycum) Peoples.

We acknowledge the financial support of the Government of Canada
through the Canada Book Fund (CBF) and the Canada Council for
the Arts, and the Province of British Columbia through the British
Columbia Arts Council and the Book Publishing Tax Credit.

25 24 23 22 21 1 2 3 4 5

Printed in Canada

*To Carol, Ruby, Maureen, Helen, Eleanor, Bev, and the staff
at Cariboo Health Unit; to Hazel, Beth, Cecile, Verna, Peter, Joyce,
Nancy, as well as the many professionals who worked so hard
and so competently in those early days.*

*To the teachers who, in remote one-room schools, brought
education and joy to their students and made me feel welcome,
alerting me to health problems and helping me organize
screening, immunization, and well-baby clinics.*

To the resort owners who fed me and gave me accurate directions.

To the truck drivers who stopped and put my car back on the road.

*To the many residents of the Cariboo who fed me, rescued me,
and made sure I didn't die out there in the wilderness.*

CONTENTS

Author's Note 1

CHAPTER ONE   Launching into
the Cariboo 3

CHAPTER TWO   Plunging into Work 13

CHAPTER THREE   Dying in the Woods 29

CHAPTER FOUR   Lessons from the Black
Creek Women 40

CHAPTER FIVE   Meeting the Rancher 53

CHAPTER SIX   Evading Officials 65

CHAPTER SEVEN   Working in the
Outlying Country 77

CHAPTER EIGHT   Nursing at Darla's
Boarding House 88

CHAPTER NINE   Manipulating the
System 98

CHAPTER TEN   Missing Narcotics,
Threats of Suicide 111

CHAPTER ELEVEN   Eviction from
Mrs. Sharpe's 123

CHAPTER TWELVE   Discovering
                 Ranch Life 134

CHAPTER THIRTEEN   Two Hundred Miles
                   into the Chilcotin 145

CHAPTER FOURTEEN   Falling in Love with
                   the Cariboo 160

CHAPTER FIFTEEN   Skidding through
                  the Winter 176

CHAPTER SIXTEEN   Combating Constant
                  Racism 188

CHAPTER SEVENTEEN   Translator Trials 204

CHAPTER EIGHTEEN   Responding to
                   Demands 211

CHAPTER NINETEEN   Arguing with a Gun 221

CHAPTER TWENTY   Learning Experiences 236

CHAPTER TWENTY-ONE   Medics in the Chilcotin 251

CHAPTER TWENTY-TWO   Decision Time 263

Acknowledgements 278

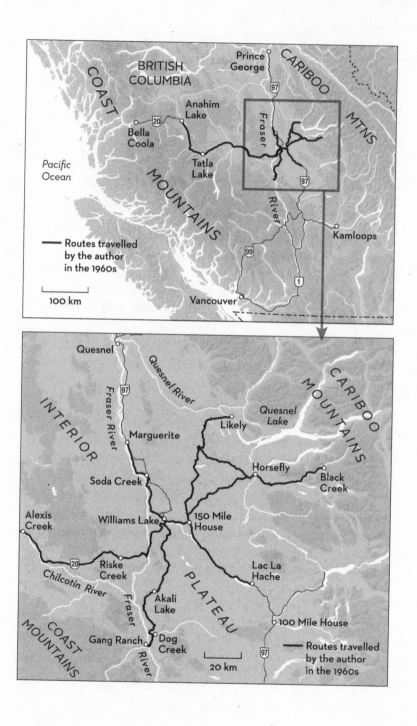

AUTHOR'S NOTE

FOR THOSE readers who know the Cariboo region of British Columbia, the town Williams Lake is a central hub where rough highways lead to the west and east. Nurses were expected to cover vast amounts of territory, so much of my new experiences in the Cariboo in the 1960s focused on getting to those remote areas. The communities and hamlets mentioned in this book still exist. The people described are real as well, but I took a few liberties, such as changing everyone's name, moving a principal from one school to another, and changing the occupations of some people in order to make them a little less recognizable. I also took two friends and made them into one, changed the doctors out of all recognition—their ages, their appearances, but not their conversations—and invented a couple of characters: Sam the doctor and Charmaine, the young girl going to art school. Everyone else was part of my life in the Cariboo. The character of Carl is based on a real person. I telescoped time, as the events did not all happen in one year.

The terminology around Indigenous Peoples has been updated from the 1960s. The words used in the past are not acceptable today, nor should they be. I raised a son who was a member of the Gitxsan nation and have experienced prejudice from behind his shoulder. I've done what I could to fight it. I applaud the changes in the language which is much more respectful now. The term "Native" was sometimes used respectfully in the '60s as it implied that the person was connected to the land and Indigenous, but it was often used disrespectfully as well, implying a person was not a full-fledged citizen. "Indian" was a misnomer and had pejorative connotations, but it was used officially and extensively. The language was part of the prejudice of those times. In 2001, when I received my PhD in education, my thesis concerned Indigenous education at Hazelton High School, the community of my son's ancestors. The teens there still used "Indian," but the educators, including the Gitsxan educators, were turning the language to "Aboriginal." Now we use "Indigenous" or "First Nations" to try to eliminate as much culturally oppressive language as possible. When I worked in the Cariboo, I used the most respectful language of the times. But using language of a bygone era is tantamount to colluding in the attitudes underneath that language, so I have changed the terminology in this book in order to be respectful of the people of today. I have left the words used by people in dialogue, but the narration uses modern terms. The language carried prejudice. As I worked in the area, I gradually came to see racism in health care and in society. It profoundly disturbed me.

I wrote about the medical knowledge as it was at the time. It was the best we had, and we relied on it. Nursing has improved; it is different today, but I did not go back in this memoir and modernize the medicine. I trust you will read it with an understanding of those days.

The incidences in the book did happen. I did live with the independent people of the Cariboo and experienced severe weather. I was not prepared and had to learn from experience and from the people in the community who often felt I needed their guidance. They were right; I very often needed their help. In the age of rock 'n' roll, Woodstock, free love, and civil rights, I nursed in the wild regions of the Cariboo, where we were less interested in social movements and more interested in staying alive and surviving the rough roads, oncoming logging trucks, and the challenges of country nursing.

Marion McKinnon Crook, writing in Gibsons, BC, on the unceded territory of the Squamish Nation, Sḵwx̱wú7mesh Úxwumixw

CHAPTER ONE

LAUNCHING INTO THE CARIBOO

I STEPPED DOWN from the Greyhound bus in the late afternoon of a hot August day, relieved at the end of my twelve-hour trip from the Coast. After four years of university, I was where I wanted to be and who I wanted to be—Marion McKinnon, Cariboo Public Health Nurse. That feeling of satisfaction lasted only a minute. The truth was, I wasn't sure of anything. I felt like a foreigner in a new country, my suitcases beside me, abandoned by the bus that had delivered me, awkward and alien.

From the coastal valley, the bus had wound through the Fraser Canyon, following the river up into the Interior Plateau of British Columbia. Even though the windows had been open, the air had been stifling, and I'd sat almost stupefied by the heat. The land was vast and seemed to roll into forever.

Get a grip, I told myself. *This is going to be an adventure.* I took a deep breath and looked around. Dust was everywhere; on the asphalt road, on the parked cars, and on the windowsills of the motel above the town that doubled as the bus station. Bits of ash floated past me, drifting on the slight breeze. To the west, I could just see a tall beehive burner proclaiming a mill site, probably the source of the ash. To the east, a lake stretched to the horizon, cradled by hills. This was the Cariboo: blue skies, a wide valley, and brown grass on the hills rolling into conifers at the skyline. It was a land of sunshine—a land of logging and ranching, remote from urban centres, and I was going to be part of it.

I'd never had any ambition to be a nurse. I'd wanted to be a vet. At twelve years of age, I'd cut open a chick to see why it had died. I didn't find out, but I was fascinated by its anatomy. My mother thought that was odd. My dad just asked if I'd learned anything. At fifteen, I'd written to Canada's only veterinary college and asked what high school courses I needed for entry. I'd wanted a career with animals and one that let me live outdoors as much as possible. I remembered their answer: "Don't bother to apply. We don't take women." I'd been shocked. It had been so unfair. I hadn't cried. I'd just seethed. There were very few career choices for me in the late '50s.

I'd entered university and studied science because that was what interested me but without a clear vision or goal. At the end of my first year, I realized I had to pick something that would give me work upon graduation. My parents had five other children. My dad told me he'd pay for whatever program I wanted even if that meant studying in Europe, but I couldn't take that much from him. He wasn't wealthy and that would have been a huge sacrifice. I picked a nursing program that had an on-campus course in Seattle, rather than a hospital course in Vancouver, because it was the sciences I had wanted to pursue, not patient care. I did find out that patients were fascinating, contrary, and challenging, and I grew to enjoy them. Still, I had no intention of working within the four walls of a hospital and no interest in working in a city or suburban community. When the Cariboo Health Unit advertised for a public health nurse, I grabbed the job.

The ranching and logging communities would give me some work outdoors. As the bus had laboured around the winding corners on its way north, I gazed at the Thompson River dashing dangerously close to the canyon road. Perhaps I'd read too much Zane Grey. Too late for second thoughts now; I was committed. Whatever was coming my way, I was not going to return home where my mother would immediately find a job for me, a safe and boring job, close by. I would manage.

I scanned the bus depot and the parking lot. Williams Lake, Cariboo District, the sign said. Why "Cariboo"? Why not

"Caribou"? Had there been caribou here in the past? I didn't think there were any around now. Then I saw a tall, thin woman standing by a farm truck, piled high with feed sacks. She beckoned to me. I waved. She called across the lot, "Welcome to the Cariboo." It could only be my nursing supervisor, Rita Browning. I had a quick impression of an athletic woman with a melodious voice.

She introduced herself, then took my two suitcases and flung them into the back of the truck with the feed sacks.

"Good trip?" she asked.

I climbed into the truck and slammed the door, twice. It caught the second time.

"It was long and hot, but I'm glad to be here." I wasn't going to start this job by complaining about the heat and the winding road that had made me nauseous. I was still influenced by the conventions of the Second World War era, even though that was two decades ago. "Don't complain, we'll get through it," my dad would say. My mother's adage was "If you can't say something nice, say nothing at all." My mother valued conformity. We were all pressured to conform and endure, but women were leaned on to be quiet and self-effacing as well. As a rule, I wasn't good at being quiet or self-effacing.

"We're delighted to have you, Marion. Welcome to Williams Lake." Her British accent was still strong, although she told me she'd been here for years. When we'd talked on the phone, I'd imagined a starchy British lady in tweed, a twin set, and pearls, not the woman beside me in well-worn cowboy boots and a denim shirt.

I knew the Cariboo-Chilcotin District in this most western province of Canada was 104,000 square miles, the size of New Zealand or the United Kingdom. I'd looked it up in *Encyclopedia Britannica*. "It's like a separate country," my mother had said, a little shocked that her chick was wandering into the bush and, as usual, dubious about my judgement. I'd had many deep discussions with my sister about our mother's lack of faith in us. Since I had faith in my sister and she had faith in me, we decided that our mother was wrong and ignored her prognosis of our future failures.

My sister and my dad were quite sure I would manage competently in the Cariboo. But I wasn't prepared for the openness, the vast expanse of rolling hills and grasslands, the miles of hillsides covered in evergreens. Were they fir? Or pine? The sparkling air fresh, dry, invigorating. The description on the printed page somehow hadn't translated to the almost overwhelming awe of the landscape. The Cariboo was huge. I was fascinated and eager to explore. This was where I wanted to be. Would there be moose, bear, coyotes, deer, mountain lions? Probably not caribou. I asked Rita about that.

"No, no caribou." She yanked on the steering wheel, piloting us much too fast for comfort through the almost empty streets. "The clinic is closed today, Marion. I won't take you there."

Williams Lake was a small town, serving the ranchers, loggers, and sawmill operators and their families, she'd told me on the phone when she'd offered me the job. She'd said I'd be responsible for the area east of Williams Lake and, at times, the vast ranching country to the west. It looked immense when we stopped for a moment at one of the road's high points. Hills sloped out for miles. I could see the faint blue of mountains.

I swallowed. I was a newly graduated public health nurse. I had the theory: anatomy, physiology, biology, chemistry, organic chemistry, mathematics, microbiology, sociology, psychology, ethics, and even philosophy... but not much practice. I would be alone out there in the far reaches of the district. There would be no one to check to see if I was correct about a diagnosis or the dosage of a medication. No books to get more information. No doctor. No other nurses. Probably no phone for miles. What had seemed like an adventure when I first applied for the job was beginning to look overwhelming.

"Let's get you settled into your boarding house, and then you can come with me to the 4-H sale. My daughter is showing, and I have to be there to shame other ranchers into buying her calf." She drove on.

"How do you do that?"

Rita was about my height and slim. She had blue eyes and blonde hair streaked with grey. She was not an imposing sight, and, with her unequivocal, proper British accent, I couldn't imagine her intimidating ranchers.

"I simply sit there and note who is bidding and who is not and stare at them."

I wondered if she could send out the "steely eye" the way my mother could.

She pulled to a stop in front of a two-storey house in the centre of town, where Rita informed me that the nurses usually stayed. I had a brief meeting with Mrs. Sharpe, my new landlady. We stood at the foot of the stairs to the rental rooms. A sharp smell of disinfectant hung in the air. From a large portrait framed in dark wood, a small man, standing by a globe and dressed in a Second World War uniform, glared at me. He had the same nose and narrow face as Mrs. Sharpe and the same disapproving stare.

"Here's your key. No men in the house. Breakfast and supper included. First month's rent is due today." Her voice was as sharp as her name. She tilted her head and leaned forward as she pinioned me with her bright brown eyes. I instinctively moved back a pace and then felt foolish. She wasn't going to harm me. Still, I had a feeling she wasn't going to be my best friend.

I nodded, wrote her a cheque, and left my two suitcases and my tiny Remington typewriter on the bed. I had to have a typewriter. My penmanship was so bad that even my parents couldn't read it. If they wanted a legible letter, I'd have to type it. My dad had bought it for twenty-five dollars and I treasured it—old and rickety as it was. Although the room was small, it would be enough. It had the essentials: a bed, a desk, and a closet. I slipped out of my sundress and hung it on one of the few hangers in the closet. Then I shook out the creases from my only other summer dress and pulled it over my head. I kept my flats on my feet. I had only my Oxford shoes, a pair of pumps, and the flats I was wearing to choose from. The flats would have to do. My dad was sending my trunk next week, but there wouldn't be a lot of clothes in it. The bathroom was across the hall and shared with one other boarder who wasn't home.

"The other boarder is a teacher, grade five," Mrs. Sharpe had said. "A silly young woman called Dorothy, but I expect you will enjoy her. All the other nurses have."

What did she mean "All the *other* nurses?" How many nurses had come and gone from this small town? Why did they leave? Overworked? Overwhelmed?

I joined Rita in the truck, and we again barrelled down the streets. When I'd worked at my public health practicum in the eastern farming district of Washington State, my supervisor had been what I had thought of as professional. Her uniform was always in place. She was rarely away from her desk and always addressed me as "Miss McKinnon." Twenty minutes with *this* supervisor revised my whole notion of a professional supervisor. Rita slammed on the brakes, and we skidded into the rodeo grounds. Here, according to the sign, they called it the Stampede Grounds. Corrals held cattle and horses. An outdoor arena contained small children and big cows, following one another in a circle.

"Good," Rita said as I followed her through the grounds. "That's the class before Millie's. We're in time. Climb up here beside me." She jumped up onto a set of stairs.

I climbed the steep bleachers behind her, trying to keep the skirt of my dress close around my legs. We sat on a bench near a tall man in work jeans, denim shirt, and a stetson.

"Hello, my love," Rita said. "This is Marion, the new nurse. My husband, Jim."

Jim raised his stetson, nodded, and then looked back at the ring. "Millie's next."

Rita leaned over to me. "He's nervous," she said.

"Sold!" the auctioneer shouted.

"That's a good price," Jim said quietly.

"Yes, it's a good crowd," Rita said. "Millie's calf should do well." He nodded.

I'd grown up on a small farm in the Fraser Valley, not far from the city of Vancouver. My family had a pony, some chickens, and, occasionally, a beef cow—only one. I was the family member who looked after the stock, but I wasn't accustomed to animals in great numbers. I looked to the pens beyond the arena and saw what seemed to be a hundred cows or calves and about thirty horses. Everywhere there was dust.

My stomach growled. Breakfast had been hours ago, and it was now past three in the afternoon. I was slim, but I had the appetite of a lumberjack. The crowd was applauding the last of the 4-H kids leading their calves out of the ring.

They hushed as the new group filed in.

"That's Millie." Rita pointed to a small girl with blonde braids leading a calf about ten times her weight.

"That's a calf?" Visions of tiny sweet-faced infant cows flitted through my mind. This calf was tall, heavy, square, and impressive.

"A heifer, Pansy," Rita said. "Good breeding stock. Millie won't have to sell her for slaughter. Some rancher will buy Pansy and keep her."

I nodded, absorbing the information.

Millie manoeuvred her heifer, planting the animal's feet in the dirt, squaring them, using a stick of some kind to push a foot until the heifer shifted her weight.

Jim grunted.

"Nice job," Rita said. "She's got those hooves shining. What did she use?"

"Vaseline," Jim said.

"Very nice."

I looked harder at Millie's heifer. The coat was a rich brown mottled with patches so white they almost gleamed.

"Took her all morning," her dad said.

"Did you help?" I asked him politely.

He glanced at me sharply. "Not allowed."

I could feel the tension around me. I said nothing more. I was still hungry, and I could smell fried onions. There must be a concession stand somewhere, but I didn't dare break the silence and inquire.

We sat quietly throughout the bidding while Millie put Pansy through the circling, stopping, positioning, and, eventually, the sale. The tension relaxed.

"Would you like something to eat?" Rita asked me.

Finally. "Yes." I tried not to sound desperate. A hamburger. Onions in butter, tomatoes. The smell conjured up the vision.

"Hello, Rita," a man, who was climbing up the stairs, called up from below us.

Rita smiled. "Sam, come on up here and meet the nurse."

I was eager to meet handsome young men—especially handsome young cowboys—but I was hungry and not happy at having my lunch delayed.

"Hello, Nurse," this vision of tall, dark, and smiling said. Then he took another look at me and fell back a step—just stepped back into the air—and dropped.

"Watch it!" Rita said, concern in her voice.

"I'm okay. Hello." Sam hopped a little to keep his balance one step below us, then climbed up again.

I grinned to myself. Imagine me, knocking someone back on their heels? I wasn't glamorous or curvy like Marilyn Monroe, and I wore glasses. Generally, men didn't fall down at the sight of me. It was heady stuff.

"Sam, this is Marion, the new nurse. Marion, this is Sam. He's a local doctor."

"Truly?" My eyes flew up to his stetson and down to his cowboy boots.

"During the week," Sam said. "Can I get you a hamburger?"

"Absolutely." If he got me some food, I was willing to be impressed.

"Beer?"

I looked around. For the first time, I noticed people were drinking alcohol, mostly from brown glass bottles. I wasn't used to beer, especially in the middle of the day.

"Coffee?" I suggested.

"Coffee and a hamburger—with all the fixings?"

I nodded, and Sam departed. I might get to like Sam.

Jim had left a few minutes before, leaving Rita and me momentarily alone, but there wasn't time to ask about the job. More people climbed up the bleachers and joined us. The conversation swirled around the price 4-H calves fetched and the price of feed the kids put into them. Rita included me and introduced me to a couple from Horsefly and another from Riske Creek. Several young men hovered in the background. Weren't there any young women here?

"And this is Michael."

Another cowboy. This one a little shorter, a little sandier, but just as eager to please.

"A new nurse?" He looked at Rita, raised his eyebrows, then turned to me. "Welcome to the Cariboo."

"Thank you."

"He's a dentist here," Rita said. "You'll probably be referring lots of kids to him." Michael was another one who didn't look like his occupation. At least, he didn't look like any dentist I knew. I was going to examine teeth? I didn't know how to do that. I'd have to learn.

"Can I get you anything, Nurse?"

"Marion," I said and smiled. "Thanks, but something is on its way."

He started to sit beside me, but Jim reappeared just then, and nodded to him. "Did your niece get her price?"

Michael moved over to sit beside Jim and talk about cattle prices, leaving the spot beside me free for Sam who appeared with my hamburger. I thanked him and took my first bite. Heavenly. I was in beef country, after all. I ignored all the talk beside me. Sam made short work of his hamburger, and I was down to the last bite when a small cyclone whooshed in beside me.

"She's gone," wailed the little whirlwind as she flew into her mother's arms. "She's gone. Pansy's gone!"

"I know. I know." Rita cuddled her daughter close.

Millie straightened, stiff as a pole, turned to her father, and shouted an accusation. "Daddy, you said somebody nice would get her! That nasty idiot from Miocene bought her, and she'll hate it there! She'll die of lonesomeness." She moaned and threw herself into her father's arms.

"There, there," Jim said. "Take it easy. She's not going out to Miocene." He patted her shoulder.

Millie sniffed, then sat up. "What do you mean?"

"I mean Henry Robinson up Wildwood way bought her off the 'idiot.'"

"He did?" Millie stared at her dad, obviously checking veracity.

I wasn't the only one listening avidly. Michael and Sam were quiet, and the people in the row in front of us and the row behind us were also suspiciously quiet.

Jim spoke softly, but we all heard him. "Henry did buy her, and Pansy will have a good home with him. You know he wants to improve his herd, and your Pansy will contribute strong bloodlines. She's a good heifer. You know that."

"Yes, I know that." Millie sniffed. "I know Mr. Robinson. He's kind."

"She'll be fine." Again, he patted her shoulder.

"Oh, that's lucky. I'm glad. Can I have some money for a hamburger?"

Jim nodded, reached into his pocket, and passed her a few dollars. Millie's eyes still shone with tears, but she had transformed from wildly unhappy to peaceful in seconds. Sam and I watched her skip down the stairs toward the concession.

There was silence for a moment, then Rita murmured to Jim, "And just how much did that cost us?"

Jim shrugged. "Pansy's her best friend."

"How much?"

"Just a couple of hundred. I could lose that much in a poker game."

Sam and I exchanged a glance. It was a month's salary for some people. I didn't know if the calf was worth the extra money or if Jim did it for Millie's happiness. Sam grinned, understanding my reaction. "It's a different world."

He was right. My parents would never have tried to make me feel better by spending a "couple of hundred" dollars. They would have helped me manage the problem and given me advice about what to do next, but I don't think they would have simply paid money to make me feel better. I found Jim's manoeuvring remarkably generous and loving and completely foreign.

The heat, the dust, the cattle, the cowboys... Tomorrow I would accept my car, my health unit keys, and the wide and wild territory of my first job. I blinked, breathed deeply, and fervently hoped I could cope.

CHAPTER TWO

PLUNGING INTO WORK

I MET DOROTHY BISHOP that night at the boarding house.

"I'm Dorrie," she said and smiled. "Welcome to the tower. I'm thrilled to have someone sharing this prison with me."

"Is it that bad?" I said. I was a little taken aback, but she was decidedly cheerful about it.

"It is depressing but *so* respectable." She stood in her doorway and beamed at me, looking like a pixie, small and compact with a delicate face, red curls, and bright blue eyes. "I hope you're the nurse for Williams Lake Elementary. That's where I teach."

She invited me into her room, which was larger than mine and contained a bigger bed and a small hot plate with a kettle resting on it.

"Tea?" she asked.

I nodded. I didn't like tea much, but I wanted to be friendly. I eyed her hot plate. "I should get one of those." It had two elements, allowing her to cook a pot of soup and boil a kettle of water at the same time. It would be handy on nights when I arrived home late from work and missed supper.

"Don't let the buzzard know you're getting one. We're not supposed to have them." She reached for two teacups with matching saucers and a tea caddy and set them on the counter.

"No?" Mrs. Sharpe sounded like a stickler. "Any more rules I should know?"

She ticked the rules off on her fingers. "No hot plates, no irons, no toasters. All are fire hazards. No telephone, no men in your room."

"Also fire hazards?"

She laughed. "So the buzzard thinks." She set out some Walker shortbread cookies. I helped myself. Then she picked up the kettle before it sang, rinsed the teapot, dropped the tea leaves in the water, let it steep, and then served it. That was a lot of trouble; I'd stick to coffee. But I accepted the tea and pondered Dorrie's name for Mrs. Sharpe. *The Buzzard.*

"She hovers?"

"She hovers with malicious intent. Keep your door locked when you aren't home."

"Why stay here?" I was curious. Surely, there were other homes that would take in boarders and other landladies who wouldn't pry into their lives. I didn't have any salacious secrets, but I didn't relish the idea of a nosy landlady.

Dorrie toed off her pumps. She unsnapped her nylons from her garter belt, rolled them down, and put them in a drawer. Then she unhooked her garter belt and stashed it with the nylons. "That's better."

I had sisters and personal experience with garter belts and nylons. I knew what a relief it was to take them off. It felt as if your legs could breathe.

Dorrie sighed, then smiled. "I stay because she's respectable— very respectable—and since I'm not, she makes me look good to the school board."

It sounded as though the school board was nosy as well. "School boards are strict with teachers?"

"Unmarried female teachers—and that's most of us."

I studied Dorrie for a moment. She was petite and pretty but perhaps too vivacious, as if she saw the world as a little brighter and more exciting than most. That could be too stimulating for some, especially principals and school board members. But she probably knew how to *act* modest and demure.

"I suppose they want a teacher who's a moral example to the kids. You have to be very quiet or very careful."

"Exactly. A single female teacher can go to parties but never get drunk. Date but never have sex. Have opinions but keep them to herself. Male teachers are required to be discreet—that's all." She didn't sound the least bit bitter. She sounded as if she was reciting the rules of a game she was playing.

"It's not fair."

"No, it isn't, and if the school board knew how I lived, they'd fire me." She poured more tea. If this was a game, I'd bet she was winning.

"So the school board can fire you if they don't like your behaviour?" I didn't think the health unit could fire me for licentious living, only for malpractice. The tea was surprisingly good. Maybe Dorrie's friendliness and personality infused it.

"Of course," she said.

"Let me guess. The school board is all men." That wasn't unusual. In my hometown, there was one female pharmacist. The rest were male—the doctors were male, the bank managers were male, the religious leaders were male, and, of course, all veterinarians were male.

"Right."

"And you get around it by living here?" I glanced around the spartan room. It definitely didn't seem like a place to conduct a secret affair, not that I'd know what that looked like.

"We couldn't have a more unexciting address. Mrs. Sharpe is the conscience of the community," she intoned with brief solemnity. Then she grinned. "Luckily, she isn't all that smart. Shrewd but not smart."

Dorrie was a combination of shocking and kind with an ironic edge. "Where are you from?" I asked.

"The good and respectable town of Langley."

I raised my eyebrows. Langley wasn't far from my parents' home in the Fraser Valley.

She explained. "Very religious, my family, as is the whole community."

"Strict?"

"Let's just say we have different ideas of heaven. Here is heaven."

I was fascinated by Dorrie but found I had to concentrate to keep up with her rapid-fire conversation. I guessed at her meaning. "There seems to be a lot of men around."

"Lots of lovely, lovely men. You should have your pick." She sipped her tea, her eyes wide and sparkling, gazing at me above the rim of the cup.

I couldn't help but be impressed with her enthusiasm. Still, I was more cautious than she appeared to be. "I'm not sure I'm ready for them yet. My job is going to be difficult at first. I don't want to be distracted."

She solemnly waved a cookie at me. "It is the nature of women to be distracted by men. You can handle your job *and* men."

I laughed. "I'll look to you for advice."

"Glad to give it."

I wasn't anxious to get involved with any man, at least not yet. Pregnancy was a big issue because birth control was not an exact science and abortion was difficult to get as well as illegal. For some reason, my nursing degree included very little information on either subject. I had studied hard at university, put off having a partner until I could support myself, and, finally, I was in a job I was going to love, but I was still incredibly naïve about sex and pregnancy prevention. I'd have to learn, as patients would expect me to be informed. I needed to know for myself as well, so I had more choices when I was ready to engage with those "lovely men." I'd find some pamphlets at the health unit, or, failing that, I'd ask Rita. She had only one child. She probably knew. Dorrie probably knew as well.

I SCUTTLED past the disapproving portrait on Mrs. Sharpe's wall the next morning.

"I call him Grampa Harry to make him less grim," Dorrie had told me.

I hadn't managed the breezy "Morning, Harry" and wave Dorrie gave him, but I did see him as a little less foreboding.

When I arrived at the health unit, one of the three office clerks handed me a package.

"I'm Ellie Carpenter," she said. "I'll type your letters."

"Wonderful. Nice to meet you." I'd never had a secretary before. I was glad my letters would be both legible and correct in grammar and spelling. Although my grammar was usually correct, my spelling was creative.

Ellie was about forty, big boned, with dark hair and brown eyes.

"Rita asked Elsbeth, a retired PHN, to leave her old summer uniform here." Ellie looked critically at me. "Should fit."

I'd come to work in a blue pencil skirt and white blouse, as close to a uniform as I had with me.

"The bill's inside." Ellie flapped her hand toward the package.

I'd have to pay the retired nurse for it. I'd started with $300 in my account, and after paying my room and board, my current balance was $220. I hoped the uniform wasn't pricey.

"Thank you." I took the parcel and headed for the office Ellie indicated.

"Incoming is on your desk," she called after me.

I nodded. *Incoming? Incoming mail?* I felt very professional with an office, a secretary, and incoming mail.

As soon as I was alone in my office, I opened the package and shook out the uniform, a blue and white seersucker shirtwaist dress. I changed quickly. It was a little loose in the waist, but came with a belt, and I buckled it tight. There was no mirror in the office, but I was sure it fit. I stood straighter and felt important. I ran my fingers over the badge on the sleeve: BC PHN. British Columbia, Public Health Nurse. I was official.

The phone on my desk rang. I answered. "Yes?"

"It's Ellie. Did it fit?"

I laughed. "It did. Just a minute. I'll model it." I put the phone back in its cradle and stepped into the hall. Ellie stood at the other end, beside the counter. A fair-haired woman stood behind her.

"Looks good," Ellie said.

"Thanks. It's great to have it." I smoothed the dress over my hips.

"Marie." Ellie indicated the woman behind her. I waved. Marie nodded.

"I put Elsbeth's name and address in the box," Ellie said. "Make the cheque out to her for five dollars."

"Many thanks." If Ellie was this efficient about everything, she was going to be a big help.

There was a small hat in the box—a blue and white seersucker cap like a stewardess's hat with a wing-like piece of fabric on the side and the same insignia that was on the dress. I tried it on. I felt ridiculous and whipped it off. With luck, I wouldn't be required to wear it.

Rita approved of the uniform, gave me a tour of the health unit, and began conducting my two-week orientation. She took me to my school, Williams Lake Elementary, and introduced me to the principal, Hannah Harbinger, a dumpy woman of about fifty, with an authoritative steely eye. If we ever had a clash of wills, she'd be formidable. I had a brief tour, and then Rita and I headed to the hospital, which stood on the top of a small hill at the edge of town. Much fundraising in the town and cooperation from the provincial government had gone into getting it built, Rita told me. It had only been open a few months and was modern, airy, and commodious.

Rita escorted me to the boardroom to attend a meeting of the local doctors. She introduced me, and they gave me their rapt attention. Apparently, I was most important as a referral agent, but they also expected me to look after their patients when needed and deal with minor communicable diseases. Sam was there, smiling cheerfully, looking much more doctor-like in his sports shirt and tweed jacket. A short physician of about sixty lolled back in his chair and eyed me up and down. That felt creepy. I wasn't getting into any corners with him. There were six doctors. As soon as we left the meeting, I wrote down their names.

"You'll figure them out," Rita said. "Watch out for Dr. Wright."

"Short, sixtyish?"

"That's the one."

"Got it."

BY THE end of two weeks, I was getting used to the town—the dusty streets, the preponderance of pickup trucks, and the friendliness of total strangers. I had a clearer impression of the demographics—few older people and a high number of young families who'd migrated here so the husbands could work in the logging industry. They produced a lot of children, which kept the nurses busy with child health clinics and school work.

I concentrated hard at work, but tried to relax when I got home. Dorrie hauled me out for drinks in the local lounge and introduced me to several men. I had turned down four invitations. I was not ready to date yet; I had enough to deal with.

I got accustomed to the rhythm of attending to my inbox first thing in the morning, reading the government bulletins and articles on public health, and organizing my day. That first forty-five minutes was quiet as few phone calls came in and no one dropped by. I had time to learn new ideas from my reading. I was constantly learning in my practice as well.

Rita was loyal and supportive with the staff and skilled at negotiating health care with the many agencies that delivered it. She lacked some background in science as she had no university education and had learned as she worked. Still, she was confident of what she did know and wasn't shy about asking when she needed information. I felt appreciated and part of her team. But it was obvious that I wasn't necessarily skilful at every aspect of public health. I had given many immunizations during my practicum, but the protocols at this clinic were distinctly different.

There were about fifteen mothers waiting in the clinic with one or more children with them: babies, toddlers, and preschoolers. A volunteer, Mrs. Anderson, a matronly woman who didn't seem to mind the din of crying and conversation wafting around her, weighed the babies, wrote the results in the blue booklets the mothers had received at their postnatal home visits, and advised them to wait their turn. We gave the immunizations in our own offices. When a mother emerged from one of the offices, Mrs. Anderson sent another in.

We interviewed the mothers. We were using Rita's office today. She had set up vaccines, syringes, alcohol wipes, and a small bottle of acetone, which we used instead of alcohol when we administered smallpox vaccine. Smallpox was live and would be killed by alcohol. I noticed where the wastebasket was, where the charts were deposited when we finished the visit, and where the chairs were. I looked for toys for any accompanying child. Being competent sometimes meant knowing where everything was. I had my own stethoscope hanging around my neck. My eye swivelled back to the syringes.

"What are these huge syringes for?" I asked Rita as we prepared.

"This is a 20-cc syringe and twelve needles. You load the DPT."

I translated that to diphtheria, pertussis, and tetanus vaccine.

"Into the 20-cc syringe?" My voice squeaked with disbelief. That syringe was huge.

"That's right. Then you take the haemostat and pull a sterile needle from the row here." She took the pincer-like instrument and did so, lifting the needle and fitting it into the end of the syringe. She instructed me as if handling this monster was a totally normal procedure.

"You give .5 mL to the baby, then use the same haemostat to remove the used needle and place it in this container." She indicated the jar on the counter. "Then attach the next one. Keep everything sterile, of course."

I was becoming more and more apprehensive as she proceeded with the explanation. The only time I'd used a large syringe was when I had drenched a horse with worm medicine. I'd never used one on a person, much less a baby! I'd worked in a health unit where syringes and needles were individually packaged. I had only to break open the package and use a sterilized, compact, individual-dose syringe. This giant syringe with its complicated set of needles was more than I could possibly handle. I took a deep breath. Other nurses did this. I really did not want to fail.

"Just watch me for the first one," Rita said.

I glued my eyes on her and tried to absorb everything she did. I listened while she interviewed the mother and watched while she used her haemostat like a delicate wand, attaching the needle to the syringe as if by magic. She immunized the infant. It looked smooth and almost easy.

"Your turn," she said before the next patient entered.

I could feel my heart rate accelerate and my shoulders tense. I had to do this. I would be giving immunizations to babies at least once a week. It was part of the job. I gritted my teeth and started. I managed the interview quite well. The mother was anxious to talk about her daughter, and I remembered the normal stages of development and assessed the child. No problems there. Then I picked up the haemostat.

The mother smiled nervously. "I hate this part."

I smiled as reassuringly as I could manage. *You and me both*, I thought.

I swabbed alcohol on the baby's arm and, using the haemostat, maneuvered the needle onto the end of the syringe, then I carefully laid the haemostat back on the sterile cloth. Now, to give the shot. I paid close attention to the indicator on the syringe. I didn't want to give too much vaccine. It could easily happen. I felt perspiration on my forehead. I concentrated, making sure the end of the needle didn't touch anything, and I picked up the soft flesh on the baby's arm.

"Take a deep breath," I said to the mother.

"Okay," she said.

I did the same and shoved in the needle. The baby screamed. I watched the indicator on the syringe, ignoring her screams and making sure I gave only the correct dosage. I withdrew the needle and set it down. The baby screamed even louder, wailing with shock.

I felt shaken myself and wished I could whisk out of the room, faint, scream a little, or even wail with the baby, but I was supposed to be the ministering nurse here. I concentrated on the child. I rubbed the baby's arm, patted her shoulder, and then attended to the records, writing down the immunization in her blue record book and in my file. The mother tucked the blue record book into her purse, comforted her baby and left.

I picked up the haemostat to remove the needle. I took deep breaths to control my nerves. I hated making babies cry.

"Just a minute," Rita said.

I paused, holding the haemostat with the needle at the end in one hand and the syringe in the other.

"That needle might have a barb on it." Rita looked at it critically. "After they have been autoclaved many times, they sometimes get rough parts on them." She took the haemostat from me and rubbed the needle on the towel. It caught on a thread.

"Yes. It's got a barb. We'll throw this one out."

"You mean I put a barbed needle into that baby?" I was horrified.

"Afraid so."

Using a needle was difficult but necessary, but using a barbed needle was barbaric.

"I'm going to test every needle before I use it so I don't get a faulty one," I said with a fierce determination.

"Good idea." Rita approved. "Maybe we should all do that. Do you want to immunize the next one?" She seemed to think she was being generous.

"No, I'll watch this time." My hands were shaking too much to hold that syringe, and I didn't want her to notice.

I'd get used to doing this, but it was going to take some time.

AFTER MY two-week orientation, I was on my own and ready for my first independent foray into the country. I'd be away for three days. I packed medical supplies, records, and my own suitcase in the trunk of the 1962 Chevy II, owned by my government employers and assigned to me.

"There are no real rules around the use of the car," Rita told me. "Just bring it back in one piece, and submit your gas bills for reimbursement." I interpreted that to mean that I could use it as if it were mine. It had been serviced and, I assumed, was reliable.

By now, the fall had begun. The temperature dropped at night, and the leaves had turned colour. As I drove east toward the Cariboo Mountains, the country spread out before me. Yellow poplar blanketed the hillsides for miles, brilliant against the cobalt blue sky. I kept stopping to absorb the beauty. It amazed me to see miles and miles of open land below the huge vaulted sky. I was a tiny presence in a vast landscape, a pristine world. Zane Grey would have loved it. The air smelled tangy and felt a little cool.

I wore my winter navy wool uniform, tailor-made to my measurements—a straight skirt, and a suit jacket with a nipped-in waist and an insignia on the pocket. It was still reminiscent of a stewardess outfit but smart. The navy hat, like an army forage cap, was easier to wear than the summer one and also had an insignia proclaiming who I was and where I worked. The uniform was supposed to evoke confidence in my patients, as if I were government-sanctioned and capable. When I put it on, I felt more competent and professional. It was amazing how delusions could be created by clothes.

I had a list of the children at the Big Lake School, a one-room school with a new teacher, about thirty miles from my office in Williams Lake. She lived in the teacherage, a small house supplied by the school board beside the school. I wondered if she came into town very often. It must be lonely out here.

I drove down a low hill into the Big Lake valley. Rail fences, called snake fences here, zigzagged over the field. Brilliant yellow willow bushes defined the paths of the streams. Copses of poplar blazed gold near the lake and dotted the fields. A few houses clustered near the road. The school wasn't far from the lake, well back from the main road, down a long driveway. Twenty students from grades one to eight attended, all in one room. The teacher was young but stricter than I'd expected. She had the students stand, say good morning when I came through the door, and then sit on command. That was unusual and made me feel uncomfortable, as if the children were being forced to show me subservience. I told her I planned to conduct vision tests and assured her I would try not to interfere with her lessons.

I measured off twenty feet at the back of the room and tacked up the eye chart. I still carried the ruler I'd used to measure off the twenty feet when I asked a little grade one girl to come up for her test. She came, but she burst into tears.

I took her hand and crouched down beside her. "What's the matter?"

She just shook her head.

A teenage student at the back of the room glared at me and then down at the ruler in my hand. I stared at the ruler. Did this teacher hit the kids with a ruler? I handed the ruler to the teenager. She took it, and the little girl stopped crying. I explained the eye test to her and told her it didn't matter if she could read it or not. If she didn't manage it this time, I'd try it again when I next came. That seemed to reassure her.

I tested all the children and wrote referrals for those who needed to see an optometrist, all the while pondering the behaviour of the teacher. It wasn't against the law to hit children. Teachers used the strap to discipline, usually big boys who were obstreperous. But it was cruel, especially cruel to torment a six-year-old. Who would stop her? The teenagers would probably report it to their parents. Eventually, the community might do something about it— if it was happening. What could I do? I'd pay attention and watch the behaviour of the teacher and the reactions of the children next month. If I suspected she was cruel, I would talk to her supervisor.

There were four mothers waiting for the well-baby clinic, which I held at recess at the back of the schoolroom. I concentrated hard on manipulating that malevolent outsized syringe and the slippery needles. I tested each needle on a sterile cloth before I used it. None of them had barbs. The babies cried but didn't scream.

I had one more duty before I headed toward the Cariboo Mountains and the hamlet of Likely, where I'd stay overnight. Rita told me to find a rancher, Tom Anderson, in the Big Lake area, and give him a TB test.

"His brother has TB, and he visited him last month. We have to follow up all his brother's contacts, and Tom Anderson is the only one in our district. The others are somebody else's problem."

The TB preventative program was province-wide and effective in stopping the spread of tuberculosis. We tested all contacts of active TB patients: family members, friends, anyone who spent time with them. When one tested positive, we sent them on for further diagnosis and then put them on a medication regime. If one contact was missed, TB could spread from that person.

"How do I find him?" The Big Lake area was huge. There were ranches, big and small, all over this country.

"I sent a letter saying you'd be around on this date. We can hope he'll be available."

"No phone?"

"No phone." She handed me the directions to the ranch. Something was missing.

"No address?" I came from a settled area where roads had names and houses had addresses.

"No address. Just directions. Second road past the school, turn left, and then it's the first right." She nodded as if the directions were crystal clear. "It's good to go now before winter."

I'd found Rita's remark about the season cryptic until I took the first right onto a farm track. With rain, this road would be mud and probably impassable for my Chevy II. I got out and opened the gate, hauling it wide, drove through, and, after getting out of the car again, dragged it closed behind me. I could hear my dad in my head. *"If you find a gate open, leave it open. If you find it shut, shut it behind you."* I didn't want to be responsible for escaping cattle.

The ranch was about two miles beyond the gate and beautiful. The log house nestled beside a small hill, which gave it shelter from the wind. A stream, just a trickle now, ran through the yard. Two black-and-white border collies raced toward my car. A woman came to the back door. The dogs, while noisy, looked friendly. Tails wagged.

I got out of the car, pulled out my black bag containing my TB testing materials and information brochures, and called, "Hello!"

"Bessie. Mike. Stop that!" The woman flapped a dish towel at the dogs. They obediently stopped barking and flounced beside me like a formal escort to the back door.

I introduced myself and asked for Tom Anderson.

"My husband," she said. "Sorry. He's out checking fences. We didn't know what time you'd be here, but he said he'd keep an eye out. I guess he got into the bush a ways. I'm Sharon. Would you like coffee?"

I would be giving immunizations at a clinic in Likely at 3 p.m., and I had to test the children's eyes at the Likely school before that. I checked my watch. I could spare a few minutes. The woman was in her late twenties, trim, athletic with long brown hair, and freckles on her nose. It was possible she was lonely and needed someone to talk to. Good mental health nursing included listening to people, and, to be honest, coffee sounded wonderful.

"Thanks. I'd love some. Maybe Tom will come while I'm having coffee?" I started to follow her into the house.

"Lean on your horn. He might hear that."

I returned to the car and hit the horn. The dogs went wild but calmed when I left the car.

Sharon was friendly, and, as far as I could see, stable and happy. The coffee *was* wonderful. Tom didn't show up.

"I'll try again next month, but I don't like to leave it that long." I gave her the date and the probable time I'd come by. I hoped the rains wouldn't have arrived by then, or I would be plowing mud to get to the ranch.

I was wrestling with the gate at the main road when a horse galloped up from a path in the bush.

"Hey, Nurse!" the rider called.

I turned and waited. They were an impressive sight. The chestnut horse, bigger than any I'd seen before, had a white blaze on its face and wore a bridle with silver fastenings. The man was compact, wearing jeans, a jean jacket, and chaps. He swung out of the saddle, the chaps flapping around his legs.

"I'm Tom Anderson."

I smiled. "I'm Marion McKinnon, the nurse. I'm glad you caught me."

"I heard the horn, but I was in the upper meadow."

That must have been some distance away. "Your brother has TB. How's he doing?"

"Doing good. Those medicines you people are giving him work a wonder."

"They do." Prevention worked well too, but we had to find the contacts.

He dropped the reins on the ground and walked toward me. The horse didn't move.

"Can you do that test here?" He removed his stetson, brushed his forehead and hair with the back of his hand, and waited.

I gazed around me. There wasn't a table, a stump, or any handy counter. I looked at my car hood.

"I guess."

I pulled out my black bag and fished out a syringe, a small one this time, individually packaged with a tiny .25 needle attached. No fussing with a haemostat. I opened the aluminum suitcase that held my clinic supplies and extracted the bottle of serum. I spread a sterile towel on the hood of my car, loaded the syringe, and placed it on the towel.

"Our biggest problem here," I said to him as I worked, "is con-taminating the test site. You want to protect that from dirt and subsequent infection."

He nodded.

"If it gets infected, it will look as though the test is positive, and you'll have to have X-rays forever."

He nodded again. I glanced over at the horse, but it never moved except to shake its head, jangling the bridle. It was as if it was tethered to an invisible stake.

I inserted the tiny needle just under the skin on the underside of his forearm and slowly pushed the plunger until a small bubble appeared. The protein serum absorbed quickly. I gave Tom a card that explained how to read the test in two days and how to measure any reaction with the circles printed on the card. I asked him to call or mail in the results to me at the health unit. I explained that the purified protein serum was derived from the TB bacillus and any reaction would show he had at least fought that bacillus. It didn't necessarily mean he had active TB.

"If the test site is red in two days, come in, and I'll give you an X-ray requisition."

"I'm pretty busy here." He pulled his shirt sleeves down to his wrists and snapped the cuffs.

I looked at him. I wanted to say: "You're not too busy to stay alive, are you? You're no good to this ranch if you die of TB." But I remembered my public health instructor's axiom: *Patients need information more than they need direction.*

"TB can move pretty quickly in some people. The sooner you follow up on this, if you need to, the better chance you have to combat it and to keep working."

He blinked. "Good point. Thanks."

"You're welcome."

He mounted his horse and cantered away.

I stood there for a moment, looking at the empty syringe on the hood of my car, the yellow poplar on either side of the road, and the disappearing horse and rider. I breathed in the spicy scent of autumn. This was my new world, and I loved it—needles, syringes, and all.

CHAPTER THREE

DYING IN
THE WOODS

THE ROAD TO Likely was gravelled and graded, but the occasional cavernous pothole, created by logging trucks with their eighteen wheels bearing giant logs, jolted the car, making me bounce and sending the metal baby scale clattering in the back seat. While it was a public road, it was narrow. One of those big semis coming at me could flatten my Chevy. I tried to repress the mental image of twisted metal, blood, and my body mashed in the middle of the mess, the baby scale lying on the road, and paid attention to my driving. I was careful on blind corners, ready to take to the ditch if a truck suddenly appeared in my windshield, and was even prepared to drop off a cliff if the choice was meeting the truck head-on.

"Don't even *think* a logging truck will get out of your way," Rita had told me. "The driver expects you to move. He can pull you out of the ditch. You can't pull him out."

I assumed nothing and stayed alert for trucks and moose. Three logging trucks came toward me on straight stretches, and I managed to move over far enough to avoid a collision. They all honked a thank you. I slowed my breathing, relaxed my fingers on the steering wheel, and kept driving.

I stopped for a moment at the top of the long hill that descended to the Quesnel River and the hamlet of Likely. From here, the settlement looked small—only a few buildings. More houses and

cabins must be scattered in the trees since there was enough pop-
ulation to support a school. It had been a gold mining centre in
the wild rush of the 1860s, and there was still a little gold panning
in some of the streams, but the main industry today was logging.
Ellie had told me the mill site was farther along the river and on
the edge of the lake. There was no evidence of logging that I could
see nearby—only those few houses and a carpet of conifers covering the mountains. Likely looked like a hamlet in the middle of
endless wilderness.

I descended the long, steep hill slowly. The road was narrow, and
there were no banks or guardrails to protect me from slipping over
the cliff. I made the sharp turn at the bottom and approached the
bridge. Somewhere, there was a dam under it or near it. The bridge
didn't seem unstable, but I breathed a little easier when I was on the
other side. A sign saying Quesnel Forks pointed to the left. I didn't
have any families to visit or any clinic appointments in Quesnel
Forks, another old mining settlement, so I turned right toward
the lodge, where I'd be staying overnight. My odometer showed
I had travelled sixty-six miles. I was a long way from my office.

Quesnel Lake, Ellie told me, was the deepest fjord lake in the
world and had 360 miles of shoreline. "It's impressive," she said,
"and cold." I'd have to travel farther along this road to see it; here,
the Quesnel River rushed under the bridge, past Quesnel Forks
and west to the Fraser River. The huge cottonwoods along the edge
of the river were still green. The frost hadn't hit them yet.

I pulled up in front of the lodge and took in my personal suitcase, leaving the aluminium one with the vaccines and supplies in
the car, and registered with Mary, the owner and receptionist. A
wiry, energetic woman, she showed me to a tiny room with a small
bed that looked clean and private. There was no lock on the door,
but there was a chair in the room. I could put the chair under the
door handle if I wanted to be secure; I'd lived in Seattle, after all. I
wasn't used to trusting strangers. The lack of a lock did make me
wonder if I was safer here than I had been in Seattle, or maybe very
few women stayed at the hotel.

Mary fed me a sandwich and some coffee and told me the school was a mile farther along the river and up the hill. A poster on the wall reminded me that the clinic was at 3 p.m. I had to get up to the school soon.

I'd left my baby scale and black bag in my car when I registered with Mary, and now I slung my purse on the seat beside me and headed for the school. Past the lodge, the road divided into a Y. The left-hand one went on to the Cariboo Mountains through a back trail, the Yank's Peak Road, to Barkerville, about thirty rough miles away. It wasn't fit for my Chevy II.

"Don't go left," Mary had said, "at least don't go far along it. You can go a couple of miles up to Keithley Creek, but after that you need a truck."

The right-hand road angled back down to Quesnel Lake and Mackenzie's sawmill where many millworkers' families lived. The school squatted at the fork where the road divided.

Mr. and Mrs. Pederson, husband and wife, both taught in this two-room school. They were friendly and helpful and seemed to have a good rapport with the students. I tested students' eyes and handed out referrals. I also checked over Mrs. Pederson's nine-month-old baby who, while I was there, helped himself to a snack by unzipping Mrs. Pederson's dress and reaching for her breast. I wondered if he did that in the classroom and what the community thought about it. This wasn't done where I came from. My mother would be shocked. So it surprised me. From a public health point of view, it was good for the baby.

Two mothers showed up for the clinic, and when school let out, I immunized their babies.

About four o'clock, I drove out to the mill site. I didn't have any business there this trip, but I wanted to stop at the mill office, introduce myself, and find out how many families lived in the surrounding area and if there were any public health concerns. I also wanted to see Quesnel Lake. I did see the lake, but I was disappointed. It didn't appear large—just a narrow strip of water with a small mountain of forest on the opposite side. Its size must be in its length.

Since the owners of the mill also owned the cabins the mill workers lived in and had a lot of influence over them, the mill manager was like a feudal lord. I pulled up to the office, a three-room newly built cabin. The new lumber gleamed yellow in the afternoon sun. I smelled the pitch from the log walls as I entered the building.

The manager, Bob Preston, hurried into the reception area. "Nurse! Thank God you're here. We need you."

That sent panic into my bones. I was not an emergency room nurse. I could barely remember emergency procedures. Airway, cardiac assessment, respirations.

"We have a copter coming in with a worker injured in the bush. Arlie. Arlie Sanders. We sent a plane for the doctor from Williams Lake, but he's not here yet."

"What happened?" I followed Bob into his office.

"Arlie Sanders. He's a faller. He got in the way of a tree."

I saw in my mind a young man and a huge fir, falling from a great height. I'd heard about fallers. They had the most dangerous job in the bush. They took out individual trees with power saws, usually working in pairs. One would cut into the tree and the other would watch for hazards, such as trees that were hung up on other trees, those that fell the wrong way, or bounced into the air when they landed. The logger I met in the bar where Dorrie and I went last week had told me all about them. They called some of those trees "widow makers." Arlie's survival would depend on where he was hit and how severely.

It wasn't five minutes later when we heard the helicopter—the engine roaring overhead as it hovered over us, then landing just below, on the soccer field.

"Stay here," Bob told me. "We'll bring him up."

Four men carried the injured logger on a stretcher. They worked together smoothly, almost running but keeping the stretcher level and steady as they pushed it into the building and into the empty office. The room, with a bare desk and empty walls, looked as though no one had ever used it. The huge oak desk acted as a hard bed, and the men gently transferred their friend onto it. I took a quick look. He was going to need a miracle. The only emergency drug in my black bag was adrenaline—almost useless in this case. I took out my stethoscope and a flashlight.

The injured man was about twenty-one, blond with broad shoulders, and muscular. His boots were large and steel-toed for safety. They hadn't saved him. He'd been a strong, vigorous man. Now, he was bleeding from the ears. A bad sign. His skin was pale, and he was unconscious. He was still alive but breathing slowly. One of the men who had carried him in, an older man, stood beside him, head bowed, praying quietly. I recognized Catholic prayers—"Hail Mary," "Our Father"—intoned quickly and in a low voice, the words running into each other like an incantation. His hands fumbled together as if he were counting imaginary beads.

I did a quick examination. Brain injury, for sure. I heard a plane engine cut out as it landed on the lake. The manager disappeared and returned in about five minutes with the doctor. Wilson. Dr. Wilson. He nodded at me.

"What do you know?" he asked me.

"Next to nothing. Slow respirations, bleeding from the ears. The only drug I have is adrenaline."

He stepped up to the young patient. I stepped back. There was nothing I could do. There was nothing anyone could do. Arlie died within three minutes.

Dr. Wilson didn't try to revive him. There was no way to relieve the pressure of the bleed in the brain; no oxygen to supply to the brain; no cupboard of drugs to prevent edema, the swelling in the brain. Dr. Wilson was about thirty, probably very experienced in dealing with many kinds of trauma. He stood there for a moment and bowed his head with the men as he pronounced death. I also bowed my head. We waited. A couple of the men were crying. The man beside Arlie continued to pray, murmuring. I wondered if he was Arlie's logging buddy, the one who was supposed to keep him safe. The immense sorrow spread through the room like a fog and settled on us all. Arlie was young. He had gone to work in the morning, and now he was dead.

The silence stretched on for a very long time as we waited: the dead boy, the older men, the doctor, and me.

Finally, Bob said, "Who knows his mother best?"

One of the men said, "I guess that'd be me."

"Can you go with me to tell her?" Bob spoke slowly.

The man said, "I'll get my wife and we'll go."

The men followed each other out of the office and into the reception area. I stayed in the office with the doctor.

"Head trauma," I said inanely. Obviously, it was head trauma.

"Yeah. He had dilated pupils when I got here. Did you see that?"

"Yes." I'd checked that while waiting for the doctor.

"Not much chance, poor bugger." He closed the young man's eyes and placed his arms on his chest. That compassion for his patient hit me like a blow. I swallowed.

"What now?" I looked away from Arlie.

"I'll take the body back to Williams Lake and do an autopsy, but I'm sure I'll find it was massive brain hemorrhage. Can you find information about how it happened and send it to me?" He shoved his hands in his pockets and turned to me. He spoke carefully as if trying to give some semblance of normality to our conversation.

"I'll try. Do you want me to telephone it to you?" My voice sounded shaky, surprising me. I swallowed again.

"Yes. The sooner, the better." He gave me his office phone number. "Oh. Lorne Wilson, by the way."

"Marion McKinnon," I responded, a little steadier now.

"You came to a meeting at the hospital."

"I remember you." He had sat beside Sam.

"I'll talk to the manager here and get back to town. The plane is waiting." He glanced at Arlie.

"I'm so sorry," I said, feeling inadequate.

"Yeah, me too. I hate this part of medicine."

We looked at each other in complete understanding. We were educated to help people. We spent our working lives trying to do that, and, sometimes, like today, we failed.

I sat in the reception area while Bob organized the removal of the body to the plane. When he had finished directing the men, he invited me into his office to await the worker and his wife who would join him on the desolate trip to the young man's mother.

I took out my record book and asked for the deceased's name and the particulars of the accident.

Bob wiped his face with his handkerchief, reached under the counter, and brought up two glasses. "Whiskey?" he asked.

I was about to refuse and then decided I needed it. "A small bit." We weren't supposed to drink on the job, but my professional ethics instructor was a long way away.

He poured a shot for himself and about a half-shot for me.

"Here's to a fine young man, Arlie Sanders," Bob said.

I raised my glass and sipped. "To Arlie."

"Ah, well. This is a vicious business." Bob tossed his drink straight back, slapped the glass on his desk, and poured himself another. This time he sipped it.

"Can you tell me how it happened?" I asked. "Dr. Wilson would like to know."

"He was taking out a fir. He and his crew buddy thought it was pretty straightforward. They didn't see that the branch from a nearby tree had caught under one of the fir branches. When Arlie cut through, the tree started to topple and then hitched, changed direction, and hit poor Arlie square on the head."

"No hard hat?"

"No. He's supposed to wear one. Workers' Compensation insists. But lots of them don't."

Was this a teaching moment? "Do you think you could persuade the other fallers to wear hard hats?"

"Might be able to now." He sounded grim.

I wrote down what he told me, and we sat there as the afternoon twilight crept in around us. By six o'clock Bob had finished his drink, but I didn't want to leave him alone. We continued to sit there, talking about the town, about the country, and about the almost unlimited trees around us that the logging company was harvesting. We heard a truck drive up.

"That's Mike and Julie." He stood and stared at me. "This doesn't get any easier."

Did that mean he had to bring tragic news often? How many other men had died in the woods?

I followed him out and watched them drive away. I dropped my black bag in the back seat of my Chevy and returned to the Likely Lodge. I noticed the bright yellow leaves on the poplars near the school, the soft green of the huge cottonwoods by the lake and along the river, but part of my brain was rolling over the dangers that fallers faced. Maybe I could set up a work safety program? I'd have to check out the research on hard hats and accidents, so I could give facts to the community next time I came. Perhaps I should talk to the women at baby clinics? Give *them* the facts about safety and let them be the advocates.

I pulled into the gravel parking space beside the lodge, unloaded my bag and my aluminium suitcase, and hauled everything up to my room.

I changed into slacks, a shirt, and loafers. It'd been a relief when my dad had sent my trunk last week with the rest of my clothes and shoes. I ran a comb through my hair, fluffed it a little, and headed downstairs to the dining room for supper. Nothing seemed to interfere with my appetite. Mary set a table for me in the corner. Only one of the other five tables was occupied, but I could hear the buzz of conversation and the occasional loud comment from the bar in the next room. Mary put a bowl of soup in front of me. There were no menus. She cooked. Customers ate. She jerked her head toward the bar.

"Filling up fast," she said. There were quite a few people in the bar. "A bit of a wake for Arlie."

"You knew him?" I asked.

"Well, of course. He grew up here." She sniffed.

I stared at her. "Oh my." That would be very hard.

She blinked rapidly and took a deep breath. "A good boy, that one. No father. Looked after his mother. A good boy." And she left me to go tend the bar.

I knew Mary was a widow. Her husband had drowned when he was out fishing right in front of the lodge. Mary had run the lodge on her own for the past ten years. She would understand loss.

She returned in about fifteen minutes with a bowl of stew and a couple of tea biscuits.

"Looks great."

"Moose," she announced.

I stared at the stew. I'd never had moose before. I nodded toward the bar. "Is everyone in town there?"

"Pretty much. We're all standing drinks and making sure Judith gets one on every round. We're planning on getting her sloshed."

"Judith?" I felt as though I was several sentences behind in this conversation.

"Arlie's mum."

"She's here?" That surprised me.

"Of course, she's here." Mary almost snapped at me. "You think she should sit alone on a night like this?"

"No, you're right." But I *had* imagined her sitting at home with neighbours and relatives, quietly grieving. I hadn't imagined a raucous wake in the bar.

"You can join us when you're finished here. Drink your coffee in the bar." Either she was making me welcome or making less work for herself. Whichever it was, I'd cooperate.

"Thanks." I might join them. I'd come to the Cariboo to have adventures, but I'd had enough adventures for the day. This was a private wake for the community. I wasn't part of it, at least not yet. Maybe it would be intrusive to go in there? Then again, wouldn't I be sorry tomorrow if I hadn't gone? And maybe someone wanted to talk or ask me questions about something? I only came once a month. Besides, I had a suspicion Mary's invitation was really an order. By the time I'd finished the stew—moose tasted like beef only tangier—I'd decided to go to the bar. Perhaps only for a few minutes.

I pushed open the door and was immediately assaulted by a wave of noise. Surprisingly, there were only about twenty people in the bar, but they were all talking and smoking. Cigarette smoke drifted up to the beams and gave a hazy, surreal look to the room, something like a painting where you know there are people in the picture, but they seem vague, without definition. Faces became clearer as I moved closer.

A large woman in a print dress, with a black sweater draped around her shoulders, sat against the wall at a far table. Eight people crowded around her. Beer glasses were stacked on the table and in danger of falling, and, as I watched, one of the men grabbed six glasses and took them to the bar. Mary thanked him. I looked for a place to sit. A man at a nearby table got up.

"Here, Nurse." He gestured to his chair.

"Thanks." I sat. Mary slipped the coffee in front of me and made introductions. "Harold." She nodded at the man who had stood. "James, Jackie, and his wife, Frieda."

I smiled and tried to remember their names. I didn't say much, as it was so loud any conversation would take a lot of effort, and I didn't know anything about the price of lumber and something called "stump fees," which I assumed were a government tax on logging.

I finished my coffee and made my way over to Judith. The people sitting with her parted to let me approach.

"My name is Marion McKinnon," I said. "I'm the public health nurse. I'm very sorry for your loss."

She nodded. "They told me you tried to help my boy." I could see the tear marks on her face, but she held herself firmly erect and had an immense dignity.

"There wasn't much I could do," I said awkwardly.

"You were there," she said. "Thank you."

That was too much. I'd done nothing, and in her grief, she was thanking me. With all my education and studying, I had nothing in my head or in my black bag to help her son. I could only watch him die. I managed a nod and got out of there.

I walked across the road to the cottonwood trees and sat on a rock near the river. I'd hoped the swish of the rushing water would soothe me, but the scurrying motion, racing by, just made me think about how quickly life passes by and how dangerous this country could be. All my frantic plans to help prevent more deaths in the woods, my concerns about teaching safety, were just a way to keep from feeling. I gave up on that. I let the sadness rise. Arlie was only a year younger than me. He'd gone to work the way I'd gone to work this morning, doing what was expected of us, trying to be productive and useful to earn a wage. We didn't expect to die. The fates were capricious, grabbing a life without any forewarning. The older man who had been praying had tried to comfort himself by putting order around Arlie's sudden, inexplicable death. He couldn't do it. There was no order. Knowledge was supposed to protect us. Arlie was supposed to know enough to stay alive. I was supposed to know enough to help him stay alive. We'd both failed. I sat on the rock, letting the river hurry by, unstoppable, predestined, like the thread of Arlie's life—and let the tears fall.

CHAPTER FOUR

LESSONS FROM THE BLACK CREEK WOMEN

I N THE MORNING, Mary had a huge breakfast ready for me: eggs, sausages (probably moose again), and toast. I ate quickly and headed outside. I stood by my car, taking in the flowing river, the blue mountains beyond, and the peace of the country. A loon called a wild demand from somewhere in the reeds to my right. Another answered far out on the water. I imagined Arlie watching me from those ancient and enduring trees. *Sorry, Arlie.* There was nothing we could do for a head injury like that. I felt sadness wash over me as I remembered the scene in the mill office. Then I collected my feelings of inadequacy and sorrow and shoved them into my mental "later" file. They would come up again. I was sure of it.

Whatever my failings of yesterday, I was the nurse for this community, and I had to get on with my job. I loaded my suitcase into the trunk and climbed into my car. I had one visit to make in the Likely area before I could head out to Beaver Valley and the well-baby clinic there.

I drove past the school, took the left-hand fork in the road, and rattled along the few miles to Keithley Creek, the baby scale producing metallic percussion from the back seat. The directions were clear: second driveway after the split tree. The tall cedar had been sliced by the heavy load of ice in the winter or, perhaps, by lightning. The top section lay on the forest floor, and the jagged broken trunk pointed to the sky. I turned up the second road, really a trail. Mrs. Kelsey was a regular patient who received a vitamin B injection every month. She had her medication with her, and I was only supposed to administer it. I pulled into a gravel spot near the front door of a small cabin constructed on pilings, so that the front steps led up to a porch about four feet above the ground. I grabbed my black bag and got out of the car. A huge woman in pants and a man's plaid shirt flung the cabin door open.

"I expected you yesterday," she complained, her voice loud in the silent meadow. Trees surrounded us in a circle, leaving a clear space around the cabin where every living thing seemed to have been leveled except for tufts of yellow grass, dirt, and rocks.

"I sent a message I was coming today." I was a little startled by her accusatory tone.

"With who?" She thrust her jaw forward. White curls bounced around her round face. Her shoulder muscles strained the material of her shirt. I wouldn't argue with her.

"On Message Time." That was the radio broadcast at noon and 6 p.m., sending messages to people with no other means of communication. I hadn't sent the message myself. Ellie had called it in on my behalf.

"Didn't hear it," she said, as if that was my fault.

She didn't have a phone. I supposed I could have sent a message to the school or the Lodge and asked someone to take it to her. I started to feel a little guilty. Then I thought she must have known I'd be here around this time as a nurse came on a regular schedule.

"Sorry," I said curtly, trying to convey I wasn't sorry at all.

She sniffed but held the door open for me. "I knew you'd be here yesterday or today, because there was a baby clinic notice at the Lodge."

"Good." I walked into a big room that served as kitchen and living room. She had a bottle of liquid vitamin B on the table. I was highly doubtful vitamin B was of any use to her. She didn't have anemia, and even if she had, I wasn't sure the injection would be efficacious. I scrambled for reasons for this visit, which I considered a waste of my time. Her doctor was one of the older physicians in the area and might be behind the current treatment protocols. On the other hand, he might be wise in the ways of the Mrs. Kelseys of the world. Perhaps he thought sending a nurse into Mrs. Kelsey's house once a month would allow him to monitor her health, without putting her to the trouble of making the long trip into town. Or that sending a nurse once a month would make her feel as if she was important. Or she might have bullied him into prescribing it. Some doctors thought it improved a patient's mood, but there was little evidence for that. I didn't think the doctor was sending me to check on her mental health. She didn't seem depressed or lonely. She was a little strange but not morose. She had lived in the middle of the bush for ten years. I presumed she liked it. She had a husband around somewhere. Vitamin B injections wouldn't harm her. As I entered the cabin, I gave a quick thought to her mental stability. Was she eccentric enough to be dangerous? I was probably safe.

"Put your bag there. Wash your hands there, and then give me the shot."

A "please" would have been too much to expect. She didn't offer me coffee, which most people would have done, but I didn't particularly want any.

"Glad you came early. Got to get out on the site." She stood by the table, clearly impatient to have me gone.

"The site?" I asked politely as I prepared the syringe.

"Gold. We're panning."

I nodded as if it was perfectly normal to live in the middle of the mountains, panning for gold. For her, it was. I was suddenly curious. What kind of panning did they do? Did they use a sluice box, shovel in gravel, and let the stream wash through it? Did they crouch at the edge of a river and dip the pan into the gravel? I put a damper on my inquiring mind. I knew better than to ask if she was successful.

"Don't ask people how many cattle they have, how much timber they're taking out, or if they're getting any gold," Rita had told me.

"That's tantamount to asking how much money they make, and it's none of our business."

In fifteen minutes, I was driving away. Mrs. Kelsey was not going to be my favourite patient, but I'd be back.

I stopped at the lodge and called in my information to Dr. Wilson's office on the probable cause of Arlie Sanders's accident as I had promised I would. Then I was off to Beaver Valley. There was a forestry service road from Likely to Horsefly that was more direct than retracing my route down the Likely road, but it was too rough for my car, and I had to stop in Beaver Valley in any case. I backtracked almost to Big Lake and then went east. It was about thirty miles to the Beaver Valley sawmill site, school, and the next clinic.

The day was bright and the trip beautiful. Poplar splattered the hills with brilliant yellow. Meadows still green and ringed with dark firs lined the low land. I stopped for a moment at the side of the road to appreciate it. The scent of pine pitch drifted on the crisp air. It was glorious country, and it was getting into my bones.

The road was gravel but fairly smooth. The lake lay along the east end of the valley. The sawmill at the far end was owned by Seventh-day Adventist people. They had hired quite a few workers from their own communities—some of them from the US. Even so, the people seemed to be used to our BC public health system and were ready, supplying a volunteer, to help me weigh the babies. The students at the school were quiet but appeared relaxed. I didn't feel the tension I had in the Big Lake School. Since I had another volunteer to help with the eye testing, I had time to check the teeth of the children. I knew Seventh-day Adventist people were conscientious about health and extolled healthy food and preventive medicine and advocated refraining from stimulants like coffee or alcohol. I hoped they'd be careful about dental health as well. As the children finished their eye tests, I asked them to open their mouths. I was only looking for holes in the teeth and gum disease, but I didn't see any. Fillings, yes. Holes, no. The Beaver Valley people seemed like a self-contained community that looked after their children.

I drove the next twenty miles to the community of Horsefly, east and a little north of Beaver Valley. My district roads formed a fat "H," with the one north arm of the H ending at Likely. It was an efficient route, with only one backtrack from the north end of the Likely arm to the Beaver Valley Road.

While there was some logging and mining in the surrounding area, most of the Horsefly community worked on ranches and in the summer tourist trade. Horsefly Lake, only about fifty miles from the main north–south Highway 97, was renowned for its fishing. As September was fishing season, there would be many recreational vehicles, trucks, and campers on the road heading for the opportunity to catch some rainbow trout.

I managed patience behind a huge fifth-wheel trailer until it pulled to the side and let me by. I fueled both my vehicle with gas and myself with lunch at the outskirts of Horsefly and arrived at the school about 1 p.m. This was the biggest school in this part of my district. It had six rooms and went from grades one to ten. After that, the high school students boarded in Williams Lake and attended high school or simply left school. I did more eye tests and teeth exams. There were many children with holes in their teeth— quite different from Beaver Valley. Maybe the parents in Horsefly didn't get the education about dental health that the parents in Beaver Valley did. I could look into bringing some brochures the next time I came. I wrote out dental referrals for the children to take home to their parents.

Rita had told me that giving dental referrals resulted in better care, as many parents complied. Some got Dr. Scot. "A drunk and an idiot," she said. "He tells parents, 'They're only baby teeth; let 'em rot!'"

"And he's still practising?"

"Not for long," she said grimly.

I didn't ask who or what was going to force him to quit. Perhaps the other dentists? His patients might object. One woman in Williams Lake told me, "He's a real good dentist when he's sober."

I'd been to Horsefly once before on a day trip when I had first arrived. The nurse I was replacing drove with me as a passenger while she checked some TB tests she'd done previously. I had accompanied her to a cabin where the Cook family lived. A woman with four children presented their cards, each with a name and the results of the test. The mother had a positive test, and the nurse filled out an X-ray requisition. The mother would take that into town and get an X-ray. The children all tested negative.

I looked at the children, and, when we were back at the car, I said to the nurse, "A negative test on a child younger than two is not reliable. The youngest child, Audrey, needs an X-ray." I had taken a six-week course in TB nursing, and I was sure of this.

She started the car. "When you come next month, you can tell her."

It would only take a minute to return to the house, but I thought she might not want to admit to the mother that she'd made a mistake. I didn't say anything more. She was driving. To insist on returning to the house would be a fight. I decided to keep the peace and deal with the Cook family on my next visit. Now I remembered that child and planned to talk to the mother.

I drove out to the cabin where the family lived. It was empty. There were no curtains on the windows, no toys on the porch. My mind went blank for a moment. I'd been so sure I'd deal with the problem this trip that I hadn't considered they might be gone. Where were they? I knocked on the door of a nearby cabin. A woman of about twenty opened it.

"No, I don't know where they went. Her husband left his job. Probably got a better one. They moved somewhere in town."

"Williams Lake?"

"Maybe."

"Thanks." I was worried about that little one. I cursed myself for not insisting on returning to the cabin on the last trip. I had checked that they didn't have a phone, so I couldn't have called, but I could have left a message with the mill office. I'd try to find her when I got back to town.

I drove about six miles to the Horsefly Landing Resort on the edge of Horsefly Lake. This is where I would stay for the night. I settled in. The owner, Marjorie Plant, gave me supper. I took my records into my cabin, finished recording what I had done today, and pulled the files I needed for the next day. Staying organized was a trick. The secret was to enter information at the end of the day. I recorded the immunizations as I did them, but I checked every night to make sure I hadn't missed any, and I added information that I wanted to follow up later. It didn't take long.

I sat outside on the small veranda in the evening and watched the night close in on the lake. I could see the Cariboo Mountains rising high far across the water. Meadows, cabins, and roads surrounded me here, but the other side of the lake looked wild.

The village of Horsefly spread out over many acres. I didn't know anyone here except the teachers and Marjorie. There was no congenial pub attached to this resort where locals congregated in the evenings, so I felt more distanced from the community here than I did in Likely. But then, perhaps it was my fault for opting to stay at the beautiful resort out of the main village area.

In the morning, fueled by Marjorie's full breakfast, I headed to Black Creek, a tiny community ten miles farther east with a one-room school and only fifteen students. After I checked on the students there, I set out for the logging camp where I would conduct a well-baby clinic. Ranches and logging operations supported the people here. Past the school, a small logging mill nestled at the bottom of a ravine with a stream running through the mill site. I drove across a log bridge to the mill yard and the main cook shack. Mrs. Sorenson, the wife of the owner and most probably a part owner of the company, welcomed me and plunked a cup of coffee in front of me.

"The women will be here for the clinic at ten," Mrs. Sorenson said. She was a short, stocky woman and looked strong. I wouldn't have been surprised to find her hauling lumber off the green chain. I'd left the organization of the clinic to her as, apparently, she managed it every month. It was clear that I was fitting into her schedule, not her into mine. We'd probably get along just fine if I remembered that.

I set up the baby scale in her kitchen. The heavy, cumbersome metal scale was awkward to carry with its metal cradle and long arm with a movable balance weight. Mrs. Sorenson weighed the babies there and wrote down the weight on a piece of paper. Each woman brought it to me in the dining room where I sat at a long table. All the women gathered around the table. If anyone had a private problem, they wouldn't be telling me about it unless they didn't mind an audience. I soon found out it was difficult for me to give any advice at all.

"The baby doesn't like mashed-up meat," a woman said, indicating her eighteen-month-old son sitting on her knee.

"Try putting some sugar in it," one of the women said before I could say a thing.

"My kid likes mustard in it," another said.

"There's sugar in that," the first one said.

"True enough."

"Try rolling it in pastry. He might chew on it then," a third said.

"Or maybe giving him a bone with meat on it. He will probably chew it," said a fourth.

The first mother looked at me. I raised my eyebrows. "It's all worth a try," I said.

I had no idea how her child could be encouraged to eat meat. No one had said anything that could harm a child, so I had no need to criticize.

"It's worth trying because he needs the iron." I slipped that in quickly.

She nodded.

Another woman took her place with her two-month-old baby girl in her arms and another child, a boy about two, at her knee.

I checked my records. The two-year-old didn't require anything. His immunizations were up-to-date. But the baby needed her first shot. I attended to it. The baby cried, but just a protest, not the wail of pain from a barbed needle. The toddler cried in sympathy.

Mrs. Sorenson handed the toddler a cookie, and the baby dove into her mother's breast and suckled while we talked. I'd never seen anyone in the city do that. It seemed like a good idea. The baby certainly thought so and was quiet.

I wrote down the immunization information in the child's blue book, gave it to the mother, and noted it in my records. We used an individual card file for each child, and this family's envelope was thick.

"How many children do you have, Mrs. Deacon?" I asked.

"Ten." She stared at me as if daring me to comment.

"Ten," I repeated, a little in awe of her. She looked to be about forty.

She jiggled the baby a little and sat straighter in her chair, her dark hair straggling down her back, her hands holding the baby red and chapped. "I tell you, Nurse, nothing seems to keep me from getting pregnant. I nurse my babies until they are almost in school, and I still get pregnant."

"Uh, nursing doesn't prevent pregnancy." I knew that much. It was surprising what a strong myth that was.

Mrs. Deacon plowed on as if I hadn't spoken. "And then nothing lets me get rid of them. I was up on the roof shovelling off the snow with this one, hoping I'd fall. No such luck." She snorted.

I had a moment of shock but recovered fast. She was cuddling her daughter. She may not have wanted the baby, but she seemed bonded with her now.

Once she started on her grievance, she seemed determined to expound on it. "There's got to be better birth control than trying to get the old man so drunk he can't perform." Her voice was flat but hard. I noticed her hands shaking, jostling the baby a little. I thought she was probably shaking more from anger than anxiety.

There were murmurs of agreement around the table.

Mrs. Deacon was still talking. "I told him I'm going to cut it off and nail it to the woodshed. I'm that tired of being pregnant." She was so emphatic I was almost convinced she'd do it. I could see the lurid headlines in the local paper: Local Woman Resorts to Primitive Birth Control.

The women laughed, but I heard her desperation.

"I'll bring information next time," I promised.

"Yeah. Yeah. You do that. I'm that fed up, I tell you."

A small woman with two children hovering around her said quietly. "I could use that information."

I nodded. "I'll bring it."

I did know about diaphragms, but I didn't know if all the doctors fitted them. Getting fitted for a diaphragm meant travelling to Williams Lake, sixty miles from Black Creek. That trip wouldn't happen often for these women. I mentally cursed my university for giving me such a scanty education about this. How could they have missed teaching us about it? It was essential information out here.

"And there's no point in telling us about condoms," Mrs. Deacon said. "My guy won't use them. Seems like it's not masculine or something. There should be a condom women could use."

I agreed. Maybe there was. I needed to find out. I felt sorry for Mrs. Deacon who had more children than she wanted. She should have more choice.

The women dispersed and the men who had been working in the mill filed in for lunch. Mrs. Sorenson invited me to join them. She served me a huge lunch of steak, potatoes, and vegetables. Her son sat next to me, a handsome guy, blond and fit. He had flown to Williams Lake and back in his own plane and told me about it. I was entranced by the idea of flying over this wild country. I wondered if I could learn to do that. It would be dangerous but exciting.

What I said was, "That sounds pretty fascinating."

He looked at me, raised his eyebrows, and said cynically, "I suppose you want a ride?"

I was suddenly embarrassed. I hadn't been angling for an invitation. "No," I said. "I wasn't looking for that."

I could tell he didn't believe me. He was about my age and good-looking, and, since he owned a plane, obviously had more money than most people. He was probably used to women pursuing him. I wasn't the least bit attracted—too blond, too gorgeous, and much too smooth. But there wasn't any way I could tell him that without being offensive. I sipped my coffee. This was awkward. Mrs. Sorenson hovered in the background. I had to conduct a clinic here every month. Better she thought I was enamoured of her son than annoyed by him. I truly wanted to prick his ego and thought of some choice insults I could throw at him, but discretion and the ethos of professional behaviour overruled my more honest reactions. I smiled, ground my teeth, and went back to my meal.

I stopped at the Black Creek School, tested eyes, and checked teeth. I spent only a few minutes at the Miocene School, another one-room school with only twelve students. When I was finished, I was free to return to Williams Lake, my three-day trip completed. I felt a lightening of my spirits, a feeling of returning from an adventure. It had been my first trip on my own, and I had managed it. About twenty miles west of Horsefly, well past the Beaver Valley turnoff, and about forty minutes from Williams Lake—just when I thought I was almost home—I felt the car lurch, heard an ominous thump, and felt the shudder of a flat tire. It's a wonder I didn`t have one earlier considering how rough the roads had been. The baby scale jangled in the back seat. I pulled over and looked at the tire. Yup. Flat. My dad had taught me how to change a tire, but I'd never done it without his supervision. I had the theory down, just not the practice.

I wrestled the spare from the trunk and laid it on the ground. I found the jack and pulled it out. As an independent nurse in the wild country of British Columbia, I was supposed to look after my own problems. I just wish I didn't have to struggle with a flat tire. I was studying the car to see where I should put the jack when a truck eased off the road and parked behind me.

A man climbed out from the driver's seat. Jason. I'd met him last week when Dorrie took me to the bar in Williams Lake. He was the one who had told me about the logging industry. He was my age, sandy hair, blue eyes, polite, and pleasant.

"Hi, Jason."

"Got a problem, Marion?" He nodded at my car.

I smiled. "Flat tire."

"Glad to fix that for you." He smiled at me and I realized he really *was* happy to help me. He found a couple of rocks and put them behind the front tires, positioned the jack, and hoisted up the car. He jerked the flat tire off the rim and put on the spare. He tightened the nuts on the wheel and then lowered the car. It took strength to do that, so I was glad he'd come along. He retightened the nuts when the car was resting on the tire. It looked easy when he did it. If I had tried, I'd be still struggling to loosen the wheel nuts. He was crouched, tightening the nuts, and almost finished changing the tire, when he turned to me and said, "Would you like to marry me?"

I stared. I'd met him once before. *Once!*

I stalled. "Um... Um. That's very flattering, Jason. Very flattering." I stalled a little more and thought hard. "You're sure attractive and a nice guy, but I'm just starting my career, and I'm not ready to get married for several years yet. I'm thinking of going back to university for my master's degree. I'm not ready to settle."

"Ah," he said. "You have a degree already? I didn't know you were so brainy."

Most nurses did not have degrees, only about eight percent of us. He'd assumed I was hospital trained as most were.

"Yeah, pretty brainy," I said. "It's a bit of a curse sometimes."

"I can see that. You might be real old before you're ready to get married."

"That's true." I might be twenty-five or twenty-six.

He dropped the jack back into the trunk and hoisted the flat tire in beside it. I gulped down an almost irresistible impulse to laugh.

"Now, you get this to the gas station right away and get them to fix it. You don't want to be travelling without a spare." He was as easygoing now as he had been when he stopped to help me.

"I'll do that, and thanks very much."

"It's no trouble. I'll follow you to the gas station." He seemed to take my refusing his proposal without rancour. Maybe he proposed to someone once a week.

I smiled. "You're a nice man, Jason."

He grinned. "I'll make someone a good husband?"

"You will." He probably would if he got over his propensity for proposals.

"See you in town."

I waved and got into my car. There must be very few eligible women in this country for a man to propose marriage after one meeting. I wasn't so stunningly attractive he couldn't help himself. Maybe he thought I was suitable. Still, I'd like to let Mrs. Sorenson's supercilious, smug son know someone thought I was irresistible. An accusation of vamping in the morning and a marriage proposal in the afternoon. Were most days going to be like this?

CHAPTER FIVE

MEETING THE RANCHER

I DROPPED THE TIRE at the gas station, beeped a thank you to Jason, and drove to the health unit parking lot at about five-thirty. Everyone had left for the day, probably on the dot of five. Occasionally a nurse stayed later, recording immunizations, writing letters, or planning programs, but not today. Quiet settled over the reception area, the clinic room, and the offices. I called out a "Hello." No one answered. Late afternoon sun streamed through the window into my office. As inviting as the room seemed—so quiet, clean, and private—I didn't stay. I dumped my records on my desk and hauled my aluminium suitcase to the lab where the autoclaving and cleanup took place. I put the vaccines in the fridge and left the suitcase open so Anna-Lise, our health unit lab assistant, could see I had finished with it. It was a treat to have someone else tidy up after me.

I was too late for dinner at Mrs. Sharpe's. "Five-thirty on the dot, or you can do without," she had said. So I stopped in at Wong's Café for a quick dish of chow mein and vegetables. I was halfway through the meal and sipping my green tea when Sam arrived. He looked as tired as I felt. He smiled.

"Join you?" he asked.

"Sure." I nodded at the empty chair across from me. The room held six small tables and one large one. Bright pictures in reds and golds hung on the yellow walls. I could hear the clatter of pots and pans from behind the divider at the back of the room and the melodious rise and fall of rapid Chinese. The spicy smell of soy sauce hung in the air.

Mr. Wong appeared at our table. He was short, wiry, and taciturn. "The usual?" he asked Sam.

Sam agreed. Mr. Wong put another cup in front of Sam and poured him some green tea from my pot.

Sam thanked him and turned to me. "I called you, but your Mrs. Sharpe wouldn't take a message and wouldn't say when you'd be home." Sam raised his eyebrows.

"I was out in the district for three days. Mrs. Sharpe is hopeless. You'd best call me at the health unit." Nice that he wanted to see me again. I could be interested in Sam.

"That's okay? They don't mind personal calls?" He gulped his tea without waiting for it to cool.

"Everyone knows what my landlady is like."

"What did you do out in the district?" He nodded his thanks when Mr. Wong put his order in front of him.

I told him about my work and the beauty of the country. I didn't tell him about Arlie Sanders. Sam had enough drama and death in his own world. He didn't want to talk about the troubles of his world either and told me about some of his trials, learning to ride a horse.

"I figure I'm in ranching country now and might as well acclimatize. I have a friend who has a ranch nearby, and he's trying to teach me to stay on the horse's back." His food disappeared as if inhaled.

"Any luck so far?"

He shrugged. "A little."

"You'll probably enjoy it, and at least no one can call you or demand attention when you're on the back of a horse." I imagined it felt like freedom to him—no responsibilities except to himself and the horse.

"That's the plan."

We ate, conversing easily until we were both just sipping tea. It was cozy and oddly intimate. Mr. Wong had replenished the pot twice.

I looked over at the people at the nearby tables. There was a family, a couple of women, and a single man in the corner. He looked a little drunk, swaying in his seat. Suddenly, he stood. He was a tall man built like one of those bulls I'd seen at the 4-H sale, all shoulders and muscle. He bellowed, "I'm gonna have me some—"

I don't know what he was after, but Mr. Wong, all five feet three inches of him, sidled up beside the man, did something to his neck and arm, and had him out the door in seconds.

I blinked. "What was that?"

Sam grinned. "Martial arts of some kind."

"Pretty effective." Mr. Wong had impressive talent.

The family in the corner looked up but went back to talking and ignored the incident.

"Most people know better than to cause a disturbance at Wong's," Sam said.

"I can see why." I stared at Mr. Wong who, seemingly unperturbed, picked up empty dishes from the man's table.

Sam pulled out his wallet. "Let me get this?"

"No, Sam, please." I smiled. "I can look after my own." This wasn't a date.

"Okay, this time. How about letting me take you out? Say Friday? There's a country and western band coming to the bar at the Ranch Hotel. Someone said there'd be dancing. Want to go?"

"Hmm. Yes, I'd like to do that." It was time I started dating.

"Great." He stood.

I put my hand on his arm to stop him. "Sam, do you mind if I bring Dorrie with us? I haven't seen her all week, and she's been really generous in taking me out several times." I'd find out quickly if he was someone who would pay attention to what I wanted.

He was silent for a moment. "That'd be fine. I'll get my rancher friend Carl to come with us. Even it out."

I was sure Dorrie would agree to that. "Okay. Just phone tomorrow at the health unit to check with me, and I'll make sure Dorrie doesn't have other plans."

"I'll do that." He waved and left.

Dorrie didn't have other plans. "Sounds like a blast. You and the doctor and me and the rancher. Ideal."

"It'll be pretty relaxed, Dorrie. I don't know Sam very well and the rancher not at all." It would be a casual date. We weren't going to be paired up for life.

"I'll behave," she promised.

"Just be yourself," I reassured her. "It will be great to have you. Make that first date easier for me."

Sam confirmed the next day. On Friday, Dorrie and I dressed in a flurry of skirts, heels, and dangling earrings. We were ready when Carl's truck arrived.

Mrs. Sharpe allowed the men into the front room, but no further.

"Don't be late," she said as we were leaving.

I turned and looked at her. I was not a teenager. She was not my mother. I hadn't left home to be treated like a child. "Mrs. Sharpe, I do not have a curfew. My hours are my own business and none of yours."

She reeled back as if I'd hit her. I felt an instant of shame—she was old, after all—and then decided that I was justified in doing something to keep her from controlling our lives.

Sam looked startled. Carl grinned.

Before we had exchanged more than brief introductions, we were settled around a small table at the bar with the music blasting away. Carl turned out to be Carl Peterson. He was about twenty-six or twenty-seven, five ten, and wore cowboy boots and a stetson, like Rita's husband. They went well with his clean jeans and sports shirt. Maybe all ranchers dressed like that. He had green eyes, ash-brown hair, and was more stocky than slim. Sam looked athletic and dark compared to him, wearing jeans and a sports shirt. Dorrie looked glorious with her auburn hair spilling over her shoulders in waves. She was slightly plump, had a voluptuous figure, creamy skin, and eyes sparkling with enthusiasm.

"I'll have a beer," she said, "and then I want to dance."

"I'd be much obliged," a stranger said as he stopped at our table, "if you'd dance with me."

"Sure thing." Dorrie bounced up and was whisked away.

Sam blinked.

Carl laughed. "I'll get the beer. What are you having?" he asked me.

"Just a glass of pilsner," I said.

He took Sam's order and disappeared toward the crowd at the bar.

"Ma'am." Another man stopped in front of our table. "Could I have this dance?"

I smiled. I had no idea who he was. "Not this one, thanks. I'd like to get my drink first. Come back in a half-hour, and we'll have that dance."

"That's a promise," he said and moved away.

"I didn't realize," Sam said, "that all the men in the bar would want to dance with you two. Maybe we should have gone to a movie?"

I laughed. "Let's just go with the flow here. I promise we'll leave with you. At least, I promise for myself."

Sam shook his head. "That Dorrie. She's a butterfly."

I noticed his eyes following Dorrie as she polkaed around the room. It was a lively dance, and she was good at it. Her partner deposited her at our table just as Carl returned with the beer.

"Good timing." She raised her glass. "To new friends."

We followed suit. It was a loud, raucous, and exhausting evening, but a lot of fun. I danced with Sam only twice but managed four dances with Carl.

"Never again," Sam complained on the way home. "I'm not taking a woman to a bar full of men, so she can dance the night away with someone else."

"Oh, stop complaining," Dorrie said. "There were two of us with you, and I danced with you three times."

"You did," Sam said. "True enough."

Carl drove into the gravel parking lot at Mrs. Sharpe's house at about two in the morning. Sam and I got out and left Carl and Dorrie in the truck.

"Thanks, Sam. That was fun." We managed an affectionate kiss. I might not be very experienced, but I knew when a kiss was affectionate and when it was passionate.

"I had fun, too," Sam said. "Uh, Marion..."

"Uh-huh?"

"Your friend Dorrie?" He looked embarrassed.

"You're attracted to her." I'd seen the way his eyes had followed her at the bar.

"Yeah. Really." And this was the man who had fallen off the bleachers when he met me. I hoped he wasn't a butterfly himself.

"Go for it, Sam. She'll be good for you, and she has a generous heart. You'll appreciate her." The kiss test made it obvious we weren't going to have a romantic future.

He smiled. "You have a generous heart yourself."

I left him on the steps and went in. Dorrie followed me a few moments later. We tiptoed up the stairs to my room and shut the door. Dorrie flopped onto the bed.

"Carl is a nice man."

"He seems to be," I said.

"Sam is an exciting man. You're so lucky." She sighed.

"Sam is an exciting man to you. He's just a friend to me."

"Really?" She looked straight at me, her eyes wide.

"Really." I nodded.

"I should go after him?" she persisted.

"Maybe let him go after you. He's interested." I was no expert on romance, but I thought Sam was interested enough in Dorrie to do the pursuing.

"Is he? There's a thought." She stretched. "What a night. I'm sleeping in tomorrow. Monday comes too soon. You're coming to my school on Monday?"

I yawned. "I'll have to check my schedule, but I think so."

MONDAY SAW me at Williams Lake Elementary where Dorrie taught grade five. The principal, Hannah Harbinger, took charge.

"Lots for you to do here," she said as she toured me around the school. "We have quite a few students whose fathers are mill employees and quite a few whose parents are ranchers, professionals, or who work in retail. A mix of people, and I try to make sure they do mix here. There will be no segregation in my school."

"No families without jobs?"

She shook her head. "Everybody's working."

She showed me an impressive library. "Books. The most important part of the community."

And then the staff room. "You can talk to the teachers in this room. They spend recesses and noon hours here unless they are on playground supervision. You do the vision and hearing screening, the immunizations, and any referrals for impetigo, scabies, and lice."

"No lice," I said firmly.

"What do you mean, 'No lice?' The nurses always check for lice."

"Not this nurse, Mrs. Harbinger. Lice are not a disease threat. They are not a public health problem. They are a pest." I had a lot of experience in my practicum avoiding examining kids for lice.

"They cause a lot of stress. That makes them a mental health problem," she argued.

I knew teachers wanted nurses to manage lice, but it wasn't a good use of our time, and it wasn't our mandate.

"I'm willing to instruct the teachers on how to look for lice, or you can hire a retired nurse, or even an interested, untrained parent to do that job. Why don't we wait until we see if there is a problem?" I held my voice firm. I had to win at least one argument with Mrs. Harbinger, or she would run my life here.

I was going to have this fight with every school. It wouldn't be much of a problem with those schools I visited once a month, but Mrs. Harbinger probably would expect me every week.

Dorrie flew in at recess and asked if I'd help with her Girls Club. She was trying to get the grade five female students interested in careers. Most students around Williams Lake—girls and boys—didn't go on to university or further education of any kind. She wanted the girls to see they could earn their own money and create their own lives. It was an uphill battle, and she thought I'd be a good role model.

"What would I talk about?" I worried a little. Grade five girls might be daunting.

"Maybe tell them about the important women you know and what they do." Dorrie had given this her attention. When it came to teaching, she was dedicated and serious.

"I'll think about it." I liked the idea of trying to instill some ambition into the young girls. Was that public health? I thought it was time better spent than chasing lice.

The days sped by with well-baby clinics, school visits, home visits to check on the health of newborns, visits to check on the elderly who were alone in their houses or their remote cabins, and travelling to find my way to all the small schools in my huge district. When I went to a school, I might find that the teacher had a message for me: someone occasionally asked if I'd stop in and make sure her mother had enough to eat and enough firewood. Technically, that was the social worker's job, but I rarely saw a social worker in the outlying areas. I looked at it as preventative medicine and made the visit. I tried to find Audrey Cook, the little girl with the negative TB test. I asked the other nurses, but no one knew the family.

I had three big schools: two in Williams Lake, and the other in Lac la Hache, which was sixty miles south, and I stopped at several small schools between them. It took a lot of organization, so I was busy.

In the middle of October, Rita asked me to dine with her family on a Saturday night.

"Come in the afternoon, and we'll get you up on horseback. You're in the Cariboo now."

I hadn't told Rita I knew how to ride, and I wasn't going to tell her. She might get an overblown idea of my competence.

"You don't mind if I invite neighbours?" she asked.

"No, not at all. I'd like to meet your neighbours."

The following Saturday, I arrived at Jim and Rita's ranch, the Lazy Seven, driving the government car. No one seemed to mind that I treated it as my private vehicle. Rita and her daughter Millie met me as I pulled into the yard. I'd worn jeans, a shirt, and my runners. I didn't own cowboy boots.

Rita frowned at my footwear. "What size?"

"Seven."

"You should have your own boots," Millie advised me critically. "You can get blisters from other people's boots."

"For today, she can borrow," Rita said. "I have a pair around here somewhere." She rooted in a bin that seemed to have about forty shoes in it, muttering under her breath and banging the shoes against the side of the bin. She came up with a pair of battered cowboy boots. I sat in her mud room and pulled them on. They fit.

"Good. You need the heels to be secure in the saddle." She dusted her hands on her jeans and nodded with satisfaction.

Feeling like someone in a western movie, I followed Millie outside.

The ranch was set in a narrow valley with fir-covered hills on either side. The Fraser River ran nearby. Fences delineated corrals and pastures, and beyond the fences lay a long ribbon of alfalfa fields. Behind me I saw cattle still grazing on the last of the summer grass.

"No snow yet," I said to Millie. The air was crisp. I wore a jacket, but I wasn't cold.

"Not yet." She flicked her blonde braids and hopped on the back of a huge stallion, saddled and waiting. "This is Captain."

My horse, Penny, was much smaller and, I hoped, quieter.

"Cattle are so stupid with snow," Millie called back to me.

I mounted Penny and followed Millie and Captain from the corral to a dirt lane.

"When it snows, they just stand there and wait for someone to feed them. Horses now," she patted Captain's neck. "They paw to get at the grass. They won't starve."

She led me up into the hills and onto a high meadow. I caught the scent of pine pitch from the stand of lodgepole pine at the edge of the meadow. It was much colder here and more open. Millie dug her heels into Captain and sent him into a gallop. I followed. My body remembered how to ride, and I thrilled to the speed of the gallop. Some horses have a rough gallop and throw you around in the saddle, but Penny's was smooth, and we flew along the trail. Trees blurred at the edge of my vision. The wind streamed through my hair. It was glorious. Millie pulled up Captain at the end of the meadow and looked back at me.

"You can ride. Mum said you couldn't." She sounded disappointed.

I shrugged and grinned. "I'm no expert."

"You're good enough. We can go a little faster going home," Millie said.

We trotted most of the way. While my body remembered how to ride, my muscles weren't used to it, and I was glad to see the ranch buildings.

"Just take her to the shed," Millie said. "I have to put Captain into the corral over there." She pointed. "We have one mare in heat, and Captain might smell her if I let him into the shed."

Beyond the shed, horses were drinking from a trough. One was thrusting its nose under the fence, trying to eat a small tuft of grass just beyond its reach. As I neared the shed, I trotted Penny into the yard and slowed her to a walk. A man stood waiting for me. Carl. Was Carl one of the neighbours?

"Hi. Have a good ride?" He smiled up at me.

"I did." I swung off Penny and held the reins in my hand.

"Looking good," he said. I wasn't sure if he meant me or the horse, or me *and* the horse.

Suddenly, I heard Captain scream, a high almost trumpet-like blast, and then Millie yelled.

Penny shifted nervously. I turned to see Captain tearing along the corral, pulling against the reins, ignoring Millie's efforts to control him.

"He's caught the scent of the mare." Carl took the reins from my hand and swung up on Penny.

Rita flew from the back door. She shouted, "Grab the fence, Millie! Grab the fence and get off!"

Captain was heading for the corral gate and the mare beyond it. Either he'd jump it or he'd crash through it. Millie had given up trying to pull back on the reins and was watching for a chance to get off. Carl sent Penny into a gallop alongside Captain. He crowded Captain toward the corral fence. Captain was still heading for the gate, but he was closer to the fence now. Carl drove Penny almost in front of Captain and forced the stallion to a sudden, momentary stop.

"Now!" Carl yelled at Millie.

Millie jumped from the saddle onto the top rail of the fence. Carl twitched Penny out of Captain's way. Captain darted past, tore to the gate, and sailed over the top. He picked out a mare and herded her away from the others. Then he mounted her—the saddle seemingly no impediment.

Millie had climbed down to the ground. Carl stopped to talk to her. She nodded. He trotted back on Penny to the shed and dismounted in front of me.

"That was close," I said. I was breathing fast and I hadn't moved. Just staring at them had spiked my adrenalin. I watched Millie walk slowly toward the porch where Rita stood waiting. She opened her arms, and Millie ran into them.

Carl watched with me then looked over his shoulder at the stallion. "I hope they wanted that mating. They've got it now."

It had happened so quickly. Millie could have been bucked off and trampled, crushed against the fence, and knocked senseless. I resolutely pushed away those thoughts. She might have been scared, but she was not injured.

Carl and I led Penny into the shed and removed her saddle and bridle, brushed her, picked the dirt from her hooves, and led her into the corral. Carl caught Captain, who was calmer now that he had been successful with the mare. Carl removed the saddle and bridle and let him loose in the pasture. Rita called us to supper. We left our boots at the door and joined the family at the table. I supposed this sort of drama occurred on ranches all the time. There must be all sorts of dangers.

Jim had been down the road, picking up an elderly couple to bring them to dinner, so we were six plus Millie. It was Millie who told the dramatic tale of Captain and the mare. I saw Jim's face turn white. He looked at Carl and raised his glass. "Thanks."

Carl just nodded.

After dinner Rita packed a piece of pie for me and one for Carl to take with us.

"Mrs. Sharpe isn't known for her cooking," she said to me. "And your mum and dad are still away," she said to Carl.

Carl walked me to my car.

"Want to go out Friday night?" he said.

"I have a date." One of the men I'd danced with last weekend had asked me to the movies. He was a new accountant in town. "I can make it Saturday though."

"I'll pick you up at six, if that works. We can go out for dinner."

I pondered my social life as I drove home. It seemed I just had to be female and new in town to be popular. I might as well enjoy it.

CHAPTER SIX

EVADING OFFICIALS

I VISITED ON AVERAGE four newborn babies and their mothers in a week. When mothers opened their doors, their eyes went straight to the heavy baby scale I toted. It looked official, as if the power of the government of British Columbia guaranteed its accuracy. It was more important than I was. That scale was my entry into their homes, so I was grateful for it, and once there, having weighed their babies, I could answer any questions the mothers had, introduce them to the immunization regimen, and address other problems, such as an older child's hearing or a mother's health. I began to feel more confident of my assessments and advice, as if I fitted my uniform more naturally. I had a place in the community, a job to do. I belonged.

Besides baby visits and child health clinics, I was responsible for three large schools and nine smaller ones scattered over 3,600 square miles. I felt a sense of ownership of that country, as if everyone was in my care, but I wasn't the only health professional they saw. People went to doctors in town, to specialists in the city, saw social workers, teachers, and other professionals. They also took medical advice from their neighbours. I overheard one man tell another, "Just use the antibiotics you got for the calf last week. That ought to take care of your pneumonia." It probably would, too.

I expanded my knowledge as I explored the trails and byways, checking on tuberculosis patients, new babies, and the occasional recluse. I loved the small schools tucked away in valleys and beside lakes. I never knew what to expect when I arrived. One teacher with grades one to six in a one-room school ushered me to a chair while the children waited, eyes bright and full of excitement. "We are going to the music festival in Williams Lake next week, Nurse, and we have a poem we are going to recite for the speech competition." They recited it for me. Sometimes they waited to put on a concert or a spelling competition until I came, and I always took the time to listen. I considered those events perks of the job—a relaxing relief.

The six nurses in the health unit met every Monday morning at 9 a.m. to ask questions, support each other, and plan immunization blitzes in the schools. When we immunized the children in a large school, we arranged a date that suited the school, sent out all the parental permissions, and scheduled at least two nurses for the work. It was efficient and disturbed the school less than if one nurse tried to do it all. While none of us enjoyed giving immunizations, we all wanted do to it as quickly and with as little drama as possible. I'd discovered grade five students, in particular, were prone to histrionics, and the quicker we could manage the injections, the better.

I was paired with the nurse Sophie Kubik for some school clinics. She was a treat to work with, and she and I helped one another with our large schools. She was about thirty-five, confident, married, the mother of two, and enthusiastic about her work. She was a graduate of a hospital training school and felt a need to constantly improve her public health knowledge to catch up to the university graduates. She also tried to improve her vocabulary and courageously used words she'd heard but didn't quite understand. I overheard her tell someone that the pain was "execrable" when she meant "excruciating" and that expenses were "perdition" when she meant "per diem." No one corrected her, partly because we were fascinated to hear what she might say next, and partly because we didn't want to embarrass her. She didn't seem to notice the momentary silence after she'd dropped one of those malapropisms as we translated the word and then carried on.

For the most part, the students at Williams Lake Elementary were quiet and cooperative. Sophie set up in one office and I set up in another. Two parents volunteered and went to the classroom and called the children to us five at a time, so no student had to wait nervously in line for very long. As I was looking at the girls waiting in line—who I knew could start egging each other on to hysteria—I failed to notice the panic in the boy whose arm I was holding. I brought the needle close to his arm, and he suddenly reared back, dragging me with him. He was strong and his movement so sudden that I instinctively reacted by holding him tightly. I shoved him against the wall with my hip, held his arm steady, and injected the vaccine in seconds. He had been distracted by the strength of my sudden movement—and I had that needle in and out quickly. I put the syringe behind my back so he couldn't see it and eased him to a standing position.

"You're okay now, Michael. It's all over. You're fine now. Take a deep breath. That's it. You're fine."

"Oh," he stuttered. "Oh. Okay. It's over."

"Take another deep breath now. You will need to take this paper to your parents." I handed him a printed form that told his parents what immunizations he'd received. "Anytime you're apprehensive, take a couple of deep breaths, and let them out slowly before you feel really scared. That helps."

"Yeah. Yeah. Thanks." He grabbed his shattered pride and managed to look normal as he left. He wouldn't want the others to know how frightened he'd been. We were behind the office door, so I don't think the girls had seen.

I sat down in a chair for a moment after he'd left and took a couple of deep breaths myself. Was that assault of a patient? If I had stopped and tried to talk to him, he might have been even more apprehensive. Better to have the injection over with so he didn't have to worry about it anymore. Still, I had physically shoved him. I suppose I'd do that again if I had to because it was easier on the child than waiting in fear.

When we'd finished, we adjourned to the staff room. Sophie set up a new clean work space there, laid out her syringes and vaccines, and asked the staff, "Who's had their tetanus shot lately?" The teachers were as nervous as the students, but they lined up to get their immunizations.

One man, about twenty-five, held up his arm. "Is there anything I shouldn't do after this? Like not play tennis?"

"Right," Sophie said as she brought the needle closer. "No tennis and refrain from sexual intercourse for two weeks," she said with a totally straight face.

"What?" He jerked his arm away and jumped back quickly.

There was a stunned silence. The teachers stared at Sophie. I couldn't contain myself and started to laugh. "It's not true," I reassured everyone. "It's okay."

I heard a collective sigh, and then the staff also began to laugh. Sophie stood waiting with the syringe in her hand and grinning.

That was Sophie, often unprofessional but spontaneous and fun. She sometimes did what I only thought of doing. I helped Sophie at her school, and we got the immunizations out of the way early in the school year.

ONE DAY, Rita made an announcement. She stood in the doorway of my office, papers in her hand.

"We're going to start a pilot project on home care. We're going to try and persuade the doctors to discharge patients from the hospital to their homes and send in a home care nurse. At first, it will just be for dressing changes, wound care, and suture removals, but it may develop into something more complicated."

"This is coming as a directive from Victoria?" I asked. Victoria, 350 miles away, was the headquarters of our public health service, and, like the tsar in *Fiddler on the Roof,* best kept a long way from us.

"It is, and we are one of two health units that are going to pilot it. I want you to hire two nurses, RNs, who can work just in the town area. Well, I'll hire them, but I want you to read their resumes and tell me who you think would be best." She left the printed material describing the goals and limits of the service on my desk.

Rita advertised, and only two nurses responded: Kate Jones, who was my age and who had worked on medical wards for three years, and Sally Roche, about fifty, who had worked as a public health nurse years ago and then, casually, at the hospital. Rita hired them both.

I enjoyed the challenge of implementing this program. It meant patients could leave the hospital many days earlier than usual. It would be cost-efficient for the health care system and more comfortable for the patients. I met with the doctors and explained it. They were interested. I talked to Anna-Lise, our health unit lab assistant, about the kind of equipment the nurses would require and how often they would need to have their bags refilled. It would make extra work for her, having the dressing and suture sets ready. The first problem was we didn't have enough equipment. For now, I'd ignore that. We had our first home care meeting in my office.

Kate was about five foot four with short red hair and dressed in slacks and a sweater. She was tidy and seemed serious and attentive. Sally was about the same height but wore jeans and a plaid shirt and seemed full of humour, as if this home care job was a new adventure.

I had a list of patients and assigned the nurses to their case loads. We organized the days they would work in order to cover the weekends. I didn't work on weekends, but I was willing to be available on the phone. That meant persuading Mrs. Sharpe to take a message—which was another challenge. She reluctantly agreed to do so. I impressed upon her the notion that it could be life and death. I doubted a dressing change would ever be that crucial, but I needed drama to get Mrs. Sharpe to cooperate.

While Victoria had provided the budget for the home care nurses' salaries, they hadn't provided any money for the equipment we'd need. I made an appointment with Nan Morrice, the director of nursing, at the hospital. Nan managed the hospital and the nursing staff. There was no hospital administrator, so she did every-thing. She was about forty, a little overweight, with brown hair and brown eyes, and wore a white uniform with a blue sweater over it. According to Rita, she was very organized. She knew about the pro-gram because Rita had explained it to her. I told her about the lack of equipment. She looked thoughtful for a moment, then stood.

"You should meet Lionel. He manages our supplies."

I followed Nan down the long corridor to a huge room full of hos-pital supplies. Nan conferred with Lionel while I waited by the door.

"Lionel will look after you," Nan said and disappeared toward her office.

Lionel, about sixty, thin, and a little hunched, was the custodian of this room. He showed me the towering shelves of equipment and supplies: suture sets, dressing sets, gauze bandages, four-by-fours. They were exactly what we needed. It was a treasure trove.

"I'm off to coffee now," Lionel said. "I'll be back in twenty minutes."

I stared at his retreating back and then at the bountiful shelves. *All right!* I opened my black bag and grabbed bandages, gauze— anything I thought necessary. I made room in my bag for dressing sets, suture sets, haemostats, tweezers, and scissors, until it was crammed full. I found a pillowcase on a shelf and stuffed it with kidney basins, tubing, clamps, and a large foot basin. We could reuse the metal equipment, autoclaving it at the health unit. I took enough of the disposable supplies to last for a month and would worry about replenishing them later.

I hefted my load and was gone before Lionel returned.

From then on, until the end of the next fiscal year, which was April when Victoria finally increased our budget, I showed up at Lionel's supply room once a month and, while he went to his cof-fee break, took enough from the shelves to keep the home care nurses in business.

By the end of October, the home care program was working smoothly. We had increased our types of patients, with injections of daily insulin for a young woman with a cognitive disorder, colostomy care for a discharged patient, and pain medication for a dying patient. The doctors liked the service, and it was their suggestions that augmented the case load. No one had called me on my off time, and no one had called Rita, who was my backup.

I HAD other nursing programs besides supervising home care and immunizing babies. I made home visits and pursued TB contacts. I still hadn't found little Audrey Cook. Maybe she had moved. Maybe the TB test really had been negative.

"It's time you went to Gang Ranch," Rita said one morning. "There's supposed to be a week of good weather. Can you leave sometime this week and spend a day out there? There's school work, and there's a teenager who is supposed to be at Woodlands, the children's mental health institution in New Westminster. He's got a low IQ, and they think they can give him some education. Anyway, they want bring him to the Coast and assess him."

"They" meant the mental health services.

"What do the parents think?" I asked her.

"Don't know. Here's his file. See what you can find out."

Gang Ranch was about forty miles from Williams Lake, along Dog Creek Road, across the suspension bridge, and on the west side of the Fraser River. It was a gravel road, of course, but through ranch country, not logging country. There wouldn't be many logging trucks. It was the biggest ranch in North America at 37,000 acres.

The topography of the country I drove through was dramatically different from the eastern part of the Cariboo. The low hills and open grasslands rolled miles through the Chilcotin to the west with no barriers until the Coast Mountains, which were out of sight two hundred miles away. The country was brown now, almost bleak, with the occasional stand of stick-like poplar trees. I had the heater blasting in the Chevy as the October day was cold, but there was still no snow. I was comfortable in my car since it was an automatic, easy to drive, and reliable. It didn't have a lot of power, but it managed all the hills. I thought about my car the way I supposed Carl thought about his horse, Pammie. It was my teammate.

I drove past Alkali Reserve, a small community about twenty-five miles from Williams Lake. The reserves had their own federal nurses and were overseen by the federal Department of Indian Affairs, not the provincial health department. I knew the federal nurse, Patricia Stone. We'd had coffee and talked about nursing, but I didn't know the community. I heard the chief and his wife were working on reorganizing the reserve and creating a safe and sober space for their people. I drove on past the Dog Creek store and followed the road high above the Fraser River to Gang Ranch.

The road was narrow, and the Fraser River far down on my right looked like a grey winding ribbon at the bottom of a trough. Gradually the road shrunk to *very* narrow, and clay hills rose to my left. I guided the car cautiously along the cliffs, across the narrow bridge over the Fraser River, and up the clay cliffs on the west side. At one point, the road climbed and turned sharply, and, since I couldn't see beyond the bend, I wasn't sure there was any road there at all. I stopped the car, got out, and peered around it. I had visions of driving around that sharp corner and plunging two hundred feet into the Fraser. But the road was still there. I got back in the car and continued carefully. Once over those hills and onto the plateau, the land flattened. I turned onto the Gang Ranch roadway along a wide bench landscape where the ranch buildings spread over the meadow.

I found the school and met the teacher, Anne Adams. She was about twenty-two, single, and very happy to see me. There wouldn't be many people—particularly young people—here. She had fifteen students, mostly children of the ranch hands whose families lived in the cabins nearby. I examined eyes, checked teeth, and sorted out what immunizations might be needed the next time I came. Anne was enthusiastic about her students and seemed creative. There were art projects on the walls and science experiments on the windowsill.

"I have one family I need to visit here," I told her. "Their last name is MacKay."

She smiled. "Nice family." She nodded to one of the students. "Gordon, when you go home at noon, would you tell your mother the nurse will be coming over?"

Gordon was a handsome First Nations boy, about twelve.

"Yes, miss," he agreed.

I got a description of the cabin where Gordon's family lived and wrote it on the outside of my file folder.

"Do the students go to Williams Lake for high school?" I asked Anne after Gordon left.

"Some of them. They board in town during the week. Most of them don't go anywhere."

We stared at one another. Not going to high school meant subsistence living for the rest of their lives—at least for most of them. I couldn't imagine facing life without some education or skill. "That's awful," I said.

I remember wanting to quit school when I was sixteen. School had become unbearably boring. My dad had lectured me. *"You can be a hairdresser or a doctor or anything you want, I don't care, but you will have some kind of certification, so you can look after yourself."* That seemed eminently reasonable to me, and I gave up the notion of leaving school. Once in university, I found that I loved school and hoped to get a graduate degree at some point.

Anne looked worried. "I feel I have to give them everything I can because that may be all they're going to get. It's a lot of pressure."

I asked her about the owners of the ranch, but she wouldn't talk about them. I got the impression she didn't like them much. But they paid her salary, and she was loyal. This must be a private school. She had to follow the provincial curriculum, though, and a supervisor would come out from Williams Lake to make sure she did.

I dropped in at the main ranch house on a courtesy call to the owners. The woman who answered the door was one of them.

"Yes?" She was trim, about thirty-five, and looked impatient.

I explained who I was. She did not invite me in, just left me standing there, bundled up in my down parka with the icy breeze cooling my cheeks. I got the idea that she saw me as one step above an insurance salesman—someone she hadn't asked to see and didn't want to waste time on. I was disappointed. She would not likely be helpful if I needed to implement health programs. That was the last time I'd stop by without an invitation.

When I pulled into the yard where Mrs. MacKay lived, Gordon was just heading back to school. I waved. He nodded.

Mrs. MacKay invited me in, hung up my parka, and gave me a cup of coffee. She had much better manners than the owner of the ranch. She was short and plump and had the smooth brown skin of her Dakelh people. The cabin was small, probably four rooms, but cozy. In this crisp fall weather, the wood stove was welcome and the smell of baking bread irresistible. While I stirred milk into my coffee, Mrs. MacKay reached into her oven and brought out a tray of baked buns with brown crusty tops. I sniffed appreciatively. She smiled.

"Here," she said and placed one on a plate accompanied by a dish of butter.

I broke open the bun and let the steam escape. Lovely.

"Want some jam with that?" She passed a dish of bright red jam. "Wild strawberry," she said.

"Sure. Thanks." It was delicious.

Another tray of buns was cooling on the counter. Half of them were gone.

"The kids." She waved at the counter.

I nodded, licked my lips, and finished the bun. I reached for my bag and the files.

"I got a letter from Mental Health Services," I said.

Although she hadn't moved, I felt her withdraw. I looked at her.

"Stanley?" I checked to make sure she was his mother.

She nodded.

"They want to send him to Woodlands for assessment."

"No," she said.

"Okay." I closed the file.

"That's it?" she said. "No telling me they know best? No telling me he'll never be able to manage?" She sat down opposite me with the thump of her considerable weight.

I shrugged. "*You* know Stanley. I don't. Is there anything about going for an assessment that you think might help him?"

"No. They wouldn't understand him. He would be lonely down there and too scared to do the assessment right, and they might keep him there. It's a bad place." She stared at me.

I didn't know much about that mental institution. Still, I didn't think an institution would be better than home, although it might have some programs that would help him.

"He's your son. You make the decisions. Want me to find out if there is a way to assess him in Williams Lake? So you can be with him?"

She thought about that.

Her voice softened. "No. He's fine. He's working on the ranch with his dad. He can help with the fencing, ride, and herd the cattle. As long as his dad tells him what to do, he does it. I've got four kids. Everyone loves him here."

And they wouldn't at the institution. She was right about that. I wondered if, when Gordon told his mother I was coming, she'd sent Stanley away. That might be her way of keeping him safe.

"I'll let you know when I'm coming again." I tested out this theory.

She grinned. "You do that."

Ah, that *was* her strategy. It was probably how she'd kept him with her all these years. Just send him off on a horse when anyone official came.

I gestured to her phone. "I could call you."

"My man's the foreman here. The boss gave us a phone." She gave me the number, and I wrote it on the file folder.

"I'll put it in the file that if anyone else comes, they should phone first." That might keep Stanley safe until the powers that be forgot about him or he grew too old to be under their jurisdiction.

"Good idea."

I didn't think Mental Health Services could apprehend Stanley. He was fifteen, after all. But Indigenous people were subjected to abuses, and one of the threats to them was police taking children from their families and putting them in religious residential schools. There was one of those just outside of Williams Lake. Gordon was lucky not to be there.

"Your kids go to school here," I said, trying to find out why.

"My man is white."

We sat in silence. Indigenous children were torn from their families, and these children were protected only because their father was white. If the parents were married, the mother and children lost their status and were no longer considered "Indian" under the Indian Act. Legally, that is. Socially, was as different matter. Where I grew up, there were few Indigenous families, but here in the Cariboo there were many, and I was starting to see how differently they were treated.

As far as I could tell, Stanley was better off on the ranch working with his dad. I didn't think any social worker or mental health worker would contribute to his happiness. Anyway, it wasn't my decision—it was Mr. and Mrs. MacKay's, and they'd made it. The advantage to living forty miles from Williams Lake on a huge ranch was that Stanley could hide out here indefinitely.

"I'll write a report recommending that he stay here and not go to the institution. I don't know if it will make any difference, but maybe they'll stop asking about him," I said firmly.

"Thanks." She was silent for a moment. Then, "Have another bun," she said.

I did.

CHAPTER SEVEN

WORKING IN THE OUTLYING COUNTRY

OVEMBER IN THE Cariboo was cold. At times the temperature dropped to ten degrees below freezing. Rita promised me it would be much colder in January. It was cold enough for me now. If there was any spot on my body that wasn't covered, the cold found it: at the wrist edges of my gloves, between my neck scarf and the top of my parka, at my ears if my toque wasn't pulled down. My Chevy gave a disgruntled cough when I turned the key to start it in the morning, in spite of its overnight connection to electricity through the block heater. I had to scrape ice from the windows.

Everyone dressed for the cold, looking like a blimp with boots. Everyone's car looked like a frost-covered alien vehicle for the first hour of the day until the interior heater defrosted the windows and then it looked like an alien vehicle with eyes. The compensation for the dropping temperatures was the almost constant sun. Bright days lifted my spirits. There was a dusting of snow but nothing like what I had anticipated until the day before I was due to go out on my three-day Likely–Horsefly–Black Creek trip. I awoke on the day I was leaving to see the countryside covered in about four inches of snow.

"I phoned the Department of Highways." Rita caught me as I was loading my car with supplies. "They've cleared the Likely Road, and they're starting on the Horsefly Road. With luck, they'll get to Beaver Valley, and it all will be clear for you when you get there."

"I hope so." November was just the beginning of the cold weather. I might as well get out in it, or I'd stay home until April.

"You have chains," Rita said. "Do you know how to put them on?"

I nodded. It was another thing my dad had taught me, although I'd rather not have to do it. It involved lying on my back and reaching for dangling pieces of cold chain and hooking them together around the tires. I'd get wet and dirty.

"Pack a candle," Rita said.

"What for?"

"If you get stuck somewhere, crack the window of your car, and light the candle. The crack will allow you oxygen, and the candle will give some heat. It's not cold enough yet to worry about freezing to death, though."

I thought about that as I drove out of town. It wasn't cold enough *yet*. That meant it would be cold enough to freeze to death at some point. I had no phone and no radio communication with me. If I got stuck somewhere, I would either have to dig myself out or wait for someone to find me. My official emergency strategy was "Pack a candle." I should have been afraid but I wasn't. Everyone who lived out in the Cariboo Mountains or in the vast ranch lands of the Chilcotin travelled to and from town under these same conditions, and freezing to death was rare. I would manage, but I'd get a candle from Mary when I got to Likely—just in case.

The grader had plowed the Likely Road, creating a clear path with no obstacles—only the usual nerve-wracking concern about oncoming logging trucks. I pulled over for a couple of them and steered back on the road without getting stuck in the snow piles on the sides. The Chevy was a back-wheel drive as were most cars, and, if I took the corners too quickly, the car tended to fish-tail on the melted snow. Dad had taught me how to drive into a skid, so I stayed on the road, but the car bucked a bit as I wrestled it into a straight line. At the top of the hill before Likely, I stopped, got out, and checked the road. It was clear and not icy. I put the car into low gear and drove slowly down to the bridge. I wondered what this hill would be like in February.

THE SCHOOL teachers were happy to see me and the school kids were cooperative. When I dropped by to see Mrs. Kelsey to give her the vitamin B injection, she was her usual morose self. I ate an excellent dinner, cooked and served by Mary, at the Likely Lodge. I was relaxing with a cup of coffee when a man sidled up to me and spoke out of the corner of his mouth.

"I need a shot, Nurse."

I looked at him a little stupidly. I didn't have a file on him and couldn't think what he wanted. He was about fifty, short, and wore a plaid shirt and heavy jeans, which had seen a lot of sawdust recently. He leaned closer. "The clap, Nurse. I've got the clap."

"Oh, sure." Gonorrhea. There was a lot of that about. "Come with me."

I took him into Mary's office, a tiny cubbyhole below the stairs, and offered him a chair.

"I'll get my bag," I said and retreated to my room.

I'd worked in the venereal disease clinic at the health unit in Williams Lake, and I regularly wandered around town looking for people who had been named by patients as sexual contacts. I checked with bartenders who were discreet and helpful. I traced relatives and asked for information. Because I was obvious in my uniform, patients approached me as I left the bar or the café where I'd been having coffee. I made sure I was available on the streets on Friday afternoons. If I was successful in tracing people, we returned to the clinic, and I gave the penicillin they needed. Most sufferers went to their own doctors for treatment. The doctors sent a report to the health unit and expected the public health nurses to find the contacts and treat them. Here so far from town, this man could pass the gonococci to others before he drove in for treatment. It was obviously best if I gave him antibiotics here.

I pulled out the penicillin I had with me and a blank piece of paper. I didn't have the correct form to fill out, but I could remember most of what I needed to know. I shut the door of the office. He dropped his trousers and I gave the shot into his glute muscle.

Then I sat down and wrote his name, age, and asked for contacts.

"My wife," he said.

I reached into my bag and pulled out a vial of penicillin tablets.

"Is she allergic to anything?"

"No."

"Give her these."

He then named a woman in Williams Lake. I recognized the name. It came up often when I was looking for contacts—so often I expect she was charging for her services. I didn't ask. Charging for sex was illegal, and I wasn't the least bit interested in bringing legal proceedings against anyone. The minute any health professional did that, word would get around, and no one would come to us for treatment.

"Anyone else?"

He shook his head.

"Symptoms aren't as obvious in women as they are in men," I said. "You'll need to be sure your wife takes these as she can get quite sick. If she isn't treated, she can reinfect you."

He looked resigned and almost pathetic. "She's going to be so mad."

I bet she was.

He stood, looked down at me for a moment, and gestured to the paper. "That girl. You'll look after her?"

I smiled at him. "Yes, I'll see to it." It was kind of him to worry about her. He might have been angry she gave him the disease, but he wanted to be sure she was helped. Then the cynical side of my brain popped out a thought. *Maybe he wanted to be sure she was disease-free, so he could meet her again?* Well, that was practical. I'd offer her treatment when I returned to town. She was going to give me a lot of work tracing her other contacts.

THE NEXT morning, the roads had been cleared through Beaver Valley, so I stopped at the school on time and went on to Horsefly without any vehicle trouble or delays. Horsefly School was in the centre of town, surrounded by a large playing field, now covered in snow. I stashed my purse, parka, and boots in the staff room and went to work. I screened students for hearing on this visit as well as the grade ten students for visual acuity.

One six-foot tall, hulky young man did not pass the vision test.

"Looks like you have trouble seeing," I said.

"I'm okay."

He obviously did not want to know he had vision problems.

I showed him his screening results. "You need to go to town and get your eyes tested for glasses."

"I'm not wearing glasses!" He drew himself up to his full height, as if he needed to be ready for an attack.

I studied him for a moment. "Do you hunt?"

"Yeah."

"What do you hunt?"

"Moose. Deer."

"Here's the thing, Jason. If you're hunting with friends, they can see the moose at 200 yards; you have to be 20 yards from it to see it. Guess who's going to get the first shot?"

He stared at me. "Glasses would let me see it at 200 yards?"

I solemnly promised him they would.

He was quiet for a moment, then jerked his head. "Okay, then."

The hearing test produced a problem with a girl in grade eight. I asked her to come to the staff room to talk to me about it, as there was no one there. It was quiet, and we could be private.

"Did you notice you have difficulty hearing?" I asked her. Most of the time kids and even adults didn't notice hearing loss as they had always experienced it and thought of it as normal. Or it had come on gradually, and they'd become accustomed to not hearing.

She could hear me speak. Her loss wasn't so severe she heard nothing. I expected that in a quiet environment, with only one person speaking, she would do fine.

I continued. "When there are many people talking, you can't figure out what they are saying?"

She nodded, her eyes huge.

"When the television is on or the radio, it's hard to hear?"

She stared at me. "That's right. If the television's on, and my mum talks to me, I don't know what she says." She looked down and was quiet for a moment and then faced me again. "Is there something wrong with my ears? You're saying I can't hear?"

I looked at her screening test, turned it around, and showed it to her.

"This is the hearing level you need. This is your result, quite a bit below the usual hearing level."

"I can't hear," she repeated.

"Is this a shock to you?" I was starting to get a little worried about her. Perhaps I should have gone home and broken this news when her parents were around.

Then she looked at me and suddenly smiled. I'd thought of her as a bit of a mouse, head bent and hair hanging over her eyes, but she straightened, threw her head back, and shoved her hair away from her face. Her bright blue eyes sparkled. "I can't hear. I can't hear. I really can't hear." She looked straight at me. "I thought I was stupid!"

What a belief to bear. I wondered how long she'd had to deal with that? I shook my head. "No. Not stupid. Just hearing impaired."

She settled back in her chair and beamed at me. "I'd rather be deaf than stupid."

I smiled. "Me too."

I gave her a form letter to take home to her parents, asking them to take her to town for an assessment.

"You'd better tell my mum about this. She won't go to town until spring if it isn't important."

I took down the directions to her house and promised to visit her mum that afternoon. She didn't live far from the school. I could make the visit before I finished for the day.

Her house was a big log one with a large porch. It probably had three or four bedrooms. Her mother was in her late thirties, a little plump, obviously busy as I smelled bread baking, and there were stacks of laundry on the floor.

She glanced at the health department decal on my car door. "Nurse," she said. "Come in."

"Mrs. Decker?"

"Yes."

"I came to talk to you about Caroline."

"She's sick?"

"No, no. She isn't."

"Oh, good, come in. Coffee?"

I sat at the kitchen table and accepted the coffee. I showed her the hearing screening test.

"You're telling me she's deaf?" She stared.

"Not completely or even severely. She just doesn't hear what others do. My screening is just a rough one. She'll need a more detailed and accurate assessment in town. Then she might need a hearing aid. I can't know what kind of hearing loss she has, so I can't know if a hearing aid will help. Perhaps even sitting at the front of the classroom or closer to the television would help. You can make sure she is close enough to you when you talk to her with the light on your face. That way she can read your lips."

Her mother seemed stunned. She shook her head, took a long drink of coffee, and put the cup down with deliberation. "Deaf. She's deaf. And I've blamed her for years for ignoring me. I thought she didn't care about me and didn't pay attention to me, and all the time she couldn't *hear* me."

I sat silently as I didn't know what to say. She felt guilty. It seemed to me being a parent often meant feeling guilty.

"I blamed her. All these years. The poor kid. How could I have been so blind?" She looked up and half-smiled. "The deaf and the blind in one house, eh?"

"Hearing loss is hard to pick up on, Mrs. Decker. People just get used to it."

"Yeah." She was quiet, then looked at me. "You told her?"

I nodded.

"How did she take it?"

I smiled. "She was thrilled. Now she knows why she's different, and it's not because she can't think."

She stared at me blankly. Her hands turned in her lap. Her eyes welled with tears. She sniffed. "I called her stupid. Think on that. I called her stupid."

Maybe Mrs. Decker *did* have something to feel guilty about. Caroline had believed her. But that was past, and Caroline needed help now.

"Mrs. Decker, no doubt you did your best. You've got a chance to help her now. Will you take her to town for an assessment?"

She took a couple of deep breaths and controlled those tears.

"I will. I sure will, and I'll bake a cake tonight to celebrate. She's going to get her chance. Dear God. How could I have missed this?"

"The important thing is to get help for her now." I tried to steer her thoughts to positive action. I didn't want Mrs. Decker to break down in tears. Tears made me feel helpless.

She sniffed. "Okay. Okay." She sat up suddenly. "The other kids. George is in grade three and Jeff is in grade five. You'll test them?"

That jolted me. I should have thought of that. "Yes, before I leave in the morning. I'll stop by the school and test them."

I left the house feeling competent for catching Caroline's hearing loss and incompetent for not thinking of testing her brothers. Hearing loss is sometimes genetic. Mrs. Decker had picked up on that right away while I, the nurse, hadn't thought of it. This job had a way of reminding me I had a lot to learn.

I had one more home visit before I could finish for the day. An American family had moved into Horsefly, and I needed to check up on what immunizations the children had and what they needed.

A thin, athletic-looking woman answered the door.

"Mrs. Carlson?" I asked.

"That's me."

I introduced myself and told her why I was there.

"I'll go to my doctor for shots," she said and started to close the door.

I was surprised. Obviously, she didn't understand the health care system here. No one had yet tried to slam the door in my face. It was a new experience.

"Uh... Mrs. Carlson." I managed to grab the door. "Doctors don't give immunizations here. Only public health nurses. You can make an appointment, and bring your children into Williams Lake to the health unit, or I can immunize them at the school when necessary." I dropped my hand from the door.

She stared at me. I wondered if she thought I was shilling for business, that somehow I got paid for the number of children I immunized. It was hard to know as she came from quite a different health care system.

She looked puzzled but said, "You'd better come in."

I did and stood inside the door. No coffee invitation here. I pulled out her children's file and put it on the table.

"You have three children?"

She stared at me and nodded.

"Are the names and birth dates correct?"

She read them and again nodded. I wondered if she felt threatened because the health unit had her information.

"We try to make sure everyone gets the immunizations they need. You have to sign a consent form. We don't simply give them vaccines." I tried to reassure her that she was still in control of her children's health.

"Who do I pay?"

"No one."

There was silence for a moment. She looked at the file, at me, and then back at the file. "I pay no one? A nurse gets consent and then takes care of the shot at school, and it's all paid for by the government?"

"That's right. That's why we don't have epidemics."

"Taxes pay for it?"

I nodded.

She let out a big sigh. "It's surely different here. I'll get their records, so you can put them in your file. Are you sure I don't have to pay someone?"

"I'm sure."

IT SNOWED again overnight. In the morning, about two more inches covered the landscape. At the Horsefly Landing Resort, Marjorie's husband, Dave, had plowed the long driveway from the lake to the main road before he left for work. He had a job nearby, but I never found out what it was, and I never saw him except as a jacket-clad figure on top of a tractor or in a truck.

The driveway was easy to navigate and the roads in Horsefly had been plowed. I stopped at the school and conducted hearing screening tests on George and Jeff. Both were fine. Then I went on to Black Creek. That road was much more difficult to drive. It was flat but curved alongside the creek, and I was afraid I'd slide off into the still-running water. Later in the year, the creek would be frozen, but right now, it looked as black as its name and threatening. I drove slowly, paying attention to the swing of the back end of the car as the tires slid on icy patches.

I tried to think of the upcoming clinic to distract myself from the driving. The women at the mill site had asked for birth control information, and I'd brought some pamphlets on my last visit. This time I had more information and some addresses and phone numbers. I hoped I had what they needed. They made me nervous. I think it was obvious I had no sexual experience worth mentioning, and they had lots. They had questions that had never entered my mind. I didn't know if feeling ignorant was worse than incompetent, but both feelings were making me breathe faster.

I stopped at the top of the hill before I drove down to the Sorensons' mill. The road looked treacherous. I forgot about the coming trial with the mothers while I looked at the evil-looking ice glinting on the road. I shrugged and hauled out the chains. I probably should have put them on earlier. I'd parked on a flat spot, so I could spread the chains and back onto them. That was a little tricky, but I managed it and buckled the chains as my dad taught me. There were about four inches of chain hanging on each side of the tires, which would rattle against the fenders while I drove. I looked in the trunk of the car and couldn't find any wire or handy widget. I finally used gauze bandages from my black bag to tie up the loose chains.

I drove in low gear down the hill, over the bridge, and pulled into the mill yard. Mr. Sorenson stopped and waited for me to turn off the engine and get out. He was a tall, thin man with bright blue eyes.

"Can I help you with anything?"

"Sure." I said, "You can take the baby scale."

He reached into the back seat for the scale and looked down. He stood back, the scale dangling from his hand, and stared at my back tires.

"What's on the tires."

"Bandages."

"You bandaged your tires?"

"I tied up the flopping chains with gauze."

He shook his head. "Wire, a clamp, electrician's tape, yes. But bandages?"

I wasn't sure if he thought I was inventive or eccentric. By the laughter I heard from the kitchen where he'd retreated with the scale, he thought I was barmy. *Fine. The owner thought I was a little crazy, and the mothers thought I was ignorant.* I tried to keep my self-esteem together. I knew about immunizations and diseases and could help them with most of their health concerns—and I was the only nurse they had.

After the immunizations were completed, the mothers sat around the table and discussed the birth control methods they'd been reading about in the pamphlets. I listened to their opinions and occasionally added something from my reading, trying to be supportive without exposing my ignorance. If these mothers had addressed my university nursing class about birth control, we would all have been better informed. I absorbed as much as I could. I'd check their facts later in the books and pamphlets at the health unit, but their practical experience was highly instructive and full of laughter and colourful language. They were chipping away at my naivety.

CHAPTER EIGHT

NURSING AT DARLA'S BOARDING HOUSE

FOR THE NEXT three weeks I worked in the town of Williams Lake—no trips to outlying villages or far-flung ranches. As well as visiting families in homes and children in schools, I supervised the home care program and attended staff meetings. I read through the birth and death notices every morning, met with Rita for any updates on community concerns, and wrote reports on the many patient charts.

Dorrie and I had a catch-up evening of beer on Dorrie's part and coffee on mine while we talked about our lives. We settled on the chair and bed in her room. Dorrie had been dating Sam while I was away. Surprisingly, she was a little shy with him.

"He's super smart. It makes me nervous, and I can't just be myself. I'm not as... I don't know..." she trailed off.

The chance to tease her was irresistible. She was usually so confident. "Breezy?" I said.

"Maybe."

"Offhand?" I suggested.

"Uh..."

"Callous?"

"Oh, come on, Marion. I'm not that bad." She straightened and glared at me.

I laughed. "True, you're not." I let the teasing go. "Maybe he matters."

"Yeah. It's a little scary."

She didn't look happy to admit that.

I didn't see a lot of Carl. He was getting ready to move his cattle to the lower pastures for the winter and was working on repairing the fences that kept them there. That left him little time to come to town.

We managed a few dates. We had supper at Wong's Café one evening and talked. He was leaving the next morning, driving a big truck to the Fraser Valley to buy a bull, and would be gone for a week.

"Isn't there a bull good enough around here?" I was curious. There were hundreds of bulls around Williams Lake. I'd seen them in the pastures by the road and heard them bellowing from far fields.

"No. I want some Charolais genes in my herd, and the ranchers here only have Herefords." He managed to talk and eat at the same time, flashing his chopsticks with amazing speed, and he ate a lot: chow mein, ginger beef, sweet and sour pork, rice, vegetables, and chop suey. I ate a lot myself and concentrated on my dinner for a moment or two and then returned to the subject of bulls. I'd noticed the cattle were predominantly brown and white. Charolais were all white. "What will the Charolais bull do for your cattle?"

"Make them bigger."

The public health nurse in me responded. "But if the Hereford cows are smaller, won't that cause birth problems?"

He leaned forward. "Not likely. The calves aren't that much bigger; they just grow faster. At least, that's what my research shows."

I'm not sure what Dorrie and Sam talked about on their dates, but Carl and I talked about cattle reproduction and the ways he could control blow flies. My mother would be horrified, but I found it interesting.

He kissed me goodnight and took his time about it. My reaction to that kiss was so sudden, intense, and overwhelming, I was startled. If the ladies of Black Creek felt anything like this, no wonder they were looking for birth control.

I WAS busy in town. I visited newborn babies and explained the health care system to their mothers. Even mothers born in Canada rarely understood the services available to them and needed some explanation of baby clinics, routine checks, assessments, and the support groups they could attend.

One mother was a surprise. She was a new immigrant from India, a tall, regal-looking woman. She spoke English as if she had been born to it, and perhaps she had. She took careful note of everything I said and all the programs the health unit offered but balked when I suggested she might like to join the mothers' group at the library.

"There are quite a few women from India who attend," I said, thinking that would be an enticement.

She raised her head and stared at me. "I wouldn't associate with those women in India. Why should I meet with them here?"

I wasn't sure how to respond. Yes, we had a class system in Canada—the richer you were, the more privilege you had, and the more educated you were, the more prestige you might gain—but I hadn't noticed enough of a social divide that new mothers wouldn't attend a parenting class because they thought they were superior, which is how I interpreted this woman's reluctance to socialize. Maybe the class system was more rigid in India. I couldn't help her with this. I just nodded.

Perhaps it took a generation to adapt to local ideas. I thought of my mother with her English china, English manners, and idioms of language. Her parents had grown up in England with the English emphasis on manners and reticence. She held onto the customs of the old country even when they didn't work here. She had rules about clothes and insisted on wearing hats—before five o'clock, but not after—white gloves in the summer, and she didn't allow us to wear jeans on Sunday. She didn't believe in showing emotions, particularly in public. I thought she was trying to maintain a notion of her "class," but I might be unfair to her. It could be she was a woman who had to have structure in her life and she created it with her rules. She did adapt to my dad's farming background and welcomed anyone who dropped in at dinnertime without fuss and simply added a plate to the table. I don't think her mother would have done that. Each generation perhaps adapted more and more to the local culture. It might take time for this woman from India to adjust, but, in my opinion, she was going to be lonely.

The home care program grew as the doctors came to understand it. One Wednesday, Sally, the oldest of the two nurses in the program, with her usual enthusiastic approach to her job and her ability to get everything done, had overbooked her appointments. Since she had more than she could manage, she asked me to give an insulin injection to Mavis Anderson at the boarding house near the school. Mavis had a cognitive disorder and could not give her own insulin. Sally visited her every day, which saved Mavis a trip to the doctor's office, the doctor's staff the trouble of fitting her into their schedule, and Mavis the tedious wait for her appointment.

I had hopes we could teach Mavis to give her own insulin, and I was going to use this visit to assess her capabilities. Maybe we could have a series of pictures that showed her what to do and use the pictures when we were giving the injections, carefully following the same procedure every time until she could do parts of it, and then, eventually, all of it. I was mulling over the teaching plan in my head and responded automatically to a "Come in," from Darla, the owner of the boarding house. I'd met her previously when I'd admitted Mavis to the program. She was about sixty, married to Mickey who seemed to be retired, or more likely had rarely worked. Darla ran the house and managed the many occupants— several of whom were sleeping on the living room floor.

Mavis was one of four regular boarders, a woman of forty-five with a cognitive disorder, who was loved and accepted by Darla and her boarding crew. Her parents were elderly now and could no longer keep her at home. Social Welfare supported her living at Darla's. There was no group-living home in the Cariboo for people like Mavis, but Darla's had some of the characteristics of such a home. Mavis was supervised, cared for, and encouraged to partake in family activities. That some of those activities might be illegal disturbed no one. The others who graced the house on occasion were people with no other place to go and likely no money to pay for a hotel. I learned that they paid for a place to stay in kind. Darla had a closetful of "hot" items, purloined by her boarders.

I entered the house, carefully stepping over one body after another. Then I froze. Someone had a firm hold of my ankle. I looked down. A huge arm with a grasping hand protruded from a pile of clothes. The clothes rearranged themselves into a large man. His eyes blinked open, and he stared at me.

"Let her go," shouted Darla from the door of the kitchen. "She's the nurse!"

The man closed his eyes and opened them again slowly, like an alligator contemplating lunch. Finger by finger, he unhinged his hand. I stepped over him and into the kitchen. What would have happened if I hadn't been the nurse?

Darla bustled around me, setting out coffee cups. Mavis was happy to see me. Her cheerful nature might be part of her cognitive disorder. Some diagnoses listed positive attitude as one of the symptoms. But perhaps she simply liked living at Darla's. She didn't seem to mind getting pricked by a needle every day. Possibly, the attention compensated for the shot. I was sure she didn't understand exactly what insulin did, but she might be able to give her own insulin. Still, if she didn't understand the reason for doing it, would she consistently do it? Probably not. Sally and I would have to talk about this.

Darla supervised the injection, smiling with satisfaction. She seemed affectionate with Mavis. In spite of all the men lying on the living room floor and the occasional one with grasping hands, it seemed a good place for Mavis. Darla watched over her.

"You come back this afternoon," Darla said. "About five. Mickey and I are celebrating our thirtieth anniversary, aren't we, Mickey?"

Mickey looked up from his paper and nodded. I'd never heard him say anything.

Darla rattled on. "We're having a party. Everyone welcome. You tell that Sally. We need her to come."

I relayed the invitation to Sally when I returned to the health unit.

Sally paused for a moment at the door of my office "We'd better go at five sharp, so no one is too hammered. A couple of hours later and the party will be a police problem."

I agreed. "I'll get an anniversary card and maybe a gift. What do you suggest?"

"Hmm." She thought for a moment. "How about chocolates? A big box—but not the hand-dipped kind, just one with lots of chocolates in it."

I had a passing thought that chocolates and alcohol wouldn't be good for Mavis but decided much of Mavis's life was out of my control.

Sally handed me a couple of dollars. I stopped at the drugstore that afternoon and picked up the card and chocolates. Sally and I met at the boarding house at five and entered together. Sally had been right. The party had not quite begun, and Darla was sober.

"Hello, hello!" she said. "You brought me a present." She beamed.

The men who had cluttered the living room floor earlier in the day had disappeared for now, and Darla was resplendent in red pants and a black sweater with scarlet flowers emblazoned across her voluptuous breasts. Mavis was dressed in black pants, a bright red T-shirt with purple sequins, and a red plastic flower in her hair. She smiled broadly at us. Sally and I in our dark work clothes were definitely the dowdy birds in this flock.

"We brought you *and Mickey* a present. Where is he?" Sally peered around Darla, checking out the kitchen.

"He's downstairs. Just a minute." Darla leaned on the stairway rail and called down to the lower floor. "Mickey, you asshole. Get up here. The nurses are here."

"Hey, hey," Sally remonstrated. "It's your anniversary. You should call him 'darling.'"

"Oh." Darla stared at Sally for a moment. "You're right." She nodded empathically and leaned over the rail again. "Mickey, you *darling* asshole! Get up here. The nurses are here."

I snorted and quickly coughed, trying to control my laughter. Sally kept a straight face. I didn't know how she did it.

"That's better," Sally said to Darla.

We stayed for a few minutes to congratulate Mickey when he finally lumbered up the stairs. He smiled at us and looked down, a little embarrassed at the attention we were giving him. I took pity on him and turned to admire the garish anniversary cake, a sheet cake with white icing almost completely covered in blue and purple sugar flowers.

Darla pressed a glass of wine on us, along with some cheese straws, which were crisp and delicious. She had canapés on the counters and sandwiches on the table. About four dozen beer bottles were stashed beside the kitchen sink. It was going to be quite the party. Sally had been wise to schedule our visit before the hordes arrived. A huge bouquet of carnations and baby breath sat in some grandeur in the middle of the table.

"From Mickey," Darla said with pride.

"Nice job, Mickey," Sally said.

"Uh... thanks. She said to get red. They just had pink."

"Looking good in pink, Mickey," Sally said.

Mickey looked away and then down at his feet, giving a clear impression that he didn't want any attention. We chatted with Darla and Mavis and pretended Mickey wasn't there. It seemed the kindest thing to do.

We finished our wine and wished Mickey and Darla another thirty years and left before the partygoers arrived.

I drove a block, pulled over, put my head down on the steering wheel, and laughed. I wasn't sure if it was Darla or Sally who struck me as hilarious. The two of them seemed to spark off each other.

I thought about my mother's parties: the silver tea set, the English bone china, canapés, linen serviettes, tasteful music, flowers on the buffet. Her carefully chosen guests would arrive with flowers or small gifts and take their places in the living room. One of us, whoever was home at the time, would act as a server and offer trays of asparagus rolls, tiny crackers with cheese, and a dish of olives. My dad would inquire what cocktail each guest would prefer and set about making it. The guests would move on to a beautifully set dining room table with sparkling silver and Spode china. No one would raise their voice. No one would holler down the stairwell. There would not be the added excitement of a horde of partygoers arriving shortly and the threat of a police raid. This had been a lot more entertaining.

MRS. HARBINGER, the principal at Dorrie's school, had ideas about what I should be doing. It seemed easier to go along with most of her plans rather than impose my own. While I continued to do immunizations and screening tests, Mrs. Harbinger also wanted me to talk to grade five girls about menstruation. The Girls' Club met every Tuesday for a half-hour and accepted girls from any grade, but Mrs. Harbinger wanted an additional class specifically on menstruation and for only grade five girls. Grade five seemed the appropriate age as most of the girls were prepubescent, and I had a film and some booklets. Still, this was a controversial program, and I expect she had bullied the parents into agreeing. No one thought it important for boys to have this information. I was sure the school board wouldn't allow me to talk to the boys about puberty.

"The parents, particularly the fathers, would have me fired if I mentioned the word menstruation to my class," Dorrie said as we were sitting in the staff room having coffee at recess. "I wonder if they think all female teachers stand in front of the class month after month never doing it?"

"You know, when I was in school, it never occurred to me my teachers menstruated. I guess I thought of them as not quite human."

She grunted. "At least we're pulling the next generation into some idea that women are normal."

"What do you mean?" I was a little startled.

"I mean 'normal' is defined in our society as masculine. Pretending girls and women don't menstruate is one way of saying that *not* to menstruate is the norm, and menstruation is abnormal."

I'd never thought about it in that way before. I looked at teaching about the body as a health program, not a moral or even a sociological one. Maybe I *should* think about it. She was right. No one talked about it. When I was a young girl, my mother had taken me aside and imparted the knowledge, telling me her mother had never told her about menstruation and she had been terrified when it occurred. Mom didn't mention it again, and everyone in my house pretended it wasn't happening. Our whole society ignored it. It hadn't occurred to me that denying the fact of menstruation was denying my femininity. Dorrie had a point. Mrs. Harbinger had thought about it and was trying to change attitudes. She had a master's degree, an intelligent view of her students, and a fierce determination. She was formidable.

Mrs. Harbinger stopped me in the hall and asked me to do a home visit to make sure a child was not being beaten at home. I noted the child's name: John Bassinger. He was ten and lived with his mother and father. I wasn't sure what I could do if he *was* being abused. It wasn't against the law for parents to hit their children. If I suspected abuse, I would let Social Welfare know. I'd met a social worker who seemed compassionate. I would call him to investigate, if necessary.

I stopped at Mrs. Harbinger's office on my way out of the school to let her know I'd try to do the home visit this week. I found her leaning against the wall by her office door, shaking her head.

"What's up?" I asked.

"You know that boy I want you to visit?"

"John?"

"Yes, John. I made a deal with him."

"What's the deal?"

"I'm laughing at my own stupidity. I told him if he stayed out of fights in the schoolyard for a week, I'd give him a dollar." She straightened her plump body and hustled into her office. I followed but stopped at the door.

"And did he?"

She thumped down onto her chair. "He did. I gave him a dollar, and it just occurred to me he'll probably get into a fight on the way home in order to keep it. He'll win the fight, but it won't teach him *not* to fight. So much for my psychology."

"You'll have to go back to those psychology books."

"That's a fact."

I drove home, thinking about Mrs. Harbinger. She obviously wanted to make good use of me, and as her goal was the benefit of the children, I did what she asked, as much as possible. For all her dictatorial ways, she had a relationship with a troubled boy, and she had let him know she cared about him. She was probably a very good principal.

And, I thought, arriving home, I supposed my landlady considered herself a good landlady. The place was clean. The meals were on time, and while they weren't tasty, they wouldn't poison me. Mrs. Sharpe wasn't required to be kind or cheerful. With her usual dour view of the world, she was forecasting snow tonight.

I sat at my window and looked over the town. Dorrie was out with Sam, and Carl was away. I had an invitation to go out for a drink with a man named Hector. Carl had introduced him to me. Hector seemed such an old-fashioned name. He was a lawyer, tall, dark, and friendly. I'd go out with him on Friday. Tonight I wanted to sit and watch the world go by.

I'd been in Williams Lake almost two months. I'd packed so much into those months, it felt like a year. There was variety in both the work and the people, as well as new procedures to master and new territories to discover. I felt bigger, somehow, as if I was expanding into the job. My Scottish background sounded a warning in my head. Self-satisfaction tempts fate. If the fates were listening, they'd send me challenges.

I could see the lake at the end of town. It was still open water— no ice, although Mrs. Sharpe had assured me it would freeze solid by Christmas. In the fading light, the lake was almost black. Dark brown earth and grey tree trunks lined the banks. The air felt menacing. Winter might arrive tonight.

CHAPTER NINE

MANIPULATING THE SYSTEM

E LLIE POKED HER head into my office one morning. "There's a woman here who wants to talk to a nurse, and you're the only one in the office."

"What about?" I looked up.

She shrugged, handed me a folder, and left. I admired Ellie. She was efficient, reliable, knew what her duties were, and confined herself to those. She handed off anything she thought of as "nursing" to me.

I rose as a woman in her early thirties walked into my office. She was shorter than me, dressed in jeans and a parka, with long brown hair, brown eyes, and brown skin—a First Nations woman. I didn't know her.

"I'm Cynthia Ludlau," she said and sat.

I glanced at the small file folder, which read: Ron and Cynthia Ludlau. The address was at the edge of town. There was acreage there. She was in my district.

As if she could read my mind, Cynthia said, "I'm not status anymore. My husband's father gave up his status, so he could buy his ranch land. That meant my husband didn't have status, and when I married him, I lost my status."

"Status Indian" meant the patriarchal oversight of the federal government. "Non-status Indian" meant no benefits from the Indian Act. That meant Cynthia was entitled to provincial health care.

"Nice to meet you. How can I help?" I sat back down at my desk.

"My daughter is in the hospital in Vancouver. She pulled a pot of boiling soup off the stove and burned herself." Cynthia looked directly at me, challenging me to comment.

I winced. "Ouch."

She moved her shoulders as if trying to shrug off the memory. "Yeah. I feel so guilty because I was watching her, but she was so quick." Cynthia eyed me warily as if she thought I was going to yell at her.

"It happens like that," I said. Toddlers fell down stairs, got their fingers caught in machinery, and toppled out of cars. The list was endless. It's a wonder most survived. "How old is she?"

"She's two and a half." Cynthia still seemed uneasy, sitting on the edge of her chair and speaking abruptly.

I looked at the file. "Charlotte?"

"Right. I'm here because I want to talk to the nurses at the hospital in Vancouver and see how she's doing. I can't afford the telephone call." It sounded reasonable. Long distance charges were expensive, and my quick glance at the file showed another five children at home. I waited. "I'd like you to call Children's Hospital and see how she is." Cynthia's voice firmed, and she leaned forward almost aggressively.

"Can do," I said peaceably. She wasn't going to have to fight me on this. Charlotte needed a concerned mother. That's exactly what Cynthia was. I'd help her all I could.

I got the number from information and called. I wove my way through the hospital switchboard to the little girl's ward. I talked to the nurse briefly and then handed the phone to Cynthia.

"Ask the nurse whatever you like. Perhaps she can let you talk to your daughter."

Cynthia's eyes lit, and she smiled. "She's okay?"

I nodded. I left Cynthia in my office and went out to the reception area. Ellie and Marie each had a desk, and Ellie pulled up a chair so I could share hers. I asked for the application form for the

Shriners' benevolent fund. That organization helped bring children to hospitals and looked after their parents as well. They were particularly interested in burn patients. Ellie, of course, knew where the form was. She fetched it for me, and I filled it out.

Ellie looked over my shoulder. "Are you going to get help for that mother?"

"I am. The Shriners can send her to Vancouver, put her up in a hotel, and let her visit her daughter. The little girl is going to be in the hospital for another four weeks, and that's a long time to be without her mother."

"But she's Indian." Ellie said.

I looked up quickly. "What difference does that make?"

"The Shriners won't send an Indian. They'll think the Indian agent should do that."

I stared at Ellie. As far as I could tell, government agents didn't lift a finger to get Indigenous people better health care. Cynthia Ludlau lived in my area. Because she was non-status, she was not eligible for Indian Health Services. I wasn't sure Ellie was correct about the Shriners. There was nothing on the form to indicate the Shriners would refuse. There was no box for "race." Still, Ellie had lived here for years, and she might be right. She was letting me know I was stepping over a boundary. I thought for a moment, and then decided I didn't care.

"Ellie, we aren't going to tell them," I said firmly. She'd better *not* tell them.

Cynthia was just hanging up the phone when I got back to my office. Tears were running down her face, but she was smiling.

"She's okay. Just lonesome," she said.

"It's good for her to talk to you even if it makes her cry. Otherwise, she'll think you've abandoned her." Feeling abandoned was devastating for a child. Psychiatrists had learned that parents needed to visit children in the hospital, even if it upset them both. That idea was changing hospital policies. In the past, parents were kept away from their child. Now parents were encouraged to visit—even if the child cried when they left. It was a new idea—to psychiatry at least; it wasn't new to parents.

"Yeah, that's right. That's what I thought." She nodded. That was what had motivated her to come to see me, even though she had expected me to blame her.

I talked to her about the application for the Shriners' fund. She filled out her part of the form, and I put it in my out basket for Ellie to process.

As she was leaving, Cynthia stopped at the door and turned to me. "Can I come here once a week and call her?"

"Sure." That was a good plan. Charlotte would have some contact with her mother.

I thought about racism after Cynthia left. I'd noticed that there was a Catholic church for Indigenous people at one end of Williams Lake and another at the other end for whites. The hypocrisy of a Christian organization dividing their worship on racial grounds irked me, and I couldn't understand how people could support it.

Rita breezed into my office after Cynthia left. "Your turn to take blood at the jail tomorrow morning."

"What for?" There was always something new for me to learn.

"Syphilis. We screen for it."

Syphilis was curable in the early two stages—and sometimes even in the later stages—but many people didn't know they had the disease. In some stages, it was asymptomatic, so screening was the only way they'd know they had it. Jail was a convenient place to test for it, but we screened for it routinely in other places, too. Applicants for a marriage licence had to supply proof they were syphilis-free. It had been almost eradicated by antibiotics, so we had very few cases. Penicillin took care of most venereal diseases, so fear of dying from infection didn't motivate people to guard against it. But we still had the rare case. The disease could seem to be cured, only to come back and attack the heart and brain.

"Do I need a signed consent from the prisoners to take blood?" I asked Rita.

"No, but you do need verbal consent. Be sure you ask each one for permission. Anna-Lise will have the equipment ready for you."

"Please God, no 20-cc syringes." I never wanted to use those again.

"No." She smiled. "Small individual syringes with sample tubes. Don't hemolyze the blood." Drawing the blood too quickly or pushing the sample into the tube with too much pressure could cause the red blood cells to rupture. That might require doing the whole procedure again.

"I'll be careful."

At 8:30 the next morning, I was at the jail, in a small holding cell in the police station. The sergeant vacated his desk, and I set up my equipment on it. Five men came in, one after another, and held out their arms. I took down their names, some contact information, and asked permission to draw the blood. They all acquiesced. They were all Indigenous. What was going on with the police that the only people incarcerated were Indigenous?

The police constable who brought the prisoners to me seemed respectful, even friendly with the men, but while I took blood at the jail every week for four months, I saw only one non-Indigenous prisoner. No one talked about racism; it was just practised. I noticed racism everywhere now, revealed slowly day by day. Experience melted my ignorant white cover like snow, and I could see the real groundwork of society. It made me uncomfortable in my own skin.

I MANAGED to carry out Mrs. Harbinger's directions to visit John Bassinger's family and see if there was any evidence of abuse. They lived in an apartment in the hotel downtown. John was an only child, according to his family folder. I had his screening tests and immunization records.

His mother invited me into her kitchen. From the apartment's entrance, we walked down a long hallway to the kitchen. Beyond the kitchen were the bedrooms. It was odd. The apartment must have been carved out of the end units of the hotel and fitted in behind a bank of rooms with the long hall connecting the apartment to the hotel corridor. Whatever the reason, that long hallway meant I was some distance from safety. In the kitchen sat a big man. A size 2X shirt would fit him.

"Mark Bassinger," he said as he stood. "John's father. What's he done?"

I looked at the lumpy muscles on Mr. Basinger's arms, at the way his wife shied away from him, keeping distance between them and at the long, long hallway back to safety.

I took a slow, calming breath. "He's done nothing. I just wanted to talk about his screening tests. He seems to be fine in hearing."

Mark Bassinger nodded. "The bugger can hear when he wants to. So, what's it to you?"

Uh-oh. I instantly abandoned any discussion of abuse. This man was dangerous. I was not in a safe situation here. Now, all I was concentrating on was getting out without getting hit. I hoped my coming here didn't set John up for a beating. Concerns for my safety and concerns for John danced in my brain. I stopped speculating and concentrated on the moment. I had to give Mr. Bassinger a reason for my visit without antagonizing him or casting John in a bad light.

"He's doing pretty well at school, I hear. I just wanted to make sure his immunizations are up to date. Would you sign his consent card? That way I can update them when it is necessary. Would that be okay?"

"Just those shots?" Mark Bassinger asked. Mrs. Bassinger hadn't said a word.

"Yes," I said. "Are you okay with that? You can object if you don't want him immunized."

"No, no. Best have the kid protected. We don't want him bringing home bugs."

"Thank you." I wrote John's name on a form, placed it in front of Mr. Bassinger, and collected it after he signed it. I stood.

"Thanks very much. That was quick, and I appreciate you doing this." I trowelled on the praise, hoping he wouldn't realize that I usually sent those forms home with the kids. I couldn't possibly do home visits to get signatures for every child.

He followed me to the door. The hallway seemed endless, and the menace behind me huge. I nodded to him as I left and forced myself to sedately walk to the stairs and not break into the frantic, headlong lope I desperately wanted to do. I swear I didn't breathe until I was sitting in my car.

I had no real evidence that Mark Bassinger was abusive except my feelings and my observations of Mrs. Bassinger's evasive movements, but I was going to call Paul Clayton, the social worker in my area. This was his problem.

"Take someone with you," I said to Paul on the phone later that day. "He's massive."

"Oh, shoot." I heard Paul gulp.

Better he was warned than walk into a fist.

"I'll leave it a week or so," Paul said, "so he doesn't connect your visit with mine."

"Good idea. That last thing I need is him waylaying me on the street."

"Or following you home," Paul said.

"That too." Dissatisfied patients could easily find me in this small town.

Cynthia came regularly every week to talk to her daughter on the phone in my office. After two weeks, she managed a visit to Children's Hospital in Vancouver, paid for by the Shriners. Her husband worked at the local mill and had four days off over one weekend. He looked after the other kids, freeing Cynthia to hop the bus.

"Charlotte's so much better," she told me over coffee when she returned.

We met at the Lakeview Café. It was a small café, and Cynthia liked it there. There were mostly Indigenous people in the café today, but they seemed to accept me. Maybe it was because I was with Cynthia or perhaps because of my position as a public health nurse. I found attitudes in common with the Dakelh people around

Williams Lake. I told Cynthia that I'd try to see her the next day, and she said, "You talk like my people We never say we will be somewhere. We say we'll *try* to be somewhere."

I thought about it. "My dad's side of the family is Scottish. They'd think you were tempting the gods to interfere if you made firm plans for the future. So we say we'll try to or plan to be there rather than we will."

"Just in case the gods are listening," Cynthia said.

"Right."

My father's family were McKinnons from the Isle of Benbecula in Scotland where my grandfather was born. They were tribal in ways that Cynthia's people were tribal—and prolific.

"I have sixty first cousins," I said.

"You might be Native."

I laughed. "When is Charlotte coming home?"

"She's coming home in two weeks. She should be fine, they say. Her face is okay. She has some scarring on her chest, but they think it will fade as she grows. I hope so. She cried when I left. I felt like I was abandoning her, leaving her in all that white: white bedding, white walls, white uniforms, white nurses..." She stared at her coffee cup.

"No colour at all?"

She smiled a little. "Her snuggly bunny. He's brown."

I laughed. Then sobered. It must have been hard to leave such a small child. "Will you bring her back on the bus?"

"No, the Shriners are going to pay for a plane ride." She brightened.

"That'll be fun." I was relieved the application had gone through successfully.

"Yeah, a treat. I haven't ever flown, and Charlotte will love it. We can tell the other kids all about it. They will be so glad to see her." She smiled thinking of the coming reunion.

"I hope it's a smooth trip."

"Me too," she said fervently. The Cariboo got some fierce storms. I hoped they wouldn't experience one when flying. I drank my coffee, which was strong the way I liked it.

"Hey, Marion," Cynthia said. "Do they know my little girl is Indian? That I'm Indian?"

I thought about my answer and decided the truth was probably best. "I don't think so."

She stared at me for a moment, then laughed. "You're sneaky. I like that."

Perhaps I was. What would happen if the white Shriners discovered that the woman and little girl they were helping were Indigenous? I don't think they would do anything. They couldn't really object, and they might *not* object. I was assuming prejudice when there might not be any. Still, the prejudice in this town was maintained by practices that promoted it. Contrary practices might attract criticism. I wasn't going to offer the information.

In any event, no one found out, and Cynthia and little Charlotte had their plane ride home.

Cynthia brought Charlotte into the health unit to introduce her to us. The little girl was beautiful. I was so glad the scalding hadn't caught her face. She wore a pink parka with a coyote bush tail around the collar and looked adorable. I noticed she clung to Cynthia. I expected that the long separation would make her afraid to be very far away from her mother for some time.

I caught Cynthia's side view. *No!* She was pregnant again. "When are you due?"

Cynthia raised her eyebrows. "Soon."

This would be baby number seven. She wasn't even thirty-five. It's a wonder her insides didn't drop away. "Let me give you some birth control pamphlets—please," I pleaded.

She shrugged but took the pamphlets.

I HEARD from Paul Clayton about John Bassinger. "I suspect physical abuse," Paul said, "but I don't have any evidence, and I think I will cause more harm than good to pursue it."

"You tell that to Mrs. Harbinger," I suggested.

He sighed. "She's a dragon."

"That's why you get to report to her and not me."

"Okay." He accepted the inevitable.

I felt sorry for John that neither of us could make a difference in his life. It was frustrating when we couldn't help. We didn't always assess the situation correctly, and we couldn't always do something about it when we did. I hoped John and his mother would survive.

DORRIE DATED Sam exclusively now, but while I was dating Carl, I was also dating other men. Hector, the lawyer, was from the Okanagan. He had attended university in Vancouver and was articled to a local law firm in Williams Lake. We went to a movie and then to a small bar in the hotel. He planned to return to the Okanagan to practise law when his year of articles was completed.

"Lots of money there," he said.

I was sure he was envisioning a comfortable life of property on Okanagan Lake, a family, and lots of skiing and travelling. I let him talk while my mind wandered. The hotel bar was a snug, quiet room with six small tables. The bartender served both the bigger and louder main bar and this smaller room. Hector suggested a Black Russian. I knew it was a liquor drink, and I agreed. I excused myself to go to the washroom while he was ordering. When I returned, the bartender stopped me just before I entered the bar.

"He spiked your drink," he told me quietly. "You're the nurse?"

"Yes." I waited.

"He asked for a double for you. I didn't think you looked like a girl who was used to that much."

"Thanks." What kind of a creep spikes a woman's drink? This one apparently.

Would the bartender have warned me if I hadn't been the nurse? I was beginning to feel like a community asset that needed protection. It was heart-warming, if a little overwhelming. He turned back to the smaller room. I gave him a moment and then followed.

"Well, let's have this drink, and maybe go for a drive," said Hector.

I tasted the drink cautiously. I had to think of something that didn't betray the bartender. "You know, this seems really sweet. I don't think I can drink it. I'll sip a bit, but sorry I can't drink it." I smiled at him. As in my experience with Mr. Muscles Bassinger, my goal was to get home safely. That meant avoiding confrontation. "I have to get up really early tomorrow, so I'll take a rain cheque on the drive this time." I smiled at him but thought firmly, *There will be no next time, you creep.*

MRS. SHARPE called me to the phone one evening a few weeks later. "It's a woman, so you can talk to her."

Really? I couldn't talk to a man? What was she thinking?

"Marion, it's Cynthia. Can you come to the hospital?"

"What's wrong?"

"Well, nothing's wrong. The baby's coming, and I thought maybe you could keep me company for a while. Ron's looking after the kids."

"Sure." It was about nine. I could stay with her for a few hours.

I stayed all night. This was her seventh baby, but she was afraid, truly afraid—shaking and fearful. She was afraid of the pain and made it worse by tensing through the contractions, and she was afraid of the uncontrolled and relentless progress of labour. She needed someone with her.

"Were you afraid all the other times?" I asked her.

"Yes," she said flatly.

"What helps?" I asked.

"Just talk."

I sat holding her hand while she went through the contractions, telling her about my life growing up in the Fraser Valley, about university, my friends, and my trips. She didn't want me to talk about Williams Lake or her life here, just stories of places and people she'd never seen.

At about three in the morning, I asked her if she would consider getting her tubes tied after this one.

"The priest says I shouldn't do that," she said.

That was another thing I'd noticed. The Catholics at the First Nations end of the lake had many children. The Catholics at the white end had two. I was really tired of the hypocrisy.

I looked around the room. "He's not having this baby, is he?"

She stared at me. "Good point."

I mentally condemned all priests to menstruation, pregnancy, and delivery. They'd probably apply for canonization after the experience.

Lorne Wilson was her doctor and had been her doctor for her last three children. About six in the morning, he examined her. "You're dilated, but the baby isn't moving along. We may have to do a C-section."

Cynthia's eyes grew huge, and she squeezed my hand.

I stood. Nurses were always deferential to doctors. We were taught to agree as much as possible and to be tactful and to avoid contradicting them, especially in front of patients. But I had been without sleep and had talked myself hoarse, so I was not particularly tactful. "You are *not* doing a C-section on a seventh multip who is fully dilated!" I hissed at him. It was her seventh baby, for heaven's sake! "You have a blasted squash game today. Thursday, isn't it? You are not doing a C-section just so you can get this delivery over with and make your squash game!"

He flushed bright red. "I'm not trying to make my squash game. All the other times with her deliveries, she's moaning and crying. She's not doing that. I think the baby's not moving down."

"She's not moaning and crying because I'm a good labour room nurse, and I'm keeping her calm. Cynthia," I commanded in a firm and, I admit, loud voice, "turn over on your hands and knees We are going to get this baby on the way."

There weren't many machines to give an accurate assessment of the progression of labour. We could monitor the baby's heart rate through the mother's abdomen with a modified stethoscope, but there was a lot of guesswork and intuition in obstetrics.

Dr. Wilson watched while I helped Cynthia kneel and lower her head onto her arms.

"Move a little," I said.

She did.

"Okay, now, onto your back." I issued another command. I was not in the mood for any argument.

She turned.

"Oh, my God," she said. "The baby's coming."

I threw out my hands, palms up, and grinned at Lorne Wilson. "Over to you."

He smiled. "Let's get you into the delivery room, Cynthia. I guess this show is on the road."

Cynthia had a daughter in half an hour.

I felt like a magician.

CHAPTER TEN

MISSING NARCOTICS, THREATS OF SUICIDE

THE HOME CARE program was packed with patients. Kate and Sally worked full time every week. Kate was a little uncomfortable in the community without supervisors or others nurses working alongside her, but she was learning to be independent. She phoned me one November morning while I was sorting files in my office.

"Mrs. Patterson has high blood pressure and her doctor wanted me to check on her twice a week. I arranged to be at her place this morning at ten. No one answers, and the door is locked."

"Where are you right now?"

"At the neighbour's," she said.

"And you're worried she's had a stroke and is lying on the kitchen floor helpless?"

"Well, yes."

I thought for a moment. "See if you can spot an open window. Find a child in the neighbourhood who can fit through the window and get him or her to open the door for you." It would be better to find out if Mrs. Patterson needed help before calling an ambulance.

"Okay. Thanks."

I expected the neighbours would watch the process and keep us from a breaking and entering charge. Kate returned in a half-hour and stomped into my office.

"What happened? Is Mrs. P okay?" I asked her.

"Honestly! Some people!" She was fuming.

"What happened?" I asked again.

"I put *myself* through the bathroom window—and that wasn't easy, I tell you. And then... and then! No one was home. When I got to the kitchen, there was a note on the fridge. I brought it." She shoved a large piece of paper at me.

I took the letter-sized paper and read: Dear Nurse. I've gone shopping.

I held the paper dangling from my fingers and stared at Kate. I could not laugh. I really could not laugh. Kate didn't see it as funny. She was angry. But the vision of Kate squirming through the window to find the message inside made it hard.

"Did you hurt yourself getting in?" I tried to sound supportive. I was her boss, after all.

"Ripped my nylons. I'm going to wear long pants the next time." She dropped the chart on the counter and headed out the door.

The public health nurses wore the uniform of skirt, blouse, and suit jacket, but the home care nurses were not required to buy a uniform. So far, Kate had dressed in a similar style in suit skirt and blouse; Sally set her own rules and I didn't interfere. Sometimes her uniform was jeans and a sweater. The supervisors in Victoria might not approve of pants, but we were a long way from Victoria, and I'd support whatever was practical.

I had thought Kate might be a little too agreeable to work in the community and that she needed to trust her own judgment more than she did. As if she could read my mind, Kate turned back and said, "I'm telling her flat out. She either stays home when she says she's going to be there, or she calls me and makes other arrangements. She wasted my morning."

I nodded, thinking that perhaps Kate would be clearer with the next patient and not make assumptions. She was figuring this out for herself, though, and didn't need me to point it out.

She wasn't decisive about the next problem that occurred, but she was aware.

"Mr. Martson's pain medication is disappearing," she stated bluntly to Sally and me in the office.

Kate and Sally had been taking turns going to Mr. Martson's house. He was dying of cancer, and they had been administering heavy pain medications to keep him as comfortable as possible and out of the hospital.

"What's missing?" Sally asked.

"There were two doses of morphine missing yesterday when I went there. He's on your list for today, Sally. Maybe you could check into it?"

Sally snorted. "It's those useless sons of his. They're stealing it, and I bet they're selling it. I'll sort them."

Alarm bells went off in my head. Sally was pushing sixty. Two young men determined to steal morphine might be too much for her.

"I'll go with you this afternoon, Sally. Let's check it out together." I might not be much help, but at least I could call 911 if I had to. Rita had told me I could call the RCMP for a police escort any time I felt a home visit might be dangerous. I was reluctant to do that as hauling a police officer along with me on one visit would make the next visit impossible, and the patient could always refuse to let us in. Except in rare cases of a patient who refused to accept treatment for a dangerous communicable disease, I didn't have any right to enter a patient's house without an invitation.

"Sure." While nominally recognizing that I was her supervisor, Sally made it clear she didn't take orders from me. I could come if I liked.

We arrived about four. Mrs. Martson was grateful for the visit. Sally disappeared in the bedroom to bathe her patient, rub his skin, and give him another dose of the morphine. He didn't have long to live, perhaps a week. I stayed in the kitchen talking to Mrs. Martson. She was tiny, not quite five feet, thin, and looked very tired. She wasn't yet fifty but looked older. Two young men, both about eighteen, thin and muscular, hung around, leaning on the kitchen counter. I noticed them eyeing my black bag.

Sally shut the bedroom door behind her, walked into the kitchen, and put her bag on the counter. Both boys slid their eyes toward the bag and then away. Sally turned to face them with her hands on her hips.

"Okay, losers. Which one of you is stealing pain meds from your dad? Or are both of you oozing around, slinking into corners, filching whatever you can find?"

"Not me," the tall one said, with a patently false expression of innocence.

"Not me," his brother agreed. Both smirked at Sally. That was a mistake.

"Hah! Thieves *and* liars!" She strode up to the tallest one and shoved her finger in his chest. Her head came to his neck. I watched, ready to jump in if I had to. I didn't think my move to assist would end well, but I sat on the edge of my chair, my hands on the table, ready to launch if they started to push her.

"I'm giving the morphine in suppositories now," Sally rapped that out. "That'll be a little harder to sell. But if any of those suppositories are missing, I'll see that you guys, both of you"—she turned and shoved a finger at the second teen—"I'll see that you get diuretics and laxatives in your coffee for the next two weeks. You'll piss and poop until you can't sleep or sit down."

"Hey, you can't—"

Sally interrupted, "Of course, I can. You'll never know when I'll do it. Trust me. You'll be very sorry."

It was against nursing ethics to harm a patient or threaten to harm one. Still, the boys were not our patients. Mr. Martson was, and Sally was protecting him. I was willing to dance around ethics or even toss them out just now.

The boys slithered out the door, and Sally spent the next ten minutes holding Mrs. Martson's hand and listening to her talk about her problems with the boys.

"THEY DON'T have enough to do," Carl said on the weekend when I was helping him repair fences on his ranch. "Teenagers need to be working or hunting or digging ditches—they're always doing something or they wander off into trouble."

I found myself telling Carl quite a bit about my work. Ethically, I wasn't supposed to talk about it, but everyone needs someone to talk to, to find ways to deal with problems, and Carl was safe. He never told me any gossip he heard, which made me think he wouldn't tell anyone what I reported to him.

Some things I didn't tell him.

I didn't tell him that my nursing colleague Sophie had come into my office with a list of contacts from our local busy prostitute. She wanted me to help find some of the men because they needed antibiotics. I saw the lawyer I'd dated on the list.

I pointed to his name. "You'd better take this one, Sophie. I know him."

"Did you date him?" she asked, a worried frown on her forehead.

I nodded.

"Need a shot?" she offered.

I laughed. "Nope. Never even kissed him. He really was a creep."

I thought about the lawyer, and how he would command respect for his social standing. I thought about the way my mother judged people by their education and occupation, never asking impertinent questions, never really knowing them. She would welcome this lawyer into her house because he was educated and urbane. She wouldn't ever discover he had the morals of an alley cat. She'd be happier not knowing. It wasn't a bad strategy for social situations, but it was impractical for me. I was glad I'd only dated him once and mentally sent another thank you to that bartender.

Sophie picked up on my attitude, and sat on my visitor's chair. She looked straight at me. "Marion, people aren't creepy because they have VD. They have a health problem we're supposed to help them with. Not everyone gets VD from a prostitute and, even if they did, we aren't supposed to judge them."

Was I being judgmental? He did try to spike my drink. But did I think a person was inferior *because* they had a venereal disease? Was that my mother's influence or a view of my own? I sat silently as she continued.

"People can catch VD from their first sexual experience. They aren't necessarily promiscuous. And even if they are, some people see sex as a pleasure they want to share, and some even see it as a sport. That's none of our business."

I should have thought about this. I'd been narrow-minded, too ready to assume a censorious attitude. What had happened to my compassion? I valued my health and would protect myself from infection, but I was ashamed of my condemnation of someone *because* he had VD. "You're right, Sophie. Sorry. I'll fix my attitude." I was humbled by her. She was right. I was not supposed to judge the morals of others.

She smiled and left. In seconds her head popped back as she leaned into my office from the door. "Not that this particular man isn't a jerk. I expect you got that right."

I laughed.

In my position, I read reports of the health of the community. I knew who had communicable diseases, who had tuberculosis, who had miscarriages, who lived and died. Birth control was illegal, although most medical care workers in the community advocated for it. Abortion was also illegal, so D & C, dilation and curettage, is what they were called. This was done for reasons of infection of the uterus or pelvic inflammatory disease (PID). An abortion was only a side effect of the PID treatment. It was surprising how many diagnoses of PID there were.

I had quite a few TB patients in my case load. The work of nurses in tracking down contacts of TB patients and getting them on treatment regimes was hugely effective in controlling the disease. We worked hard at finding everyone. I hoped I would eventually find the toddler Audrey Cook. Most people were very cooperative, but I had one patient I worried about.

Mr. Bob Chan was a young man, about twenty-five, married, and living in a large apartment above his father's dry goods store. I'm not sure where he worked, perhaps in the store, but I got the notice he had active TB. His doctor was the egomaniac Dr. Craisson.

"I'm not going to the sanatorium," Mr. Chan told me, staring hard as if I was going to snap handcuffs on him any moment. "I'm not going."

That seemed a bit defensive. I hadn't suggested he needed to go to the sanitarium.

"I have your pills here," I said, handing them over. The health unit supplied the medication, and the nurses distributed it. It was my responsibility to monitor his case. "They've been sent from TB Control in Vancouver. Start taking the pills today. In two days, I will collect a sputum sample from you and send it to the lab." I handed him the glass bottle. "And I don't see why you would have to go to the sanatorium if you take your meds."

"Is that true? My doctor said I'd have to go." He obviously didn't believe me.

I thought he might be convinced if I was careful to set out my rationale. "You take the medications. We'll see if they are effective. If the results show they're working, you won't be contagious. If you aren't contagious, you won't have to go to the sanatorium. That's just for people who don't take their meds, or for whom the meds aren't effective—and I've never seen the meds fail."

He looked relieved.

I went to his apartment two days later and did a TB skin test on his wife, a tiny woman who said nothing at all. I got a list of Mr. Chan's contacts; I'd do skin tests on them or give them X-ray requisitions in the next few weeks. I also picked up the sputum sample. I thought he was more relaxed about his diagnosis when I left, but he came storming into my office a few days later. Ellie showed him in and, behind his back, raised her eyebrows as if to say "Well, this is a live one" and left.

"Mr. Chan, do sit down."

He didn't sit but paced back and forth in my small office. Then he stopped, faced me, and burst out with "Dr. Craisson says I must go to the sanatorium. I will kill myself if I have to go. Do you know how much money I owe?" He threw up his hands.

I shook my head.

"I have to pay my debts, so I have to work. *And* I have to gamble. It's in my blood. I can't do that in the sanatorium. I'll die there, so I might as well die here." His voice rose.

"Please, Mr. Chan, sit down. You do *not* have to go to the sanatorium." I pulled a letter from my pending basket. "I was going to call you today. I got the results of your lab tests. You are not infectious. If you are not infectious, you cannot be forcibly confined in the sanatorium. As long as you take your medications, you will not be infectious. Do you understand?"

I'd worked for six weeks at a TB sanatorium when I was a student nurse, learning about the disease and the ways in which it was controlled. I was sure of myself on this.

"But the doctor said I had to go, that the police would take me if I didn't go willingly." He sat on the edge of the chair and stared at me intently.

"That's not true," I said.

"You tell the doctor," he demanded.

"I'll do that."

He left then, a little less agitated.

I arranged with Dr. Craisson's receptionist that I would meet him at his office at four o'clock. I brought Mr. Chan's file with me. I showed the doctor the sputum test results and the treatment plan sent to me from Vancouver.

He was livid. "You are wrong, and you had no business telling my patient *I* was wrong!"

"He was threatening suicide, and he needed the correct information." I wasn't backing down on this.

"I'm going to phone TB Control and you will see how wrong you are." He glared at me.

Go ahead, I thought and sat back. I knew more about TB than he did.

He called the operator and, with a furious glance at me, charged it to the health unit. I didn't care. I wasn't paying the bill, but I did think it revealed a petty mind. He talked to a doctor at TB

Control in Vancouver while I waited. He took the file from my hand and read off Mr. Chan's patient number. We both waited, and Dr. Craisson listened. He hung up the phone.

He threw the letter back at me. "He can stay."

I picked up the letter and walked out without another word. He'd probably hate me forever for being right. But the patient needed to be supported. Craisson was more concerned about his ego than his patient.

I TOLD Carl about that as I held the fencing pliers while he pounded staples into a fence post. It was a cold afternoon. There were two places where the wires were sagging, and Carl wanted to repair them before one of the cows or steers or whatever they were shoved through them and disappeared. Carl had promised to make me dinner, and I knew he'd put stew on before we headed out to the pasture. Not far from this fence line, the cattle were snuffling in the hay bales we'd tossed to them from the back of the pickup truck. They were predominantly brown and white. Herefords, Carl said. His Charolais bull hadn't yet had time to influence the herd with his white coat.

"Fencing must be never-ending." I looked down at what seemed like a mile of barbed wire.

"Pretty much." He pounded in another staple, then smiled at me.

It was a lovely Cariboo fall day. I breathed in the crisp air. The sun was low in the sky but still strong enough to glint off the ice on the trees. It looked like a Christmas card except there was very little snow on the ground. Ice in the trees but bare ground. The snow that had come in October had melted in the few warm days we'd had at the end of the month.

"We need the snow cover," Carl said. "We'll get it for sure in January."

"Winter doesn't come this month?" I asked him.

"The ground will freeze and sometimes the water pipes, but we'll get some warm days when the temperature rises to just above freezing. Most of the time, it stays below freezing—but not far below.

It will get colder later on in the month with the occasional storm. It's late December and January when winter drops in and stays."

"How cold does it get then?"

"Minus forty."

I stared at him. "Can you work in minus forty-degree weather?"

"Not for long," Carl said.

I'd better enjoy being out on the land while I could. The ranch looked like a park, but I was fascinated by the way Carl viewed it. He appreciated the beauty, but it was a business, and the books and charts and research articles that were strewn over his desk showed how much studying he did to make the business pay. He had a file on every animal, and there were hundreds of them. He knew their breeding lines, and he had expectations of their growth rates. He had listed the overall costs of the ranch, and assigned a percentage of those costs to each cow, calf, heifer, and steer. When he sold them, he knew how much he needed to make in order to keep solvent. Ranching required the office work of any business.

He had shown me his new acquisition. It looked like a flat board with numbers on it.

"It's a calculator," he said.

I'd turned it over in my hand. "What does it do?"

"It adds, subtracts, multiplies, and divides. I don't have to do it in my head anymore. It's much faster than I am, and it's accurate."

I played with it, interested in the way it worked. "Was it expensive?"

"Yes. It was seven hundred and fifty dollars, but it will keep me from making mistakes that will cost me more. I can use it at the sales as well to calculate prices. I wish I'd invented it."

That was about two months of my salary. I hoped it would be worth it to him.

I found myself in Carl's company often. He was easy to be with and listened to me. He respected my work but had his own concerns and dedication to his own world so didn't need to be with me with any kind of desperate longing. In spite of the many romance novels and poems about obsessive love I had read, I thought a man who desperately longed for me would be mighty annoying.

But Carl was the one I ran to on the following Friday when I received bad news. I'd been routinely going through my morning's inbox papers, reading the birth and death notices. One name leaped out at me. "Audrey Cook, aged twenty-six months. Cause of death: Tuberculosis."

The little girl I couldn't find. The little girl whose TB test was normal and whose TB test I hadn't trusted to be accurate. I looked at her address. Four miles away. She was that close all this time. I'd known she'd needed an X-ray. I'd known she needed more testing. I hadn't found her. I hadn't been motivated enough to find her. I prided myself on knowing so much about TB, and I'd let this little one die.

I left work and drove out to Carl's ranch. I found him in the barn, grooming his horse, Pete.

I leaned over the wooden stall divider.

"What's the matter?" he turned to look at me.

"I just killed a child." I know that was dramatic, and maybe even theatrical, but I felt horror at her death, at the idea that I could have prevented it. I could almost see her, a wispy face floating near the rafters, a chorus of her wailing family behind her. She was dead, and it was my fault.

He dropped the curry comb and stepped around the wall. "You what?"

"I knew she needed an X-ray. I just didn't look hard enough for her."

"What did you do?"

"I tried to find her in Horsefly, but she'd moved. I checked the records here, but I didn't check with Indian Health. I thought about her off and on, but I got busy with other tasks, other people, other problems, and I didn't do enough!"

"Your tried," he said. "You did try."

"I didn't try hard enough. I'm guilty of what I *didn't* do," I wailed and told him about my neglect. "I didn't call all the doctors' clinics and ask if she was a patient. She must have had a doctor. It would have taken me an afternoon, only an afternoon, to do that. I could have put a message out on the radio on Message Time. I could have checked all the school rosters. I knew it. I didn't decide *not* to look for her; I just didn't put any effort into it. Did I think she would magically appear at my office door? That fate would look after her? Did I hope she'd be one of the toddlers who really did have a negative skin test when I knew that test might be wrong?"

I had been so sure I understood TB. Right. I did. I knew a lot. But that hadn't helped Audrey Cook. I'd needed to get my knowledge to her, and I hadn't.

Carl didn't say I hadn't been responsible. He didn't say I couldn't have done more. He just held me and said, "We all make mistakes."

That was true. I'd made a mistake, a dreadful one. Regret, sorrow, shame, and guilt washed over me, leaving me in tears. I could have done more, and I hadn't. It was a bad mistake, and Audrey had died.

CHAPTER ELEVEN

EVICTION FROM MRS. SHARPE'S

I SAT AT THE kitchen table and cried. Carl puttered around the house, stirring stew and perking coffee. He patted my shoulder and set the food in front of me. For once I wasn't hungry, but I did manage a little. When I gave up on eating, he took the bowl away and refilled my coffee, then sat across from me and listened. I told him again that I'd gotten so involved in other parts of my job that I hadn't done enough to find Audrey.

"How could I have forgotten her?" I asked for the seventh time. I'd betrayed her and my own vision of myself as someone who helped others. I was a danger to the community. I was a flawed person.

It was all true, so there wasn't much Carl could say except, "Take some deep breaths, Marion."

I wound down after a while. The emotions drained away, and I was left with the facts. We talked about how I could establish a follow-up system for cases like Audrey's, so no child was ever missed again. At the very least, I would learn from this.

About ten, I phoned Mrs. Sharpe and said I wouldn't be home and to tell Dorrie. I didn't want her to worry.

"Where are you?" the Buzzard squawked.

"Not at home," I said firmly. I wasn't having any criticism from her tonight. She sniffed and hung up.

I saw Dorrie at the school the next day at recess. She was making the most of her break, nibbling on a cookie and sipping tea.

"The Buzzard is flapping," she told me.

"What's up with her?"

"You didn't come home. You weren't on your regular overnight in Likely or Horsefly, therefore you must be *up to no good.*"

I was still feeling emotionally bereft and didn't have any energy to worry about Mrs. Sharpe. "Doesn't she have anything better to do than poke her nose into my affairs?"

"Is that the operative word—affair? Where were you?" Dorrie asked with some curiosity.

"At Carl's," I said.

"Aha!"

"Nothing happened. I was just worn out." I thought about how kind Carl had been and how much I needed that last night. Then I thought about Mrs. Sharpe and her prurient imaginings. "She's really too much," I complained.

"She's going to kick you out tonight." Dorrie peered into her cup. She sometimes studied the tea leaves for prophetic instructions.

"Can she do that?" I'd never been evicted from anywhere.

"Sure she can. She owns the place and likes control—in case you hadn't noticed."

I was insulted for a moment, and then I thought of the upside. It would be a relief to get away from Mrs. Sharpe. No more nosy questions, constant disapproval, and tasteless meals. Still, it might take time to find another place. "I guess I'll start looking for a room."

"How about we both leave? Maybe get an apartment?" Dorrie's eyes brightened.

"Really?" I perked up. That would be fun.

"Hey, my time with the Buzzard is over. I'd like to move into an apartment," she said.

"There's only one apartment building in town. The chance of there being a vacancy isn't high." Williams Lake was a town of houses.

"We can check. Or maybe rent someone's basement suite or something."

"I'll ask Rita." I was enthusiastic about the move now. We'd have to do our own cooking, but the freedom from Mrs. Sharpe's scrutiny would be worth it.

Just as the recess bell rang to end playtime, Mrs. Harbinger poked her head into the staff room and asked me to check in with the grade six teacher. I knocked on Mrs. Beecher's door. She left her class for a moment and stepped into the hall to talk to me. Mrs. Beecher was about fifty, almost as wide as she was tall, and lurched from side to side as she walked—probably from arthritis in her hips. That would hurt.

"Mary Ellen wants to talk to you," she whispered.

I answered in the same low tones. "Mary Ellen? Do I have her name on my class roster?"

"You do, and you have the address." She was quiet for a moment, then said, "She didn't *want* to talk to you, but I persuaded her."

I looked straight at Mrs. Beecher. "Abuse?"

"I think so. Her stepfather. She hasn't told me, but I see the signs."

Teachers and nurses were trained to look for signs of abuse in children: wearing clothes that concealed their bodies, isolating themselves from friends, emoting a sense of tragedy, a brittleness, and often a sense of hopelessness.

"Okay. Send her out."

Mary Ellen had some of the symptoms: head down, eyes darting away, shoulders hunched. She was small for her age, with black hair, white skin, and dark eyes. I didn't touch her—abused kids are often afraid of touch. I kept my voice calm, low, and friendly.

"Let's go to the small office at the end of the hall, Mary Ellen. There's no one there."

She followed me. I wasn't sure she would. She was like an edgy cat, ready to run at any moment. I sat down beside the desk. She hesitated, then sat in the chair near the door.

"Tell me about it," I said.

She stared at me for a long moment. Slowly at first, and then more rapidly, she painted the picture of a stepfather who came to her room at night when her mother was asleep. I kept my rising rage under control, nodded, and said all the things I'd been trained to say. "It isn't your fault. Your stepfather is the one with the problem. We will protect you. This will stop from now on."

"Promise," she demanded shakily.

"I promise," I said. If I had to stand outside her mother's house with a sign blazoning her stepfather's name as a child molester, I'd see this girl was helped. I felt as if I was promising Audrey I'd never let another child slip through my fingers. This child would not have one more day of terror. I found some peppermints in my purse and gave them to Mary Ellen, then escorted her back to her classroom.

Mrs. Beecher looked at me over Mary Ellen's head. I nodded. She came to the door after Mary Ellen returned to her desk.

"I'll see her mother," I told her, "and then I'll talk to Social Services."

I was supposed to do it the other way around—report to Social Services and then see the mother, but I wanted to talk to that mother before the stepfather came home from work. She lived in the centre unit of a townhouse complex, not far from school.

I pulled in front of the townhouse and took a deep breath. Mary Ellen's mother came to the door. She was a big woman dressed in jeans and a man's shirt.

"Mrs. Archer?"

"Julia," she said and shook my hand. Most women didn't shake hands. Men did and European women did, I'd noticed, but not women who had grown up in this society. Perhaps it was a sign of confidence.

"Marion McKinnon, public health nurse."

"What's the matter with Mary Ellen? She hasn't been herself for quite few months. The doctor can't find anything wrong. Do you know?" She ushered me into the hall.

She sounded concerned. I hoped she was going to help. I told her clearly, "Your husband has been sexually abusing her."

She stared at me. Her mouth fell open, her dark eyes grew huge. I was afraid she was going to faint. I put my hand on her arm. "You'd better sit down."

She turned and walked into the kitchen and slumped onto a chair. I sat opposite her.

"How could I have missed that?" Her voice was full of shock. "Oh, the poor wee one." Then she straightened. Her eyes grew hard, her voice firmed. "That bugger. He's out the minute he comes home. I'll have his clothes packed and at the door. He's gone as of this minute. Ten years we've been together, and I'm wondering If I ever really knew him. I'm glad I never married him. Easier to get rid of him without the marriage lines. I don't care where he goes. He's out." She seemed cold and resolute.

I wanted to cheer. Mary Ellen would not have to face her abuser when she came home. "That will certainly let Mary Ellen know you'll protect her."

"Damn right, I'll protect her." Julia turned to me, her face suddenly stricken with sadness. "I haven't done such a good job so far, have I?" She seemed almost despairing, as if she was facing her failure and finding it hard to bear.

I bit my lip. I thought about Audrey. "Sometimes we don't get a chance to make up for our mistakes. I think you have a chance."

Julia blinked and stared at me. "I'll have to help her. It will be up to me. I'll take her to town and get her some pretty clothes. This isn't about *her* being a girl, this is about *him* being a prick. She's got to see that."

I was impressed. She'd quickly understood what Mary Ellen needed, and it was Mary Ellen she was concerned about, not herself and not her partner. "Good start."

"I'll do that today. Right after school."

"I have to report this to Social Welfare," I said. "Sexual assault is a criminal offense."

"Hah! A fine thing that law," she said sarcastically. "And when's the last time anyone was prosecuted?"

She was right. Rape and sexual assault of children were rarely prosecuted. It was as if the women and children were possessions of men and could be used and abused. Social Welfare sometimes did remove children and try to protect them, but they didn't take the men to court.

"I'll report it anyway because I should and because I must by law. You may have a few official visitors over the next few days." I explained my position and the responsibilities of the Department of Social Welfare and the police.

"I'll be ready for them. You tell them to come here during the school hours. We can talk when Mary Ellen isn't here. When they need to talk to her, I'll make sure she's ready, and I'll be with her. No one is going to talk to her without me there! You can tell Mrs. Harbinger to keep them out of the school. It's a brave social worker who'd get past that woman."

I smiled. "I'll tell her."

I stopped at my office and called Paul at Social Services. He wasn't in. Collin O'Brien was taking his calls. I reported the sexual assault.

"I'd better get out there," he said.

"Her mother is not going to let the stepfather back in the house, so there isn't any emergency," I said.

"Still, I need to talk to her. Why didn't the girl disclose this to me? The school should have called here. Assaults on children is *our* program."

I waited a moment, absorbing his reaction. He didn't ask about Mary Ellen. He seemed more concerned about his jurisdiction. I tried to speak calmly.

"She's Paul's case. You are taking it on in his absence. I'm sure you wouldn't want to do anything Paul would complain about," I said. "You are *not* going to talk to Mary Ellen because you're a man, and men are scary to her at the moment." Which should have been obvious to him.

"It's my job," he shot back.

I mustered as much patience as I could. "Surely, you are not telling me you're going to frighten this little girl because you have a need to be involved?"

There was silence. I pressed on.

"Her mother has invited you to come to the house during the school hours to talk to her. You will need to inform the RCMP. I will leave that part to you."

I could hear him breathing heavily, probably choking back an angry retort as he absorbed the fact I was not going to let him near Mary Ellen.

"All right. I'll see the mother." His tone was laden with petulance.

"That's good. Please put a note on the file that I'd like Paul to call me when he returns." This was my reminder that the case did not belong to him.

I stopped at Mary Ellen's house the next afternoon, first checking to make sure there was no Social Services' car parked nearby.

"I spoke to the idiot social worker," Julia said. "I sent him away to deal with the police. He's useless as a child advocate."

"That's Collin. There might be a niche for him somewhere, but I agree, not as a child advocate. Paul will be your case worker when he returns." I wanted to say Paul would be better but just said. "You'll like him."

Julia snorted. "Maybe. I sent Mary Ellen back to school. She's not going to stay home feeling terrible and maybe pick up on how mad I am." She shrugged. "And she likes school."

"Did she like her new clothes?" I asked, trying to make sure Julia had followed through on her plan.

"Loved them. She went to school in a pink top and red jeans. Quite the sight."

We smiled at one another.

"You did the right thing," I said.

She sighed. "Yes, I know. But I spent ten years with that bugger, and I loved him. It makes my skin crawl just thinking about it."

"Are you working?" I asked her, suddenly realizing that the "bugger" was also the breadwinner.

"No, but I'll get some temporary help from Social Welfare—the idiot was at least good for that—and then I'll get a job. I can waitress. Maybe get a receptionist job. There's lots of jobs going in this town."

That was true. Retail outlets, offices, restaurants—all were looking for workers.

"Life will be different, that's all," she said.

There were a few tears in her dark eyes, but she smiled. She was courageous, and she was right.

I managed to get back to the school just after three and dropped by Mrs. Harbinger's office. She settled me with a cup of coffee and sent a student to fetch Mary Ellen's teacher, Mrs. Beecher, who would be joining us. Mrs. Harbinger passed around cookies. It was homey and relaxing.

I told them about Mary Ellen's stepfather, what Julia had done about him, and how she was treating her daughter. Mrs. Harbinger nodded.

"Excellent. Sensible mother."

"She wants you to keep the police and the welfare people away from Mary Ellen," I said. "She seemed to think you could do that."

Mrs. Harbinger sent me a steely look. "No doubt about that," she said.

I could trust her. I did trust her. Mary Ellen would be safe in the school.

COMING HOME to Mrs. Sharpe seemed anticlimactic. She was miffed. She was indignant, she was judgemental—and I didn't care.

"You will have to leave. This is a respectable place—"

I cut her off. "Fine," I said. "Dorrie and I will be out at the end of the month."

"Dorothy is leaving as well?" Her voice faltered. I expect we were her only income.

"That's right. We'll get a place together, but you'd best talk to her." I pushed past her and almost ran up the stairs. Having my own home where I could come in, kick off my shoes, turn on the radio, and make my own coffee without being surreptitious about it would be heavenly.

Dorrie gave her notice to Mrs. Sharpe that evening and reported to me.

"Hoist by her own petard, that one," Dorrie said with satisfaction. "Serves her right."

I felt a small twinge of sympathy for Mrs. Sharpe but repressed it.

"Did you hear anything about an apartment?" I asked.

"I asked Janet Clayton—she teaches grade one—if there were any vacant apartments in her building near the school."

"She's Paul's wife?"

"She is. She said there are none at the moment, but she thinks the people in apartment 312 are moving into a house at the end of the month."

Dorrie went to the apartment building the next day and secured the apartment for us with a deposit. The tenants agreed to leave the beds and the kitchen table. We didn't have any pictures or living room furniture, but I expected I could pick some up somewhere. We'd worry about that later. I was anxious to get into the apartment.

"Maybe we could buy a frying pan, some saucepans, and some cutlery?" said Dorrie.

"And a few dishes."

We laughed, excited about setting up on our own. Both of us had always lived with someone: with family when at home and with classmates in dorms at university. We weren't used to stocking a kitchen. And we'd have to clean the place. Maybe we could hire that out?

Moving day came quickly. I recruited Carl, and Dorrie recruited Sam, who could only come after five as he was on call at the hospital until then. She also recruited Janet and Paul Clayton and two male teachers to haul our few belongings up the stairs and into the apartment. After the first trip, the workers brought in contributions. Carl and Paul carried in a sofa.

"It was in the barn," Carl said. "My mother threw it out a few years ago."

It wasn't modern, but it was comfortable. "We'll put an afghan on it," Dorrie said. "When we get an afghan."

We'd bought bedding for each of the beds. It was great to have two bedrooms.

The two male teachers left once the heavy lifting was over.

About six o'clock, Sam arrived with a dozen beer. Janet followed him bearing a steaming casserole. She walked across the room to put it on the stove. The tantalizing scent of chicken wafted through the room.

"Wonderful," I said.

Paul followed her with a bag of bread buns and some butter.

Carl had gone to his truck and came back with a chocolate cake. "My mum sent this."

I hadn't met his mum yet, but she obviously knew about me. She and Carl's dad had just returned from an extended holiday to the warm southern States. I'd meet her soon, since they lived on the ranch adjacent to Carl's.

"Thank her for us."

We found some napkins, opened the beer, sat on whatever was handy or on the floor, and feasted.

Mrs. Sharpe seemed a long way away and in another life. Dorrie caught my eye and raised her beer bottle.

"To Mrs. Sharpe and her respectability!"

I grinned. "She's done us a favour."

Paul and I had a moment later in the kitchen when I asked him about Mary Ellen. He promised to keep Collin O'Brien away from her, so that was a relief. It seemed to me that being a successful public health nurse meant learning to work with competent allied professionals and avoiding the incompetent ones without ever transgressing the professional ethics that prevented me from criticizing them. Professionals made mistakes, but some made more than others. We let the problem drop. Tonight was a party.

We toasted, talked, and laughed until about ten. No one came and told us to go home or pipe down. Carl collected all the garbage, bagged it, and took it away with him. Dorrie and I had only a few plates and dishes to wash. When everyone had gone, we settled into the quiet.

"It looks a little poverty-stricken," Dorrie said, eyeing the bare walls and the mismatched chairs.

"We need a plan," I said, "or we will end up with castoffs from everyone's attic and stuff we hate."

"A plan. Okay. What's our colour scheme?" Dorrie unearthed her school supplies: paper, coloured pencils, and crayons.

We sketched the rooms and tried out the colours. Dorrie like brighter colours than I did, but as long as my bedroom was a cool green or blue, I could live with orange and red in the rest of the apartment. They were only accent colours anyway. We couldn't paint the walls. The apartment manager told us the walls were white and must stay white.

"Do we need rules about men?" I asked Dorrie, yawning. It had been a long day. She was draped over a chair with her head against the back and her feet hanging over the side. It was too small for her, but the previous owner had left it, so it was free. I stretched out on Carl's couch.

"I hate rules," Dorrie muttered.

"Okay. How about an understanding? We have two bedrooms."

"Yeah," Dorrie said. "But I want our apartment to be just for us"

I was relieved. I knew Dorrie was more sexually experienced than I was—well almost anybody was—but I didn't know how I would feel if she brought men home to the apartment. I'd learn to deal, but I was glad I didn't have to.

"What about Carl?" she asked.

"Not an issue, yet," I said. "And he has his own house."

"True. So does Sam."

We smiled at each other. "Okay, this place is just ours."

I lay in bed and looked out the window. We didn't have drapes yet, so I had a wide view. Snow was falling softly. Big flakes. Carl said that kind of snow didn't last, and we wouldn't have deep snow until January. We rarely had snow in the Fraser Valley where I grew up, and then it disappeared in a week. Snow here would come in January and last until April or even May. It would be different. Snow, ice, cold. I snuggled into the flannel sheets, in my own bed, in my own apartment. I was going to enjoy the coming winter.

CHAPTER TWELVE

DISCOVERING RANCH LIFE

I PARKED MY GOVERNMENT car in Carl's barn. There was no sense leaving it in the yard. Seen from the highway, it would advertise to the whole community where I was.

The fields Carl owned near the river produced alfalfa and oats in the summer. By September, Carl had harvested those fields as well as the hay meadows on the higher elevations. Now all the hay was stacked in the barn ready for winter. Carl had moved his cattle to the lower pastures where they continued to graze.

"Right now, it's wood harvesting time." Carl looked with approval at my jeans and winter parka. "I'll get you some gloves."

We were after dead fir and pine. I considered the trees on the hillside: tall, straight pines with dark green needles.

"Lodgepole pine," Carl informed me. "Good for fences, poles, and firewood."

We climbed onto his big green John Deere tractor, a mammoth machine with wheels taller than I was. I stood beside the seat, holding onto the fender and examining the controls. It had two clutch pedals, which were hooked together with a small bar. I suppose Carl could unhook the bar and use each one separately. I suspected that meant only one wheel would turn, but I wasn't sure. I studied the gear shift. It had low and what my dad called "bull low"—a very slow speed. Driving this would be much different from driving a car. Carl turned the key and pushed a small switch up. The engine wheezed, then chugged a rhythmic beat.

The exhaust pipe sticking up at the front coughed and rattled the tin cover. We headed toward the hills.

The ground was hard for it had frozen every night and thawed only a little during the day. Clusters of cones on the pines looked like flowers. I sniffed the air. Something was giving off a spicy scent. Maybe pitch from the pines. Keo, Carl's Australian cattle dog, followed behind us. Carl sometimes invited him up to ride on his lap, but Keo was too impatient and energetic to stay there long.

"He's a cattle dog," Carl had told me. "He has an instinct about cattle. Knows how to bunch them, separate one and bring it to me, and let me know if there's trouble."

"You trained him for that?" I was impressed.

"Can't say I did. More like, I just came to understand what he wanted to do."

Keo spent most of the day with Carl and his nights curled up by the woodstove. He wasn't going to be any help getting wood, but he liked company.

"Does he have any faults?" I asked Carl.

Carl turned his head, so he spoke into my ear above the almost musical chugging of the tractor. "Picks up chickens... and birds."

That translated to "picks up chicks" in my mind, and I had a vision of Keo chatting up a chicken. "Picks up?"

"He doesn't kill them. He just picks them up and delivers them to me as if he's giving me a present. One of these days, a bird is going to peck his face."

I studied Keo as he loped along beside us. Most days he was a worker, but right now he looked carefree, happily revelling in the freedom of the country.

During the summer, Carl had noted fallen trees and ones that were leaning or looked diseased. Today we were searching for them. We followed a dirt trail up into the hills and stopped at a stand of sub-alpine fir. They were larger than the pines and clustered closer together. Several dead trees with grey trunks and orange needles stood at the edge. Carl fired up his heavy chain saw. The rattling *brrr* was loud and almost sacrilegious in the silence. He took down the firs and several other trees that were standing dead or leaning, then cut all the fallen trees into two-foot lengths. I loaded them onto the small trailer we were towing behind the tractor. When we had a manageable load, we returned to the barnyard and transferred all the wood into a shed, armful by armful. Keo supervised us but didn't get in our way.

"I'll come out in the evenings and split them," Carl said.

"With an axe?" I envisioned him standing in the woodshed in the evening light, arms raised, rhythmically smashing the wood.

He nodded at the axe with a long blue handle, leaning against the wall of the shed.

"I'll do some with an axe, but I have a splitter." He showed me the small machine that could slam a wedge into a chock of wood and split it into pieces small enough to fit into a stove. It would take hours of work to create firewood from these chocks. No wonder he had the biceps of a football player.

I rode on the fender of the tractor, back and forth into the hills, all afternoon. I had to hang on when one of the huge tires rolled over a log or into a pothole. When I bounced on the fender, Carl reached out to grab me. There was a handhold in the tractor fender, a cut-out piece with rubber on the inside, so I could grip it firmly. But I didn't object to him grabbing me. Once he slammed his feet on the clutch and the brake and managed to pull me onto his lap for a few moments of bliss. It was odd: the tractor rumbling beneath us, the crisp snow around us, contrasting with the warmth we created between us. It was a brief interlude, and I scrambled back onto the fender, flushed and very pleased with life.

The poplar without their leaves were sticks of grey and looked half-dead, waiting for spring. I saw very little life, though Carl told me there were rabbits, coyotes, deer, and bear nearby. The noise of the tractor probably frightened them. Few birds flew—just some chickadees and crows.

"If birds land on the ground, Keo will stalk them," Carl said. The wise birds stayed aloft.

We drove through a grove of fir trees, shorter than the lodgepole pine with vibrant, almost yellow-green needles and a sharp smell of pitch. A few small birds flew up from their branches.

"Nuthatches," Carl said. "They sit on the trees upside down."

I stared at the tiny birds, flitting away. How did they feed themselves in the winter? Seeds from the pine cones? I'd buy a bird book.

Carl had put pork chops in the Crock-Pot before we started gathering wood. By supper time, an appetizing smell met us as we opened the door. It was a log cabin with two bedrooms, a living room, kitchen, and bathroom.

His bathroom was an experience. I shook my head as I emerged from it. "Your bathroom, Carl."

"Pretty primitive, eh?" he said. Keo had finished his dish of dog food, and Carl was setting out cutlery and some homemade bread.

"Was it designed in 1920?"

He grinned. "Pretty much. I keep thinking I should do something about it."

The toilet worked, so I suppose that's why he didn't improve it. But the shower!

He returned with a tea towel over his shoulder and the Crock-Pot in his hands.

"How do you manage? With a bucket on a stand?" I shuddered. The bathtub was rusted and didn't have a plug. "Do you fill up the bucket, stand in the tub, and dump the water over yourself?"

He nodded. "And then every so often I go over to Mum and Dad's and soak in their tub."

"Ah." I sniffed the bread appreciatively. "Your mum?"

"Yeah, I can't do bread." I looked around the cabin. Someone cleaned this place. He lived on his own, but his parents kept him comfortable. Bread and baths. He was a lucky man.

He looked straight at me. "I'll do something about the bathroom. A white tub? Built into a frame, so you can put bath salts and stuff around it? Shelves? A new toilet and sink?"

I swallowed and hesitated. This wasn't a proposal, was it? I didn't want a proposal. Not yet, anyway, especially not one that involved a toilet and sink.

"That sounds good. White's always easy to decorate around." I concentrated on my meal. He said nothing more, and I relaxed.

While Carl couldn't make bread, he could certainly make pork chops. His mum had sent over some butter tarts, so we had a gooey and delicious dessert. Just as we were starting on coffee, I heard truck tires on the gravel outside. Keo got up and stood by the door. He didn't bark.

Carl headed for the front door. "That'll be Jim and Rita and maybe Millie. A few of their steers got into my herd. I cut them out and put them in the corral. I've been feeding them until they could collect them. Jim said he'd be over. It's probably them now."

It was. Rita and Jim halloed from the front of the house, and we grabbed our parkas and boots and went outside to meet them.

"Millie stayed home," Rita said. "As much as she loves to see you, Carl, she's got her once-a-week TV program on tonight, and she didn't want to miss it."

We had TV in the Cariboo. Carl didn't, but most people did and watched the one channel available here, the Canadian Broadcasting Corporation, or CBC.

"I thought the hockey game was on?" Carl said. Saturday night was *Hockey Night in Canada* all over the country.

"Yeah, she's watching that." Rita walked beside me and the men moved in front of us. We crunched over the slight skiff of snow that had blown into the yard toward the pens near the barn. Jim and Carl looked over the corrals, and Carl indicated the gate.

"You back the truck in here, and I'll saddle up Pammie and herd them toward you."

"Where's Keo?" Jim asked.

"Right here." He must have a reputation as a good cattle dog for Jim to ask if he was going to help.

Rita and I huddled against the cold at the side of the barn. With the oncoming evening, the temperature had dropped.

"Millie likes hockey?" I said. I'd noticed more women in Williams Lake talked about hockey then they did in the south. Williams Lake had its own amateur team and hosted games that attracted a crowd. There was so little live entertainment that a hockey game was an important social occasion.

"She likes hockey, but she likes *Reach for the Top* better, and it comes on after the game."

I watched Carl ride through the open gate, Keo behind far too close to the horse's hooves. Rita hurried over and shut the gate.

"No sense in losing those cattle at this point," she said, returning to the side of the barn.

We watched Jim back the livestock truck to the gate.

"Pammie?" I asked Rita. Carl and the horse started, stopped, dipped, and sidestepped as they bunched a group of cattle and slowly moved them toward the gate. Keo took care of any independent thinkers who tried to bolt.

Rita shrugged. "I'd guess there was someone he dated years ago named Pam. The guys around here tend to call their horses after old girlfriends."

"What about Pete?" I asked, thinking of another of Carl's horses.

"Well, just the mares have girl's names," Rita said. She turned to me. "Carl's a decent sort. No old girlfriends threatening suicide or slapping him with a paternity suit." She wrapped her scarf more snugly around her neck and tucked her gloved hands into her pockets.

I hadn't even thought of that. "Good to know."

The cattle shoved at each other and made a couple of attempts to dart away, but Keo changed their minds and Carl and Pammie kept them moving inexorably up the ramp. Jim slammed shut the cage door and the tailgate, and Carl returned Pammie to the barn.

Rita and I had the coffee poured when the men stamped the snow from their boots and hung up their jackets. Keo gulped water from her dish and lay down beside the fire.

"Butter tarts?" Jim's eyes lit up, and he turned to me.

I held up my hands. "Carl's mum," I said.

"Ah, Betty Jean. She makes the best." Jim smiled in anticipation. Rita rolled her eyes.

Jim looked stricken. "Um... yours are good too, Rita."

Rita smiled. "Betty Jean is an expert. Better have some before your tongue ties itself in knots." She pushed the plate of tarts toward him.

Betty Jean did make great butter tarts—brown sugar, butter and raisins, very sweet. I had two more as we sat around the table and talked. As usual, the talk was about fencing.

"Any idea where those beasts got through?" Jim asked.

"Maybe by the creek. I'll get over there on Monday." Carl likely knew exactly where those cattle had come onto his ranch.

"I'll give you a hand. About ten?" Jim suggested.

"I'll corral any more that get through before then," Carl said.

Talk turned to Range Patrol, the new program that the Department of Agriculture had created.

"They're asking us to pay attention to strange vehicles on our land," said Jim. His hand inched toward the plate, and a butter tart disappeared.

"Rustlers?" Carl said. "We always pay attention to them."

"Are there rustlers?" I asked. It sounded like something from a Hollywood movie.

"There's always someone who thinks they can get a winter's supply of meat for nothing. We can't watch every animal all the time. We all lose a few every year," Carl explained. "They take anything. Might even take a cow in calf. Pretty damaging to herd management."

"Sometimes all you see are tire tracks and blood," Rita added angrily.

"So what's with this program?" Carl asked. "I've been busy and missed the last Cattlemen's meeting. What's up?"

"They gave us these cards." Jim rose and went to his jacket hanging by the door, fished in his pocket, and returned with a pack of printed cards.

Carl reached for a couple and passed one to me. It was a warning: Your vehicle has been observed, the licence plate noted and passed on the RCMP. You are trespassing. Leave at once.

"What are we supposed to do with these?" Carl sounded disgusted.

"Well," Jim leaned back and toyed with the remaining cards. "We're supposed to put one of these on the windshield of the next truck we see on our land."

"And that's it?" Carl said, incredulous.

"No. there's more. We're supposed to report the licence plate number to the Mounties," Jim said seriously.

Carl snorted. "By the time the Mounties get the information and send someone out, those rustlers will be long gone—with the dead steer. When the Mounties follow up on the licence plate number, the thieves will just say they were lost and got out as soon as they realized they were on someone's private land. They will deny they took the steer, and they'll be back the next week for another. What do you think?"

"About the same as you."

"Have you tried it?" Carl asked.

"Yeah. Sure. I found a 1962 Ford, nice truck, parked back behind Lone Lake Hill last Tuesday. You know the spot."

Carl thought for a moment. "Yes, I know the place. Good dirt road into there."

"Yeah, that's right. Easy for rustlers."

"You put a card on their windshield?"

"Sure did," Jim said.

There was silence while they looked at each other.

I said, "What's to stop them from just taking off with your dead cow before the police get there? I mean they shot the cow; they may even have butchered it, and they'll come back to the truck and load it. Why don't they just take off with the meat? What's to stop them?"

Jim looked at me and said slowly, "A 303 bullet in their radiator."

I looked at him, stunned for a moment, and then erupted in laughter. He had backed up the Department of Agriculture's program with an effective strategy of his own. Jim hadn't threatened the men with his rifle, just left them stranded about five miles from the highway with no way to get home except to walk. If they'd shot a steer, they'd have had to leave it there. Perhaps Jim had phoned the police, perhaps not.

I drove myself home about ten, still full of the glow of hard physical exercise, good food, and good company. I shouldn't have been surprised Jim carried a rifle. He had to deal with bear and he'd probably take down a deer for meat if he saw one. Ranchers, hunters, and the police were the only people who carried guns here. Carl hadn't carried a gun when we went for wood. But then the tractor and the chain saw made so much noise that no deer, bear, or rustlers would have come near us. I'd noticed he had a gun scabbard on his saddle. Perhaps he took one with him when he was off in the hills alone.

NOVEMBER TRIPPED into December, and there was still no significant amount of snow. It was as if the countryside was waiting—just waiting—for the heavens to dump several feet of it. I made the rounds of my schools, trying to complete as much work as I could before the students disbanded for the holidays.

Mrs. Harbinger sent a little girl named Sarah Hockley to me who had a skin rash. I was getting quite good at diagnosing common skin infections and decided with some confidence that it was scabies. I didn't tell Mrs. Harbinger that. I just said it looked like a minor problem. If there were more kids in the school affected, I'd talk to her about it, but if it was just Sarah, I'd only tell her family. Some people considered scabies a disgrace. I told Mrs. Harbinger I'd talk to the mother.

The girl lived with her mother and father in a small trailer at the edge of town. The stairs to the door were scrubbed clean. That was quite an undertaking in this world of dirt and mud. The door itself was painted a bright white. Mrs. Hockley invited me in.

"Is something wrong with Sarah?" she asked as she ushered me in and offered me a chair.

"She has a rash, Mrs. Hockley, and I've had a look at it," I explained.

She nodded. "Yes, I was going to take her to the doctor. Nothing seems to work on it."

"It's scabies, and this medication will work." I started to pull a pamphlet from my black bag with the instructions of how to treat scabies with benzyl benzoate. It was quite a common affliction and a common over-the-counter treatment.

"My child does *not* have scabies!" she almost screamed at me.

I looked up to see Mrs. Hockley had risen to her feet and was seething with indignation. *Uh-oh. She was one of* those *parents.* I should have paid attention to the ultra-clean front steps.

"How *dare* you say my child has scabies?"

"Many children do, Mrs. Hockley." I tried for a calm tone.

"I will take her to the doctor, and you can rest assured he won't tell me it's scabies."

She probably thought only dirty children were infected. In fact, scabies liked clean skin, but I didn't tell her that. She wouldn't have listened.

"Certainly." I stuffed the pamphlet back into my bag, stood, and moved toward the door. "That's good idea. You take her to the doctor."

I was curious how Mrs. Hockley would handle it when the doctor told her what it was.

"Not scabies," she told me triumphantly when I returned the following week.

"Oh, really?" I said. "What was it?"

"Just a rash. He gave me a prescription for it, and it worked just great." She spoke with a certain smugness, as if she had defended her daughter against me.

"Could I see what it is he prescribed?"

She brought me the tube with the prescription data on the label. I copied down the prescription number.

"Thanks so much," I said. "I'll need to know about this."

"That's for sure. You can't go around insulting people and telling them their kids have scabies when they don't."

I just nodded and said. "That's good advice. Thanks."

I left. When I returned to the health unit, I phoned the pharmacist.

"What is this prescription?" I asked her, giving her the number

"Just a minute." I could hear pages rustling. "That's benzyl benzoate."

"Thanks." *Hah!* Benzyl benzoate was the treatment specific for scabies. Dr. Wilson had seen the mother was upset with the idea of scabies and told her it was something else. Of course, he sacrificed my credibility in the process, but I'd forgive him for that. Sarah got treated and that was the important thing.

CHAPTER THIRTEEN

TWO HUNDRED MILES INTO THE CHILCOTIN

W E HAD our usual monthly health unit staff meeting the first Monday of December to plan our upcoming work, and, since Christmas holidays fell in this period, we sorted out the assignments. Most of the staff would be away for at least a week, and we needed to plan for the continuity of services. We had to consider the weather. Another drift of clouds had left snow over the Cariboo country, just enough to cover the fields but not enough to impede driving. The Department of Highways sent graders out to the country roads and cleared them. I hadn't had to use my chains for weeks, but winter would become more intense and make it more difficult to travel.

Rita coordinated our schedules. "Highways does a good job," she said, "as long as they don't get a huge dump of snow in a short period. If that happens, it might take them days to get out to some of the more rural roads. Travel to your country districts before we get that snow."

"I'm going east in the third week of the month," I said.

"That'll work. Get Ellie to send out messages to announce the clinics, so the people know you're coming. They might not be expecting you because no one does any business around Christmas."

I had a vision of Williams Lake totally quiet—no traffic, no people in the streets, just the pale winter light and deep snow. I'd planned to take the week between Christmas and New Year's as holiday time to go home to my parents. Carl would have Christmas with his parents—not that I'd worry about him. I might miss him, though. Dorrie was going home too, and Sam was going to visit her for a few days after Christmas.

Rita scanned the papers in front of her. "Someone has to go out to the Chilcotin soon. They haven't had any service this fall because we're one nurse short. We'll get a new nurse in January, but I need a volunteer for a four-day trip out to Anahim Lake and back—as soon as next week." She looked directly at me. The other nurses were married with families. I was the one who could spare four days away from home.

"Fine," I said, accepting the inevitable.

"Are you sure?" Rita asked me.

"Yes," I said with more enthusiasm. "It will be an adventure." This wasn't really a choice. She was couching it respectfully, but there was a directive behind that request—she was my boss.

"Be sure you..."

"Pack a candle," we chanted together. It was a joke now—that the only equipment we had to fight off death by freezing was a candle.

"Stay on the main roads," Rita cautioned. "Don't go off visiting ranches in the back of beyond, because if you get stuck in a snow-bank no one will know you are there."

I nodded. No one carried any kind of communication except truckers and police who had radios. When I was in my car, miles from anywhere, I was truly alone.

If Ellie got the radio messages out on Message Time people would know I was coming and would look out for me. I would pack warm sweaters.

I WAS sitting in the staff room of Sophie's school a couple of days later. I'd helped her with her grade five immunizations, and we were having a welcome coffee. The radio was tuned to the local station, and everyone stopped talking to listen to Message Time.

My favourite message was "To Johnny Joseph of Tatla Lake. Bring my car back. Your holiday is over." Everyone had their favourites, and we waited to see what gems the announcer had for us this day.

I heard the announcements for my clinics. "To all the people of the Chilcotin. The nurse will be at the following sites for baby clinics and for any other concerns." Then it listed all the stops I would be making on my four-day trip.

"That's you," Sophie said.

"It is." I felt a small glow of pride that what I was doing was important enough to notify a vast community.

The teachers asked me how I would travel and what I would take with me.

"Take a sleeping bag," one teacher said.

"Good idea," I said. "But I don't have one."

"I'll fetch mine and give it to Sophie. You can borrow it." The teacher was young, about my age. I didn't know her and was impressed by her generosity.

"Thanks."

"That's magmatimous of you," Sophie said.

There was a short silence. We knew she meant "magnanimous."

I headed west out to the Chilcotin the following Monday. The roads were clear. The weather forecast was sunny and cold. By cold, the forecasters meant ten degrees Fahrenheit—twenty-two degrees below freezing. I would not want to have any kind of car trouble.

Carl had given me a bottle of gas-line antifreeze. "If any water gets in the gas, it can cause engine trouble. If the engine is coughing or hesitating, pour this into the tank."

I stowed it in the glove compartment with the candle, matches, and some chocolate bars—my emergency stash.

The distance from Williams Lake to Anahim Lake, my far west destination, was about two hundred miles. I had clinics over the next four days in Alexis Creek, Tatla Lake, and Anahim Lake and a lot of driving in between. I passed over the Fraser River on the narrow bridge and then up Sheep Creek Hill. It wound skyward in harrowing switchback curves from the river ravine to the Chilcotin

Plateau, an area of the great Interior Plateau. The Department of Highways had gravelled and sanded the road, and my tires gripped pretty well. Going down might be a different experience—any ice, and I could slide. Ice formed when a sudden warm spell melted the snow and then the temperature dropped. Not today, though. It was too cold for that. The car felt secure on the road.

On top of the hill, the plateau rolled out in front of me. Miles and miles of white snow, covering the grasslands. Grey sticks of willow along the ditches and bare grey branches of poplar groves in the white fields created the only colour accents on the land. The sky was cobalt blue and immense. It was such a contrast from my eastern district where the sky was confined by the evergreen-covered mountaintops. Here, it was as if the world was mostly sky.

Lee's Corner Store was the solitary commercial building in the Hanceville community, the first settlement on my trip. The log cabin was a post office as well and served the ranches in the neighbourhood. I stopped to buy a chocolate bar and to use the bathroom. That was a euphemism as it was an outdoor privy at the back of the log cabin—no bath and no room. Exposing my backside to the freezing air was an experience and made this bathroom break lightning fast. Was it possible to get frostbite on my exposed skin? I didn't linger. In my eastern district I could pull over, dart into the bushes, and relieve myself. But here on the open prairie, I didn't have any place to hide. The truck drivers didn't bother to hide. They stood by their trucks.

When I spotted the first trucker in this position, I didn't know where to look. The driver stood at the edge of road, staring out over the plains, sending a stream into the snow. I had seen him for some distance away on this wide plateau where the road was straight and treeless. He knew I had seen him. This was the country. I couldn't just drive by without some kind of communication. I finally raised my hand as I passed and waved. The trucker took the cigarette from his mouth with the hand that wasn't engaged and waved back. So that's what I continued to do whenever I met truckers so occupied. My mother would have pretended he wasn't there. Somehow, that didn't seem right or practical. There was a different social order here. Everyone waved when you met on the road, whether you knew the person or not. Who knew when you might need each other?

I followed the Chilcotin River, although I could only occasionally see the river down in the ravine. When I arrived in Alexis Creek, there were seven mothers with babies waiting for me at the school. I sorted out the immunizations. One of the mothers weighed the babies for me, and everyone gathered around to listen to my advice on each child. No one was going to tell me any secrets with all these listening ears, but since I was only coming once, I would be of limited use as a confidant. I let them know I would be staying at the hotel that night. They could visit me there if they had anything urgent or private to talk about.

There were two women from the nearby Stone Reserve who brought their babies for immunizations. I would send my records to Patricia at Indian Health in Williams Lake, so she could add this information to her records. I didn't know why there was a federal health system for Indigenous people and a provincial system for non-Indigenous people. I didn't know why such an inefficient and prejudiced set of systems had been established in the first place. It was strange.

All the babies seemed normal and healthy. The kids in the school seemed healthy as well. I examined teeth, wrote out referrals, tested eyes, and gave immunizations. I did hearing tests on children the teacher referred to me and found only normal hearing.

"Just not listening," the teacher concluded.

Before going to dinner at the hotel, I drove over to the Red Cross Outpost Hospital. I didn't have any work to do there. This was a courtesy call. I thought the nurse might like the company of a colleague. Sister Robert (pronounced the French way, *Ro-baire*) managed the tiny hospital with great competence. She served all the people, Indigenous and non-Indigenous. The Red Cross didn't discriminate. Doctors from Williams Lake came periodically to help her. She was a short, thin, highly energetic woman dressed a little oddly in a mid-calf shirtwaist grey dress. Perhaps it was issued by the order of nuns she represented. She wore a white band near her face, holding back her hair with a short head scarf. She bustled around, slapped a cup of tea in front of me, and then shoved an X-ray into a viewing compartment and asked my opinion on a pair of lungs.

"Do you think we've got TB here?"

While I was knowledgeable on the prevention and treatment of tuberculosis, I was not the least adept at reading X-rays.

I shook my head. "No idea."

"Now, look here," she said, pointing to an area in the lower left lobe. "It looks mucky to me. Just not right." Her competence made me feel humble, reminding me of my instructor at university who had pounded into me the fact that as a new graduate I was a beginner and had a lot to learn.

"Any TB symptoms like four o'clock fever? Night sweats?" That I knew.

"Just coughing and chest pain," she said.

"Could it be a bacterial infection?" That seemed likely to me, but I wasn't going to diagnose it. Sister Robert was a much more experienced and expert nurse than I was.

"Well, yes, it could. I'll knock some antibiotics into him and take an X-ray in a couple of weeks. No improvement, and he goes into Williams Lake for another X-ray and a couple of GPs to look at him." She studied the X-ray again.

"That sounds reasonable," I said. "Did you do a Mantoux test?" Those skin tests were easy to do.

"The man's been positive for years. A positive skin test wouldn't mean a thing."

A positive response only meant the individual had fought off TB at some point, not that he or she had an active case of the disease. Once positive, people usually stayed positive. No additional skin tests helped identify the problem.

"Too bad. That makes it harder to diagnose," I commiserated. I wasn't going to be of any help to her.

"That's right. Still," she mused, "maybe I should test the family? Just in case."

She clicked off the light on the viewing box and with that seemed to dismiss her patient from her conscious thought. She visited with me, politely pouring tea, but I could see she was not accustomed to sitting for long. I left her and drove to the hotel.

My hotel room was small, but the bed looked comfortable. There was a wash basin in the room. The bathroom was down the hall. I noted there was a lock on the inside of my door. No lock on the outside, so I couldn't lock it when I left the room. I shrugged philosophically. No one was likely to steal from me. I left my luggage and headed for the bar to get a meal. One end of the bar seemed to be full of people eating, the other end of men drinking— all white men. It was against the law for Indigenous people to drink in a bar or even at home. I supposed only white people could get drunk at home or in public places. I headed for the eating section.

"Stew?"

I looked up as a man with a heavily stained apron leaned toward me. I assumed he was either the cook or the owner, or both.

"Is that's what's offered tonight?" I wondered if any café in the Cariboo or Chilcotin ever offered another choice.

He took his cigarette from his mouth and blew smoke away from me. "Yeah, stew. It's good. We can do you an omelette if you'd rather."

"What's your name?" I asked.

"Mike."

"Marion." I smiled at him. "I'll take the stew."

"The bread's fresh. My old lady makes it." He jammed the cigarette back into his mouth.

"Are you the owner?" I was curious.

"No. Just friends of the owner. They're away right now, so me and the wife are pinch hitting." I supposed it was nice of him and his wife to give the owners a holiday, but I expected Mike knew little about food safety. I eyed the cigarette with its ash dangling precipitously over the table. Oh, well. I was hungry and would trust my immune system.

"Want a drink?" he asked.

"Just coffee."

"Comin' up."

The stew was good. I didn't ask what it was made of. Probably deer or moose. The coffee was good as well. Whoever his "old lady" was, she could cook.

I unloaded my records onto the small table in my room, then sat down and caught up with my paperwork. The child health clinic work was quick because I'd kept the files in front of me when I gave the immunizations and recorded what I'd done immediately. It was the school records that could get into a mess. I carefully checked the class lists against my notations on a piece of paper and wrote in all the screening results. Ellie would transfer the records when I returned.

I visited the bathroom and had a quick wash—what my mother called a lick and a dash, no such thing as a bathtub here—and was preparing for bed when a furious bang on my door startled me.

"Hey, Nurse," a man's voice called. "Hey, Nurse. Want to party?"

I darted to the door and flipped the lock shut. Whoever he was, I did not want to party with him.

"Hey, Nurse," he called again and in a drunken tenor began, "My darling, my darling I've wanted to call you my darling." That was a song from *Charlie's Aunt*, an old musical. He got through a verse, wavering a little at the end.

I found him funny—like something from an old cartoon, the loveable drunk from the comics—until he started banging on my door again. I could see the boards give a little as he hit them. I was about to yell at him to go away and then thought, if I stayed quiet, he might think I was out.

I could hear him mutter. "Maybe she's not there." He yelled. "Hey, Nurse? Are you there?"

There was, of course, no phone in the room. If I dragged a chair to put under the lock, would he hear me? Probably. I stayed still and hoped he would leave.

My drunken suitor started singing again: "If you were the only girl in the world..." He had a good voice. I wondered who he was. I wondered how old he was, how big he was. Should I be prepared to run from the room if he broke the door down?

"Hey, Archie." I heard a voice from down the hall. "Your wife is looking for you."

"Oh," said Archie.

"Come on now, boyo. Let me take you back to your room."

"The nurse might be lonely," Archie persisted.

"I don't think so," my rescuer said.

"Nice-looking girl like that. Must be lonely."

"Hey, buddy. She's not lonely. She's got a big lumberjack boyfriend. Come on. I'll get you home."

Archie started singing again, but the sound got fainter. I felt my shoulders relax.

I shook my head. It was a good thing my mother couldn't see me now. I could laugh about Archie because he hadn't gotten into my room. It wouldn't have been funny at all if he had broken down my door, and I'd had to deal with an amorous drunk. I was grateful to whomever had led him off. Probably Mike. I put the chair under the lock and went to bed.

In the morning, Mike cooked me a full breakfast: sausages, eggs, fried potatoes, homemade bread, and lots of coffee. I noticed two couples eating at the other end of the bar.

Mike went over with the coffee pot. "More coffee, Archie?"

I snuck a quick glance at my predator from last night. He was about fifty, bald, and red-faced. A stetson lay on the bar beside him. His wife was thin, much younger, and talkative. She was pouring a steady stream of words into Archie's ear. He didn't seem to hear her. I looked away. I didn't want eye contact. I paid my bill, pocketed the receipt, and slipped away.

The hotel had a gas pump, and Mike filled my tank.

"Fill up wherever you can," he said. "You don't want to be caught without gas. A full tank keeps the condensation out."

"Good idea." I supposed condensation in the gas turned to ice in cold weather.

"Thanks, and thanks for the rescue last night. I guess that was you." I smiled at him.

"Yeah. Yeah. That's okay." He seemed a little embarrassed. "Archie and his missus go to town every so often, and they stop here on their way home to their ranch. We're used to him here. There's no harm in Archie. He's just loud. He would probably have just shaken your hand and sung to you."

"Okay," I said, but I wasn't sure about that, and I was grateful I hadn't had to find out.

I headed farther west through the Chilcotin Plateau. The heater worked, and the air was so dry, my car windows stayed clear. I drove past Redstone Reserve and Chilanko Forks to Tatla Lake. Here, the Chilcotin Plateau met the Coast Mountains. To the south was the Tatlayoko Valley, a place of outstanding beauty, or so I'd been told. Farther south was Chilko Lake—even more stunning, according to Carl—but I was not going off the main road on this trip.

The sun lit the tops of the Coast Mountains to the west, shining a brilliant white on those soaring peaks. They were a dramatic and awe-inspiring contrast to the flat land I'd been travelling through. I stopped the car to simply stare. I wished passionately I could paint. Someone should record this beauty. It sifted into my bones and made me ache. It was dramatic and overwhelming. I stood watching until the cold forced me to move.

I held a clinic at the Tatla Lake school, where three mothers were waiting for me with their healthy babies. When I was finished for the day, I retired to the Graham ranch. The owners supported the community by hosting whatever nurse arrived, providing bed and board. They invited me to join them for dinner. Stew again. The Cariboo and Chilcotin must live on stew. This was an active cattle ranch, and the family needed to get up early to tend to their stock, so everyone retired soon after dinner. At this time of year, they fed hay to their beef cattle and kept the chickens from freezing. The woman I assumed was Mrs. Graham told me that while they had close to a thousand head of cattle, they only had enough chickens to feed the family.

"As much as I need the eggs, it's a crying shame the way they take so much time. They're stupid, you know. They almost send out invitations to fox, coyotes, and martin to come and help themselves to eggs and a chicken dinner. It's like I'm feeding the coyotes."

She showed me the large bedroom off the kitchen that would be mine for the night. It looked comfortable, and I said good night as the family left for their bedrooms somewhere distant in that large log house.

"I'll let the dogs in. They're half-wild, but they won't bother you if you stay in the bedroom," my hostess said.

I planned to drop right off to sleep but soon found the comforters on the bed were no match for the freezing cold that settled over me. There was no heat in the room. Mrs. Graham had told me that the temperature had dropped to twenty-five degrees below freezing, so she'd put another comforter on the bed. It wasn't enough. I thought about the sleeping bag I had left in my car. Going to the car meant dressing and going through the kitchen past the dogs. I cracked opened the door. A low growl emanated from one corner of the kitchen. I shut the door and retreated. I only dozed through the night.

Mrs. Graham made up for the uncomfortable night by feeding me enough breakfast to keep a logger moving all day. She even gave me a hot bun in a napkin to take with me. I'd plugged my car into an extension cord hanging from a wooden post. All vehicles in this country had engine block heaters, and this morning I was glad of it as the car started without difficulty.

I drove past Kleena Kleene and Nimpo Lake and on to Anahim Lake. This was a much larger community of about a thousand people. I worked in the school, held a child health clinic, and finally made my way to the local hotel for a meal. I was tired. It seemed I spent more time driving than nursing, but I felt I'd accomplished some things: I had stayed on the road, not slipped in a ditch or over a cliff; I'd been on time for all the clinics; and I'd done what was asked of me. On top of that, I was seeing the country—albeit in the cold and snow.

An older Indigenous woman approached me at my table. Behind her a young woman of about seventeen stood quietly.

"Nurse?" the older woman asked.

I nodded and gestured for her to sit down.

"Coffee?" I suggested.

She smiled and sat down on the chair opposite me. The younger woman stood behind her and a little distance away.

"No thanks," she said. "I have a favour to ask."

"Go ahead."

"This is Charmaine, my niece. She is going to art school in Vancouver."

"Congratulations," I said.

The young woman smiled. She was beautiful.

"Yes." The older woman almost glowed with pride. "She's very talented, and she won a spot."

"What can I do?" I knew absolutely nothing about art. I hoped I wasn't going to be asked to give an opinion on her work.

"She needs a ride to Williams Lake. My brother, her uncle, will meet her there, keep her with his family overnight, and put her on the bus the next day. She has her ticket," she assured me. She fell quiet and waited.

This was the way my own aunts would ask for a favour. They'd put the problem in front of me and let me offer what I could.

"I'm not supposed to take passengers in a government car," I said.

The woman held her face still.

"But I will."

She smiled.

"If you don't write the health department and tell them, I won't either." I hoped the insurance my dad had purchased on the car would cover Charmaine if we got into an accident.

Her eyes lit with amusement, and she shook her head. "No fear of that. What time will you be leaving tomorrow?"

"About eight."

"Charmaine will be here." She nodded briskly, stood and left, Charmaine trailing after her.

Maybe tomorrow I would find out if Charmaine could talk. *Maybe Charmaine will be the artist who paints those mountains*, I thought.

SHE WAS on time the next morning and helped me load the car. She didn't talk much the first two hours but slept as I sped away from the Coast Mountains and back onto the Chilcotin Plateau. The road followed the Chilcotin River part of the way. Ice had formed on the riverbanks, but a black ribbon showed open water in the centre. Charmaine awoke when I stopped for coffee, more gas, and a break at Redstone Reserve. Like most places in this vast country, it was beautiful. The Chilanko and Chilcotin Rivers meet here, the perfect spot for a settlement. We could see the white Coast Mountain peaks, white in the distant sky. Charmaine gazed at them. Her home was at the foot of those mountains. We would lose sight of them soon.

The air seemed a little warmer, but I was not tempted to unzip my parka.

Charmaine and I munched our doughnuts and sipped our coffee as I drove east toward Williams Lake. Charmaine told me about her plans to be a great artist and make her mother and aunties proud of her. She was going to live with yet another aunt in Vancouver.

"Will you be lonely?" I thought about the beautiful, wild country we'd just left and the crowded city of Vancouver with its constant rain.

"Yes," she said simply. "But I must do this."

We drove in silence for a while, then she said. "You left home to go to school so you could be a nurse?"

"I did."

"Was it hard?"

I thought back to those days, not so long ago. I'd left my home and family to go some distance to university. My family hadn't seemed real. They had seemed as if they were living outside the authentic world and not quite in it, and I'd wanted something different. I'd felt when I'd left, I was finally jumping into real life. Charmaine, I suspected, would see her home in Anahim Lake as the real world where love and support held her close. Any other place would seem cold and uncaring. I didn't tell her that.

"It's hard, very often it's hard. It'll help to go home as often as you can."

"My mum will come and visit me." That seemed a comfort to her.

"Yes, but you will need to see your own country." I was sure of that, although I couldn't explain it.

I was tired when we finally arrived at Sheep Creek Hill, the last dangerous part of our trip just before the Fraser River and only about thirty miles from Williams Lake. The temperature had warmed still more, but I hadn't realized the sun had melted the ice on the road until my tires skidded on the first turn.

Charmaine gasped and braced her hand on the dashboard.

I let the right wheels slide into the snow at the edge of the road, which slowed the car. I quickly shifted into low gear and inched my way back onto the road.

Except for that first gasp, Charmaine was silent. Good, because I couldn't think about her and drive.

On every switchback, the back end of the car swung out. I used the snow at the edge of the road, the low gear, and a judicious touch of the brakes to negotiate that damn hill. My heart was beating at double time, and I was breathing fast when I finally coasted to the flat stretch before the bridge. I crossed the river and stopped in the middle of the road on the other side.

"God," Charmaine said, letting out a long breath. "You can drive."

I glanced at her. "Thanks."

I swallowed. There was no one on the road but us. I wiped my hands on my pants and stared at the hill in front of me. This side

of the river was in shadow. With luck there hadn't been any melting on the road here. I put the car in second gear and attacked that
hill. It was easy. No sliding. No traffic, no cars, or logging trucks
looming at us.

I pulled into the health unit about six, and Charmaine's uncle
was waiting. He had probably been waiting for an hour or so.
Charmaine hugged me, thanked me, unloaded her suitcase, and
dropped it into the back of her uncle's truck. He shook my hand
and thanked me. I managed a nod and a wave to Charmaine.

I dumped all my equipment into the lab for Anna-Lise to deal
with in the morning, put the vaccines away but left everything
else. I dropped my records on my desk and headed home to my
apartment.

"Hey," Dorrie said as I turned the key and walked in. "You made it."

I shrugged out of my parka and hung it up. "I did. Is there any
supper?"

"Sure." she said. "Stew."

CHAPTER FOURTEEN

FALLING IN LOVE
WITH THE CARIBOO

I WAS LATE GETTING to work the next day. No one complained. Ellie had started recording all my notes, and Anna-Lise had cleaned up the mess I'd left for her.

"Thanks for trekking out there," Rita said when she stuck her head into my office. "Any problems?"

Flashbacks of driving through the vast Chilcotin with an underlying fear of freezing, the drunk pounding on my door, and the slide down Sheep Creek Hill flitted through my mind. I shook my head.

"Great," she said and left.

I had paperwork to fill out on the home care program that included statistics: how many visits we had made, the nature of the visits, and how much time each nurse had spent with each patient. This was a pilot program, so we needed to prove it was effective. I understood the necessity for collecting data. I just found it tedious.

Sally and Kate arrived with their reports on their patients. Three of us in my office filled it. Kate stashed her purse and black bag on the counter behind her. Sally dumped hers on my desk. She leaned over and flicked her finger at one chart.

"Mrs. Beaminster," she said. "High blood pressure, lonely. Doesn't eat well. Neglected by her son who lives in town. She's going to get rip-roaring drunk at Christmas."

I scanned the chart and then looked up. "Won't her son take her to his house for Christmas?"

Mrs. Beaminster lived in an apartment building with many independent seniors, but Christmas could be lonely.

"Nope. Says he doesn't 'do' Christmas." Her voice dripped scorn.

"Can you pressure him in any way?" I asked her.

She was quiet for a moment. Sally had connections all over town. She would know someone who knew the son. "I'll see what I can do."

We planned the next week's work, and Kate left to start her rounds. I turned back to my charts and my records. Sally didn't leave, just sat staring at the pile of charts on the desk.

"What is it?" I asked.

"I had a problem yesterday." She still didn't look at me.

"Yes?"

"You know Mrs. Akron out in Pine Valley?" She looked out the window. I was getting worried. Sally never evaded.

I searched through the charts and found the correct one. "Right."

"I've been doing the dressing changes on her colostomy, and she called me on Wednesday. She had some bleeding from the site, so I changed the dressing."

I snapped my head up. "Did you let her doctor know?"

Sally bit her lower lip. "Not on Wednesday. I took her to the hospital on Thursday because the bleeding hadn't stopped."

A colostomy was not a common procedure here. Surgeons removed part of the colon and sewed it to the abdominal wall, giving the operating site a chance to heal. Usually, they reconnected it weeks later. Bleeding from the site was not something we were supposed to diagnose. Sally should have reported it immediately. The air in the office was still, almost oppressive. Sounds from outside—cars crunching by, the occasional truck horn—receded into the background. Sally waited.

Finally, I said, "Did you tell Rita?" Rita was my backup on the program. She should have known about this and reported it to the doctor if Sally hadn't.

"No. I took Mrs. Akron to the hospital on Thursday, and Dr. Anderson was furious." She looked at me. Tiny lines fanned out from her eyes, crinkling the skin around her mouth. She'd been nursing for years. She was reliable, knowledgeable, and conscientious. But she'd made a mistake.

I sighed. "He was angry."

"Yeah. He called me in and tore a strip off me in front of the patient. Said I was responsible for making his patient live with a colostomy for the rest of her life. If I'd brought her in right away, he might have been able to reverse the operation, but now he couldn't." Sally stared at me. "I feel really, really bad."

Reversing the operation meant putting her colon back inside, stitching her up, and allowing her to lead a normal life. The colostomy emptied into a bag on her abdomen and was supposed to be temporary. This was major.

It was true Sally had made a mistake, but Patrick Anderson had harassed her in front of the patient. I was furious. I was sorry for Mrs. Akron, for sure. Still, I doubt if Sally made that much difference to the outcome for the patient. Even if she had, Dr. Anderson was unprofessional to blame her in front of the patient. This was something medical professionals talked about in private, decided who was to blame, and then delegated the responsible person to talk to the patient.

Sally bit her lip. "I'm worried about Mrs. Akron, and I'm worried about me. Do you think Anderson will ask the RNBC to pull my licence?"

The Registered Nurses Association of BC wouldn't do anything if they didn't get a complaint, but I understood Sally's worry. Anderson or the patient could complain. Sally's income was necessary for her family. She had three kids and a husband who didn't make a lot of money. Her licence was her livelihood. But I doubted Dr. Anderson would complain about her. He'd have to admit he hadn't been monitoring his patient.

I snorted. "Not likely." I reached for the phone.

I got through to the receptionist who passed me along to Dr. Anderson, and I started in with a polite, but determined inquiry.

"Dr. Anderson, we have a problem. I hear you blamed my nurse in front of your patient, Mrs. Akron, for not getting her to you on Wednesday and consequently for ruining her life... No, I agree, however, that was highly unprofessional. I can hardly believe you did it." I was fired up and didn't want to listen to any excuses. Sally had spent an anxious night.

"She should have called me right away." He sputtered with indignation.

"True. She should have. And where were you yesterday at"—I glanced at the chart—"three p.m.?"

There was silence. "I thought so. Your day off, right? You weren't even in town. Let's be reasonable here. Sally could have taken Mrs. Akron to the ER. She should have done that. She will be more conscientious about this kind of surgery in the future. But, remember, you also have made a mistake or two in your medical practice." I was safe assuming that. Everyone in the medical field has made mistakes. "You can accept and help others who also make mistakes. No one is perfect. It is unprofessional to blame a colleague in front of a patient. Absolutely unacceptable. I am considering taking you off our home care list. You can look after your patients yourself—" Oh. I'd gone a little too far there. That was pressure or maybe, more accurately, blackmail. I didn't even know if I had the authority to do that.

"Wait. Wait." He interrupted me before I could give him more sanctions. We looked after several of his patients and saved him home visits and hours of time. "All right. All right. We all make mistakes." He said that quickly and then laughed. "Sorry. Tell Sally I'm sorry. It was upsetting."

"I can understand that. I'll tell her, but hey..."

"Got it. I'll restrain myself and won't do that again, but..."

"But yes," I said with some compassion. "It was upsetting."

I stared at the black telephone in my hand and noticed that my hand was shaking. I did not like confrontations. I carefully hung up. I took a deep breath and let the tension drain away. The air crackled with emotion. I looked up. Sally was staring at me as if she'd never seen me before.

"Marion," Sally said. "Thank you." She was biting her lips and shaking a little. "Did they teach you how to be that... that... *force-ful* at university?"

"No," I reflected. "They taught me how to inquire into a problem, not just accept it. But the pit-bull attitude comes from growing up with five siblings. It gets me into trouble sometimes."

"Thanks. Really. Thanks. You stood up for me, even when I was wrong."

"The only way to avoid mistakes is to do nothing, and even then, that can be a mistake." I thought of Audrey Cook, my own heartbreaking mistake. "Go have a coffee," I said. "The patient is not likely in as bad a shape as he said. I'll check on her later."

I drove out to Mrs. Akron's house that afternoon. She lived in a trailer in a small subdivision nestled in a valley alongside the highway. Snow covered the hills on either side. The dried yellow grasses poked through bright white snow along the ditches; in other places it was blue-grey, blending into the grey of the sky. The road was clear and sanded.

"How are you?" I asked Mrs. Akron as I settled into a chair in her kitchen.

"Better, I think," she said.

"I'm sorry our nurse didn't get you in to the doctor sooner." It seemed best to get the problem out in the open.

She shrugged and smiled a little. She was a tiny woman with short grey hair and blue eyes. Her reading glasses lay on a book on the table. The trailer was warm. It had good heating, despite the frost on the windows.

"Yes, the doctor seemed to think that made a big difference, but I don't know. It seems to me the doctor is responsible, not the nurse. He could have come out to see me. I left a message at his office. He never called back."

Well, well. That was interesting news. "He didn't?"

"No. I left it in the morning before I called Sally."

I thought about the timing. Anderson had been told, or at least a message had been left for him, *before* she called Sally. There were mistakes on both sides here.

"My husband is taking me to Vancouver tomorrow," she continued. "We're going to consult a doctor my daughter recommends. She's in nursing at St. Paul's Hospital."

"Sounds like a good idea." She would get better care. Dr. Anderson was going to lose this patient, but he would want the best for her, and I didn't think he would mind. "But right now?"

She settled back in her chair and patted the dressing on her abdomen. "Right now, everything is under control. The bleeding's stopped. The surgical site looks the same. I'm looking forward to being with my daughter and getting those specialists in Vancouver to check me out. It's at times like this Williams Lake seems a bit isolated. In Vancouver I'll have my choice of specialists and surgeons. My daughter will know what to do."

"I wish you good luck." I rose.

"Thanks for coming. Tell Sally I'll call her when I get back."

"I'll do that. Sally was worried." Desperately worried, but I didn't say that aloud.

Mrs. Akron smiled. "She's a good woman."

When I told Sally, she sagged a little and let out a huge sigh. "She's talking to me?"

I'd caught Sally at the health unit door as she was leaving to see a patient. She took a step to the side, so we could talk without blocking the entry.

"Yes, she is. She doesn't blame just you."

Sally stared at me, waiting.

"She left a message at Dr. Anderson's office, and he never responded."

"You mean," Sally said, "he knew about it?"

I reached for the door and spoke over my shoulder. "Let's assume he didn't know about it until Thursday morning because *his* nurse didn't think it was important enough to tell him."

"He hit out at me because he felt guilty?"

I nodded. "He's quick to anger but fast to return to normal. Basically, a reasonable guy."

"Sure."

Sally was doubtful, but I thought Dr. Anderson was doing the best he could and only occasionally lost it.

I SPENT the weekend with Carl at his ranch. It was peaceful. A faint hum came from the cars on the highway on the other side of the fields and a soft gurgle from the nearby river, still free of ice. I heard chickadees calling from the willow bushes and, occasionally, a cow demanding a response from her calf. Ranch sounds and ranch activity. There always seemed to be a lot to do here, including feeding the cattle. There was enough snow on the ground now that the cattle refused to graze.

I knew how to drive a tractor but only the small Farmall Cub Dad kept on his acreage. Carl taught me how to drive the big green John Deere behemoth. The steering wheel was huge but fairly easy to turn. The two clutches were clipped together, so I treated them as if they were one. As well, there was a brake so far below me that when I pushed on it to the bottom of its capabilities, I had to stand and pull back on the steering wheel to keep the brake engaged. I learned to drive it well enough to haul the trailer while Carl stood amongst the hay bales. When I stopped the tractor, he slipped the strings from each bale, then threw it in such a way the compacted hay flew apart in the air and spread on the ground. The cattle followed us, munching on the fallen hay but still pushing forward, looking for their next bite. I stopped while Carl tossed several bales in a circle. Occasionally, Keo loped off to bring in a cow that was wandering away from the herd.

Carl lobbed some snowballs for Keo to chase. For such an intelligent dog, he either couldn't figure out that the snowballs disintegrated when he caught them, or he took some delight in destroying them. His sleek black and brown body dashed over the fields, chasing snowballs and biting at the air. He stopped once in a while to look over at the herd—a proud guardian posing against the white background.

It was a beautiful day. The air was crisp and cold, the sky an intense blue, and the clumps of snow on the evergreens sparkled in the winter sunlight. My breath condensed in tiny clouds. A whiskey jack hopped onto a fence post close by. These big grey jays were intrepid, coming close to people as if they assumed allegiance. The whiskey jack was joined by two more, apparently happy with the temperature and the sunshine. Their white breasts and grey caps and backs looked like formal dress as they chattered and squawked at me.

Carl came up beside me and reached into a container near the gear shift. He brought out a handful of seeds and threw them onto the snow. Immediately, the jays swooped down near the seeds, then hopped on top of the snow, pecking rapidly, occasionally cocking their heads and staring at us. They'd been waiting for Carl. Perhaps he did this every day. I spotted Keo, belly to the snow, inching toward the jays.

"Carl." I nudged him.

He yelled at Keo, and the jays flew up in an explosion of feathers. Keo jumped into the air but missed them. I laughed.

I looked down at Carl, standing watching the jays, his back to me. He was what Dorrie would call a "find." Just being himself, he was compelling. But I liked the life he lived as well—the country life, the hard work of the ranch, the community of men and women who were fellow ranchers. He was opening up another world to me, a new way of living, and I was learning new things, such as how to drive this beast of a tractor.

As long as I was driving straight, I could manage. I could also back the tractor but not with the trailer attached. It seemed that common sense didn't operate when backing trailers. I was supposed to turn the wheel exactly opposite of what I thought would work. I'd figure it out eventually, but I might scrape a fence post or two or put a few dents in a shed while I was learning.

SAM CALLED Carl on Saturday afternoon and invited us to skate on Williams Lake.

"It freezes every year," Carl told me, "but it doesn't usually freeze without snow mucking up the surface. Right now, it's clear and it's frozen solid. Want to go skating?"

I bundled up, and about 9 p.m. we drove back to my apartment, so I could root through my trunk and find my skates. Then we drove over the causeway to the island on the lake where we met Sam and Dorrie. We parked by the lake on the far side of the island. Sam had a bonfire going on the shore, but it seemed only a small glow in the vast dark in front of us. Behind us the lights of Williams Lake sparkled in the cold air, but in front of us the black lake stretched five miles into the night. There was a moon in the clear sky. We would be able to see a little, once we got away from the fire.

Sam gestured to a log where I could sit to put on my skates.

"How is it," he asked me, "that a Coast girl knows how to skate? We prairie boys and cold winter people learn from birth, but how could you learn in lotus land?"

I laughed. "My dad taught us. For about six months of Sundays when I was ten, my parents drove us to the city and paid for us to skate around and around in the arena until we could do it." I remembered that half-hour drive, the car full of kids and skates, and the two hours of skating in a wide circle.

"Good parents."

"They have their points." I appreciated them most of the time. "And occasionally the flooded fields—what we called the flats— froze and we got to skate outdoors." Those days were special. The air was never very cold, at or just below freezing. The fields were wide and the ice a clear sheet where we could skate freely in some areas and a treacherous challenge in others where grass and sticks poked through and caught the unwary.

"*I* took figure skating lessons, so watch out, you guys." Dorrie crowed as she laced up her skates.

"I brought some sheets," Carl said.

The three of us stared at him.

"Uh, Carl," Sam said, "it's pretty cold out."

Carl looked at him blankly, then laughed. "For sailing. We'll check the wind when we get out on the lake. If it's strong enough, we can skate aways up the lake, spread out the sheets, and sail back."

"No kidding?" Sam was intrigued. "We can do that?"

"We can if the lake is clear and the wind strong enough."

The lake was clear, and there was a breeze. We skated out onto the wide expanse of black ice. Once I was used to the dark, I could distinguish the ice from the night air and even see a little way down into the ice. Moonlight revealed occasional white cracks that snaked deep below us. In spite of Carl's reassurance that he could drive a tractor on ice this thick, I felt uneasy, as if the ice was fragile and would collapse beneath my feet. I heard a boom and felt a slight shudder under my skates.

"What's that?" I stood still.

"Just the ice expanding and contracting with the change in temperature," Carl said. "It won't melt. It won't break. I'd let my cattle onto this ice."

Logic warred with emotion, but I managed to hold onto my rational brain. I wasn't going to fall through the ice.

The wind against my face was cold but not biting. I felt my earrings against my cheek. "The first thing that will freeze," Rita had said, "is your ear lobes. So don't wear earrings in freezing temperatures." I removed them and tucked them into my pocket.

I was competent on skates, and Carl must have been skating since he was a child, but Dorrie and Sam were experts. They danced together to imaginary music. Dorrie gave us an exhibition of complicated swoops, turns, and jumps. I couldn't see everything she did because she would dart out of my range of vision and then glide back into it.

"Lovely," she called out to me on one of her glides past me.

The ice was like glass—clear, smooth, and endless. We skated on it as if there were no obstructions—no twigs, no grass, no bits of debris. So far, nothing had tripped us.

Carl had given each of us a bedsheet.

"Unfold it until you get the size you want for a sail," he said as we gathered far out in the middle of the lake. I could see the light from our bonfire flickering, a tiny pinpoint to guide us back.

I didn't think the wind was strong, but once I had my sheet unfolded and refolded to the size I wanted, the lower ends tucked into my waistband, and the top ends held in my widely spread hands, the wind caught my sail, and my feet began to move. I kept my arms wide apart and immobile. The wind pushed me down the lake. I gained speed as I travelled. It was so quiet I could hear the hiss of my skates on the ice. Glorious. Flying must feel like this. I skimmed over the ice as if I were a part of the wind, dark night on each side of me, dark ice below, and moonlight above.

"Marion," I heard Carl call to me from somewhere on my right. "Are you okay?"

"Whee!" I called back.

His laugh floated to me on the night air.

We met at the bonfire, removed our skates, and packed up for home. The men extinguished the fire. I felt a little sad watching that. The moments of joy I'd felt when flying down the lake were wonderful and so hard to hold onto. Those feelings would disappear, snuffed out like the fire. Still, I would remember the unexpected magic of this night forever.

I TRAVELLED to Likely and Horsefly the following week. The snow held off and the roads were clear. I made it to the Black Creek mill site on Tuesday afternoon. The ladies met again in Mrs. Sorenson's dining room. Mrs. Deacon announced she had given herself a Christmas present.

"I told my old man I had to go to town to get presents, and I was going to stay with my sister." She settled her bulk on one of the dining room chairs.

"And?" one of the women asked. "What did you *really* do?"

"I booked myself into the hospital and had my tubes snipped. That's it for kids." She looked at us with a satisfied smile.

After ten kids, who could blame her? One might think she would have done this after five or even four.

"How did you get Joe to sign the papers?" Mrs. Sorenson asked.

Women could not have a tubal ligation without the consent of their husband.

"I asked the doctor to leave the papers with me, and I brought them back signed." She raised one eyebrow, as if daring us to ask for details. No one asked for any more information. No doubt she'd forged Joe's signature.

"Isn't he going to notice the scar?" one of the women pursued.

"It's that tiny, you can hardly see it. Dr. Wilson does a good job." She hauled up her shirt and pulled down the waistband of her jeans and displayed her surgical scar. It *was* tiny. "I'll tell Joe it's a stretch mark. He'll never know the difference."

She was trusting the women not to tell her husband—and they wouldn't. I expect she had information about them she was harbouring. As well, at some point, they might want to use her strategy. It didn't say much for complete honesty in a marriage, but the laws were restrictive, and women had to find ways to look after themselves.

I thought about Mrs. Deacon as I drove home through the sparkling afternoon. Sunlight glinted off the snow-clad fields. I reached for my sunglasses as it was dazzling. The weather, capricious as Carl had said it would be in December, had warmed and melted some of the snow, leaving patches of bright ice on the fields, but the gravel road was safe enough. There was no other traffic, and I felt relaxed. I thought again about my last clinic in Black Creek.

Mrs. Deacon handled her problem of constant pregnancies by circumventing a law that treated her like a possession of her husband. She wasn't having that, and she had worked out how to get what she needed. I'd thought Shakespeare's plays, the fiction I studied in school, and the romances I'd read exaggerated the importance of sex in society. I'd been blind. I was starting to become much more educated, thanks to my clients and my own burgeoning dating life. Still, in some ways, it would be a welcome break to go to my parents' house where it seemed they'd never heard of sex and certainly didn't discuss it.

That didn't mean I was going to ignore the practicalities of my own life. I would make an appointment with Dr. Wilson before I left for Christmas.

"You need to get fitted for a diaphragm," Dorrie had said. "Honestly, Marion. It's no big deal, and you have to look after yourself."

When I returned after Christmas, I would have to make some decisions with Carl. I needed to be ready.

"Romance is fine," Dorrie had advised, "but protection is even better."

When I thought of Mrs. Deacon and her long-delayed effective birth control, I shuddered. She was instructive. Highly motivating.

At 150 Mile House, I turned north onto the highway and headed for Williams Lake. I had the lake in view when an approaching semi-trailer truck reminded me to check my speed. I lifted my foot off the gas, and suddenly the back end of my car swung around, skidding into the path of the oncoming truck. It happened in seconds. The front end of the car followed and I was hurtling backward into the truck's lane. I was going to be killed.

Steer into the skid. I could hear my dad's voice in my head. I directed the car at an angle toward my own lane. I couldn't see where I was going, but I could feel the direction as the car slid backward. The truck must be hurtling closer. The driver wouldn't be able to stop, and I was flying back toward him. If I was still in his lane, he was going to smack right into me. I thought, *At least I have my seat belt on.* A totally irrelevant idea. Any moment now, the truck would leave me a pulpy mess, still strapped in. I did not want to die.

I felt the shudder of the car and a rocking motion as the huge truck passed me with perhaps two inches to spare. I had missed the truck but didn't know if there were other trucks behind it. I had to stop the car. I hadn't touched the gas pedal or the brake throughout this whole manoeuvre, but now with the truck safely past, I carefully tapped the brake. Without gas and with the encouragement of the brake, the car slowed quickly. I steered the car, still backward, onto the side of the road and stopped on the shoulder, facing the wrong direction. I switched off the motor, took a deep breath, and looked up. The truck had stopped, and I saw the driver drop down from his high seat. He rushed toward me. I got out and walked toward him. My legs were weak, but they worked. I didn't know if he was going to rage at me, call me stupid, or threaten to report me for careless driving.

"Are you all right, miss? God! You damn near gave me a heart attack. There wasn't a thing I could do. You were coming straight at me." He sounded more worried than angry. I got a quick impression of dark hair, a dark beard, immense shoulders, and big brown eyes.

I nodded, unable to say anything.

"Black ice," he said. "You must have hit black ice. We get the cold, then the temperature goes up, and then it freezes again, and you can't see the ice on the pavement. Did you hit the brakes?" He patted my arm.

I shook my head and swallowed. "I... I... I..." I croaked and then tried again. "I just took my foot off the gas."

He moved his hand from my arm and patted my shoulder. "That's all it takes sometimes. Did you steer that car backward?"

I nodded again.

"Good job. Friggin' good job. Are you okay?" He stepped back and stared at me. I supposed he was checking for signs of injury.

I tried to smile. "I think so." I reached out to shake his hand. He reached past it and grabbed me in a huge bear hug. It felt wonderful. I breathed a little more slowly.

"God, that was close. You're a lucky woman, and I'm a lucky man. I'm glad I didn't kill you."

He was squeezing the breath out of me, but I hugged him back. "Me too."

He laughed, patted my shoulder again, and stepped back. "Better get heading the right direction before we get more traffic."

A ranch road intersected a few hundred yards south on the highway. I pulled into the side road. It provided a sanctuary for a few minutes.

The trucker gave me a couple of toots on his air horn and was gone. The comfort he'd given me disappeared with him, and I was again reliving that spin and near miss. I sat in that roadway for about fifteen minutes, getting my heart rate back to normal, and waiting until my hands stopped shaking.

I HAD another week of town work as I tried to wrap up everything before I left for my holiday at Christmas. Sally would look after the home care program with Rita as a backup.

"We have to do something about Mrs. Beaminster," Sally informed me.

"Did you get her son to invite her for Christmas?"

"I did," she said with satisfaction. I didn't ask what kind of blackmail she'd employed. "But I think she's going to drink herself blind between now and then."

"Hmm." I thought about it. "What do you suggest?"

"Well." Sally looked at me. I could tell she was trying to decide if I was open-minded enough to deal with her proposal. "I thought we could buy her a bottle of whiskey," she suggested.

"And how's that going to help her?"

"I thought we'd invite all the old people in her complex to come to a party on the twenty-third." Sally let me in on the rest of her plan.

I was flying home on the evening of the twenty-third, but I would be here during the day.

"We'll bring the bottle, and we'll invite all those people to help her drink it. With luck there won't be much left for her." It sounded counterproductive to me, but I didn't have a better plan.

"Worth a try," I said. "Unorthodox, but it might work She'll have company and maybe make some friends." I hoped the head office in Victoria never heard about this.

That's what we did.

Sally brought the whiskey. I brought napkins and a couple of tins of shortbread and set out the glasses. Sally, who seemed to know everyone in town, welcomed people and made sure they were introduced to each other. She'd brought her portable record player and had Christmas music playing. I handed out the drinks, making sure there was only half an ounce in each glass. Older people can't take much alcohol, at least some of them can't. Those used to it came back for seconds. The noise level went up as the whiskey level went down. I thought about my public health nursing instructors. They would have never envisioned such a scene. They probably wouldn't approve of it either. I liked to think it contributed to Mrs. Beaminster's mental health and prevented her from dying of alcohol poisoning over the holiday.

I looked over at Mrs. Beaminster. She was beaming at an elderly man who, Sally whispered to me, lived only three doors away.

"Who knows?" she said. "Maybe they'll get together for crib," and she winked at me.

Sally was irrepressible. I grinned. I loved working here.

I flew home ahead of another storm. My dad promised to meet the plane and "hear all about your adventures." I don't think I'd tell him about most of my adventures. Some, perhaps. He'd want to know about the country and the industry. He'd like to hear about the Cariboo Mountains and the Chilcotin grasslands. It would be raining in the Fraser Valley—a depressing, relentless rain. I could deal with that for a week.

Carl had given me a pendant on a chain, which I was wearing. I'd probably not take it off. It was a gold jay. Just beautiful. I'd given him a framed picture of Keo. He'd hung it on the wall near his desk. I trusted Rita to keep my programs going and to prevent any disasters from striking while I was gone. Everyone told me that the Cariboo weather had been mild up to now, and in January and February it would get cold, as in minus forty. In that temperature, tires were square for the first hundred yards, air was so crisp you had to breathe through a scarf, lakes froze, the river froze, and water pipes froze.

I was looking forward to it.

CHAPTER FIFTEEN

SKIDDING THROUGH THE WINTER

CARL PICKED ME up at my apartment to drive me to the New Year's Eve dance. The Soda Creek Hall was about twenty miles north of Williams Lake along the Fraser River. Carl's ranch was halfway, so we would drive to the dance and return to his place. I packed a small bag and was ready for him when he rang the apartment doorbell.

I'd started out feeling feminine and pretty. I wore a silk party dress in a multicoloured flower print that puffed out at the hem. My mother had given me perfume, "Apple Blossom." I'd never used it, and I wasn't going to use it tonight. I borrowed "Evening in Paris" from Dorrie. It had a musky scent that seemed perfect for New Year's Eve. During my Christmas visit, my mother had taken me to the dress shops and bought me several beautiful dresses. I had felt feminine, pretty, and seductive. By the time I was completely dressed, though, I'd lost the mood. Underneath my dress I wore long wool pants. On top I wore a parka and winter boots. My dancing shoes were in a small bag with a drawstring. The minute I went from a cold room to a warm one, condensation formed on my glasses. So, in addition to being dressed like a Russian doll; I looked blind. I'd never make the cover of *Vogue*.

The hall was decorated with Christmas wreaths. Red and green crepe paper streamers looped near the ceiling from corner to corner. The windows were dark and covered in frost—on the inside.

A stage at the far end had a faded red curtain pulled to the side. A drum set, a piano, and a couple of chairs awaited the musicians. About twenty people had already arrived when we entered and were moving from group to group, chatting and smoking.

"Spring," Dorrie said as she shoved her boots under the bench on one side of the hall and opened her shoe bag. "Spring," she repeated, "means wearing only one pair of shoes when you go out." She flipped her hair with her left hand.

I grinned. After her engagement to Sam at Christmas, Dorrie flashed that substantial ring whenever she could.

"What happened to flitting around and savouring life?" I'd asked her when she'd told me she was marrying Sam.

"Going to do it," she'd said. "Only with Sam. He's not as staid as most people think. He's up for adventure." She seemed happy, so I expected she knew what she was doing, and I liked Sam. I felt a little sorry for myself though. The apartment would be too big for me when she left. I'd have to move again.

Tonight her blue eyes sparkled as she gazed around her. She looked beautiful in a deep cobalt blue chiffon dress with its pleated bodice and softly pleated skirt that swirled mid-calf. Her auburn hair caught the light from the bare bulb above her and glinted with gold streaks. Her shoes were typical Dorrie—the same blue as her dress with rhinestones flashing from the heels.

"Are you getting any flak from the school board about you and Sam?" I meant disapproval of her obvious cohabitating with Sam.

"Nope. They might fire *me*, but they don't want to offend Sam. Doctors are hard to recruit. I think we'll be all right. What about you and Carl?"

"No one's said anything. Nurses are hard to recruit as well." We had more freedom than most young women in this area because the community needed our expertise, and we knew it, though we *could* be asked to leave "under moral grounds." There would be no appeal. Both the school board and the health unit could hire and fire as they wished. I'd have to move, probably find a job in the north. I pushed the thought away.

The hall looked fifty years old with wooden floors and wood-panelled walls. There wasn't much insulation, but a wood stove behind the stage pumped out some heat. When everyone was dancing, it would be warm enough. I looked up as the orchestra tuned: two violins, two guitars, a drum, and a piano. It should be fun.

It was. We danced with our partners and danced with anyone else who asked us: jive, polkas, waltzes, schottisches, and something called the Chicken, which involved a lot of hopping and arm flapping. There wasn't a bar, but men and some women went outside in the freezing cold to down a drink and then return quickly. All alcohol consumption here tonight was illegal, which added some excitement. Sam and Carl had small flasks in their suit pockets. They discreetly shared with Dorrie and me throughout the evening.

Everyone was dressed as if going to the opera in the city. For the most part, the men wore suits, although there were one or two in jeans and pressed white shirts. The women wore dresses of chiffon, silk, or soft wool and were substantially bejewelled, making them sparkle as they danced. Dorrie was the only one whose *shoes* twinkled.

The local Women's Institute had provided the eleven o'clock supper, and we made short work of the casseroles, homemade buns, many layered cakes, and dessert squares. At midnight we kissed our loved ones, had one last round of dancing, and then piled in our cars and headed home.

It was wonderful, and I felt as if I'd had a timely escape. My mother had asked me to stay over New Year's as she was having a small party.

"You remember Matthew and Marie and her sister Della?" she had asked me.

They were my parents' friends since forever. Worthy people, but I didn't want to spend my New Year's with them.

"You'll have a nice time without me, Mum," I had assured her.

"Della's bringing her son, Johnny. He's home from university. You remember Johnny?" she pressed. My mother was good at pressure.

"Of course." Johnny and I had been in the same grade in elementary school. He was agreeable and smart. I think he got an engineering degree. I was not going to spend New Year's with him. I was firm. My mother was disappointed in me again. I thought about her pleasant, quiet New Year's party with lovely food, calm games, and conversation and then about the wild music and dancing I'd just experienced with the frisson of illicit drinking. No contest. Then there was the difference between Johnny and Carl. Again, no contest.

Keo was delighted to see us, prancing around as we entered the cabin. I hung my parka near the door and headed for the bathroom. I shut the door, turned around, and just stood there in shock.

"Carl!" I yelled. "What have you been doing?"

In front of me was a gleaming white bathtub, a new toilet, and a sink. The uneven wooden floor had been replaced or covered with shiny porcelain tiles, and he had installed a heater. An electric heater! I opened the door. Carl leaned against the jam, grinning down at me.

"Do you like it?"

"Of course, I like it. I love it! Be still my heart." I fluttered my hand over my chest. "This is fabulous. You must have worked every minute I was away."

He leaned in. "How about a reward?"

"Go away. I'll be out in a minute." I looked around, "Or maybe fifteen."

He laughed and left me to enjoy myself.

ABOUT THE second week of January, the cold everyone had warned me about settled over the country. With the cold came our new nurse for the Chilcotin. Her name was Alice, and she was an experienced nurse from Prince George, which was even farther north. She was short, a little plump, and knew what she needed.

"I want a winch installed on the front of my vehicle and four new snow tires," she said firmly at our first staff meeting. "I'm not going into the Chilcotin until that's done." She didn't get the winch, but she got the tires.

Rita was a hands-off administrator who mainly relied on our good sense, but she had some advice.

"I don't need to tell Alice this, but you Coasters who aren't used to the deep cold need to know a few things: Don't touch anything steel," Rita said. "Don't leave your car unplugged. Don't go off the main roads." With those few injunctions, Rita left us to manage our districts as best we could.

I drove out to Likely and Horsefly in the third week of January. The roads were crunchy with cold, the air still. I passed a house near the road where sheets hung on the line, frozen stiff. The dry air sucked moisture from them, even in this freezing weather. The first two weeks of January had been warm enough to deposit several feet of snow. The graders and plows had piled it at the side of the road, making the narrow road to Likely even narrower. If I met a logging truck, I would have no place to go except straight into those snowbanks.

I didn't meet any trucks, but they'd been travelling before me because they'd carved two deep ruts in the road. I wondered what the trucks did when they met each other. Perhaps radioed ahead and pulled into a driveway? I followed in the tracks they'd left, and that's what got me into trouble. I'd finished at the Big Lake School and was on my way to Likely when, after following the ruts down a hill, I drove along the straight stretch at the bottom—on ice. Halfway along this stretch, the car jolted to a dead stop, knocking me forward over the steering wheel and rattling everything in the car. It wouldn't move no matter how much gas I gave it. I shut off the motor, got out, and peered under the car. The bottom of the car was resting on the hump between the ruts. The tires were about four inches off the ground.

Truck wheels had slammed into the ground so often and so heavily they'd dug into the ice and gravel. I looked around. I needed a ramp, a log, or a piece of plywood to provide a grip for the back tires. There were poplar trees and firs but no useful wood anywhere that I could see. I hadn't seen any other vehicles since I'd left Big Lake, and there was no one around. I'd better rescue myself. I would have to climb the snowbank to see what I could find beyond the road. Maybe a piece of a wooden fence. It was cold and only going to get colder as the afternoon moved into evening. I climbed up the bank. I was just at the top when I heard a truck approaching down the hill from town. The driver would be able to see my car for some distance. I heard the gears change, the hiss of brakes, and saw a huge Kenworth cab towing an empty trailer grind to a halt a few feet from the back bumper of my car. I scrambled back down the bank and met the man getting out of the truck cab.

"High-centred are you, Nurse?" he said. I didn't recognize him. He was tall, thin, and about fifty. The decal on my car door announced who I was.

"Is that what it's called?" I stared at the car, immobile as a stranded turtle.

"Yeah." He joined me in contemplating my vehicle.

"Good name for it." I said. "That's just what it is."

"It's okay. I'll push you out." He turned back to his truck.

"Thanks."

He called over his shoulder. "No trouble. Next time keep one wheel on the side."

I nodded. Sound advice, especially now I knew those ruts could be deep. I got into the car and waited. The truck filled my rear-view mirror like some giant monster. It could plow me into the sides of the road; into oncoming traffic, if there was any; or simply roll over me. I took a deep breath, started the car, and put it in first gear.

I felt a gentle push, then I was moving. As soon as the tires made contact with the road on the other side, I accelerated and scooted up the hill. I tooted a "thank you" and ran ahead of the truck until I got to a ranch driveway where I pulled off and let the truck rattle past.

He air horned his goodbye, and I was on my way again, not even ten minutes delayed. I was not going to think about what would have happened if I'd stayed there all night.

The long hill down the mountain into Likely Valley and the bridge across the river were a little slick but manageable, if I went slowly. I unloaded my luggage at the lodge and went on to the clinic at the school.

The schoolteachers welcomed me. The kids were practising a play and wanted me to be their audience. After the clinic was finished, the mothers and I settled in front of the kids, all of us crammed into one of the two rooms, to watch the play. It wasn't exactly public health nursing, but it was fun.

Mary fed me supper and breakfast in the morning, then I was off to Horsefly via Beaver Valley. First, I had to negotiate the long hill out of Likely.

It gave me a different driving challenge this morning. It was icy, and climbing it meant I had to get momentum and keep going. I thought I could manage without chains if I got a good run on the straight stretch. I was moving along nicely and expected to reach the top when I rounded a curve and saw an old car stopped diagonally across the road. I would not be able to get past. I pulled over into a pullout and shut off the motor. I got out and went up to the vehicle. A boy of about seventeen was standing beside the car.

His face brightened as I approached. He was good-looking— dark hair, brown eyes, about five feet eleven, broad-shouldered, and smiling now. "Oh, good. I need a hand. Do you have chains?" he asked.

"I have chains," I said, "but *I'm* going to need them to get up the hill. Don't you have any?"

He shook his head. He shouldn't have left Likely without chains, especially in such an old car, and—I looked more closely—with such smooth tires. There wasn't any research that I knew of that said the brains of teenage boys were not yet capable of logic, but many of us in the health care world suspected it. Planning ahead didn't seem to be important to them. I doubted that this young man was safe on the roads.

"Have you put a warning signal up the hill to indicate you're blocking the road?"

He gaped at me. "Uh, no."

The curve was sharp enough that anyone coming from town would not see him until they were almost upon him. The cliff dropped off about sixteen feet straight down beside us.

"You should do that, and you should get your car off to the side of the road." I gave directions.

He stared at me and turned and looked at his car.

"I'll get some of the gravel from the wooden box over there and throw it under your tires," I said.

He looked where I'd pointed. The Department of Highways had constructed a huge wooden box they filled at the beginning of winter with sand and gravel. I hoped there was some in there as this clueless driver was going to need it.

"I don't suppose you have a shovel?" I asked him.

"Uh."

Obviously, no shovel. "Never mind. I'll get mine." I tried to keep exasperation from my voice.

He needed to get that car out of the way of oncoming traffic, or at least put up some kind of warning, but he didn't move. I had the shovel and was at the box when I heard an approaching truck—a big truck.

I looked up. The boy stood by his car staring at the huge semi coming at him.

I could see this tragedy unfolding. We were both going to be crushed. The truck would hit the boy, his car, and then me. I was going to die this morning. We both were. I stood frozen. There was nowhere to escape. The rock wall behind me was too high. I waited. My breath almost stopped. My eyes were wide as the truck got closer. Then, the driver pulled his steering wheel to the left and flew off the road. It was as though the truck with the trailer behind was driving on air. I heard the crash, like a loud thump, and ran to the edge of the embankment. The truck, right side up, was sitting on an old roadway below me. While I watched, three men got out of the truck, looked at one another, and started up the bank.

They were uninjured, but if I was any good at reading body language, they were raging mad. The boy had almost killed them—and me. I took a moment to be grateful I was alive, then decided I was best out of the way, coward that I was, and retreated to the sandbox. The men lumbered up to the boy and surrounded him. I gave up trying to help with the sand. No one wanted any at this point. I took my shovel and returned to my car, opened the trunk, and got out my chains.

I heard no sounds of a fight—no fists crunching or thumping. I cautiously snuck a look. The men had pushed the boy against the car and were haranguing him. Well, he deserved that. He was shaking his head, probably still unable to grasp what he had done.

They shoved the boy into his car, put their shoulders against the car, and pushed it to the edge of the road. I was afraid they were going to push the car over the bank, but they left it on the shoulder. If the boy had any sense, he'd stay in it.

I'd put chains on one tire and was working on the other when one of the men came and crouched beside me. He was short, about five feet eight but stocky and muscular. I imagine, if he decided to, he could give that boy quite a beating.

"You okay, Nurse?" His voice was even and polite.

"I am. Thanks."

"Need any help?" He waited.

"I seem to be getting the chains on okay." I felt as if the air was prickling with emotion: anger, fear, and relief. None of it directed at me, but almost palpable all the same. I didn't want to nudge those emotions in any way.

He sat on his heels, quietly watching me, then said. "You know we saw you at the sandbox."

I nodded. I wondered how the accident had looked from the point of view of those in the truck.

"I said to Gary, 'That's the nurse.'"

I raised my eyebrows. Had I met him before?

"You look after my kids," he explained.

I didn't remember him, but he'd probably seen me in Likely. "Ah, I see."

"We were going to hit that goddamned idiot." His voice was calm, but I still felt the underlying fury. "But we saw you. If we'd hit him, his car would've slammed into you." He paused. "So we didn't."

I looked at him. "Thanks."

He nodded.

I was quiet, thinking about the decisions they'd made and how quickly they had made them.

The man jerked his head toward the boy in the car. "He owes you his life."

I didn't say, "He's young," which equates with stupid in some kids. Or "You wouldn't want to kill any one." I just kept quiet.

He straightened. "So you're okay here?"

"I am. Thanks." I patted the chains. There was loose chain hanging, but I wasn't going to take the time to bandage it tight. I stood and looked up the road. The other men had gone, and the boy was still in his car. At least he had some notion of self-preservation.

"The truck?" I asked.

"A miracle," he said, crossing himself. "Still running. We landed on the road bed. Of course, Gary knew it was there. But still, a miracle. We can drive it out."

Trucks were very expensive and could cost as much as a house. Those men not only spared my life and that boy's, they put their livelihoods at risk—as well as their own lives.

"That's a relief." I tried a slight smile. I wanted to scream with relief, pour effusive gratitude all over him, and make him realize that I understood his bravery and self-sacrifice. But I didn't. He was keeping a tight rein on his anger, and I didn't want my emotions to undermine that control. I smiled again and tried to appear calm.

He grinned. "Yeah. We'll probably be tightening bolts on the sucker for weeks, but like I say, a bit of a miracle. See ya."

I waved.

I imagined what the results would have been if they hadn't taken that risky flight off the road. The road would have been strewn with bodies, or parts of bodies, until someone found us. Then they would have called the fire trucks and the police, and it would have taken many hours travel from Williams Lake to clean up the mess. I almost couldn't believe no one had been hurt.

I did not look at the boy. I heard the big semi start, and I heard the churning of the tires as it moved away. They'd managed to get onto the main road. I got into my car, pulled onto the road, and, with chains flapping, clanked up the hill past the young man. That walking disaster could walk back to Likely and get help. It was only a mile. His car was out of the way, and it was probably better if he was not able to drive for a while. I realized I was very angry.

I took the chains off my car at the top of the hill, stowed them in the truck, and spent a moment just breathing until I was calm. I still had another two days of work ahead of me.

I managed the rest of the Likely road driving carefully through the deep ruts with one tire on the shoulder and the other in the middle of the road. I did not slip off into the deep furrows. The road through Beaver Valley was flat, and the valley fairly wide. I could see approaching vehicles for quite a distance. It definitely wasn't the heart-thumping challenge of the Likely road.

I spent the night at Horsefly and was back in Williams Lake on Wednesday night. Dorrie was cooking again and had invited Sam and Carl as well as the social worker Paul and his wife Janet. I made a batch of baking powder biscuits, which was one of my few culinary achievements. Janet brought dessert. Sam brought wine, and Carl brought chocolates.

Paul and I traded stories about travelling the back roads. I told them about the incident on the Likely hill. By now the fear of imminent disaster had receded a little, and I could talk about it without gulping with anxiety.

Paul told us about searching for a house where he was supposed to do a social welfare visit and driving for hours in circles in the

Peavine Ridge area, only to find the family had moved to Quesnel and out of his district. Janet was a teacher in Dorrie's school, and they told stories of the kids, some of which were hilarious. In their stories, it was usually the student who knew what was right and the teacher who hadn't understood. Sam didn't share anything about his patients, but he talked about his riding lessons. Carl was teaching him to ride, and the two of them had had some mishaps and adventures at Carl's ranch.

Everyone left about ten. I tumbled into sleep instantly.

CHAPTER SIXTEEN

COMBATING CONSTANT RACISM

FEBRUARY WAS even colder than January. I managed to keep my car running by plugging in the block heater whenever I could. Cold attacked the minute I stepped outdoors. Breathing through my scarf prevented a sharp cough as the cold hit my lungs. Cold smacked fiercely at exposed skin—menacing, but exciting. I worked in town for the first two weeks of the month. Mothers brought their babies in and the communicable disease quotient stayed at its regular status: flu, colds, some measles, chicken pox, a little TB, and always venereal diseases.

Sophie came to my office one morning. "I'm upset. I'm agitated. I'm preeturbed."

Perturbed, I mentally translated.

Her hair was wild today, tumbling around her face in ash-blonde fly-away curls. She brought with her a sense of urgency and even sadness.

"Sit down." I gestured to my spare chair. Sophie usually faced the world with equanimity. Something was definitely wrong.

She slumped onto the chair and shoved her hair away from her face. "I just heard Annie Mahan lost her baby."

"I'm sorry. Do I know her?" I couldn't conjure up a face.

"No, I don't either." She was so impatient to tell me the story, the words tumbled out quickly. "She's the sister of one of my patients and has problems with randy priests."

I'd heard some of the religious men in the nearby Indian Residential School were abusive, but I didn't have any evidence. I was beginning to notice a raised eyebrow here and a snide remark there. But there was nothing I could pin down and report. "What happened?"

"Apparently, the priest told her sex with him was holy, but birth control was wrong. So she got pregnant, and he said she had to give the baby up for adoption. *His* baby, mind you."

"She got pregnant," I repeated.

"Sixteen. She's sixteen!" she cried.

I sat perfectly still. I didn't want to hear this.

Sophie continued, "She said she wouldn't give the baby away, and he said he'd send Social Welfare after it. This is all from her sister, who isn't helping much."

"That's hard." I hated this. "And nasty. I take it Annie Mahan didn't buckle down and do what he wanted."

"No. She went off into the Chilcotin bush and had the baby by herself. Gutsy girl! But so alone!" Sophie pushed her hair back again and frowned at me.

I stared at her. It was February. The Chilcotin was a cold wilderness. "Oh, my God! That poor kid. Is she okay?" I imagined a young woman, a girl, facing childbirth alone. It was unthinkable in this society. How could we let this happen? Why didn't Patricia, the federal nurse, do something for this girl? Maybe she didn't know about her. "Is Annie still out there?"

"She's okay. She came back alone."

Without the baby, she meant. I watched Sophie. "What do you think?"

"I think the baby died out there. It wouldn't take long in this cold." Her lips thinned, and she frowned. I couldn't tell what she was thinking.

No prenatal care, no one to support or help her, and then going off to have the baby alone. It must have been terrifying. She would be in no condition to make good decisions after the birth. She may not have harmed the baby deliberately, but with no one attending to her or the baby, it was impossible to know what really happened without talking to Annie.

"What are you going to do?" I asked.

"I'm going to get that social worker, the one with sense."

"Paul?"

"Yes. He can find Annie a place to stay away from that priest, get her on some financial support, and into high school here."

"The Indian agent won't like it."

"We won't tell him."

I wondered what kind of bureaucratic shell game Paul would have to play to make that happen.

"What if the priest comes after her?" I asked.

Sophie's eyes narrowed. She looked truly formidable. "I will call that priest and tell him that I'll report him to the Mounties if he contacts her."

"On what charge?" I was fascinated.

"Harriment."

Harriment? This time I corrected her. I didn't want her to use the wrong word in her tirade. "Harassment," I said. "The charge is harassment."

She repeated the word slowly. "Harassment. Thanks."

"Good luck, Sophie. That poor girl."

"And she's not the only one," Sophie said.

"Tell me more," I said grimly. If there were more infant deaths, I needed to hear about them, however horrible.

"You know the group of people from India who live near the mill?" She waved toward the north side of town.

That was Sophie's district. I had some of them as patients since they came to the clinic periodically. I nodded.

"Two babies have died there in a year, sudden infant death syndrome—*both girls.*"

I wasn't sure at first what she was insinuating, but then it dawned on me. Sophie was implying, not too subtly, that these babies had died not of natural causes, but that they had been killed because they were girls. I looked at her incredulously. Surely she was seeing intent where there was nothing but tragic coincidence.

"These people are not educated like the ones from India who live on the other side of the mill." Sophie began to rationalize her assumption to me. "This group has very little schooling and some un-Canadian beliefs. The babies were girls—that's the reason they died. I can't prove it. I don't *want* to prove it. I just don't want them to do it again." She almost howled with frustration. I could understand her grief at the senseless death of two babies. But she had absolutely no evidence to back up her claim. She couldn't accuse these families without evidence—to do so would put them at risk. She couldn't even put her suspicions in their charts.

"You might be wrong," I said carefully. She might be wrong about Annie, and she might be wrong about these families. It was all supposition, based on little more than a cultural stereotype. However, I was conflicted. Sophie was wise about people and noticed behaviours more than I did.

"I might be wrong," she admitted and sat forward in her chair. "But in case I'm not, I'm going to start an education program that makes sure those people know the sex of the child is decided by the man. I bet that will stop this." She banged her fist on my desk.

I jumped. "Hey." I'd never seen her like this.

"Sorry." She sat back, blinking at me, fighting back tears. "I'm upset."

"What difference will it make to know that the man's sperm decides the sex?"

Sophie's eyes lit up. "If it's a choice between saying you really *want* a girl child or saying it's your *fault* you have a girl child, the men will go for accepting the kid. They're gubbulous."

She meant credulous or maybe gullible. I wasn't convinced by her argument, but I didn't think it would do any harm to mention this information. As long as it didn't go any further than that.

"And if they know I'm watching them, they'll be less likely to do it. You bet I'm getting into those homes immediately postnatal. They'll walk into their house with the baby girl, and I'll walk in right behind them."

I didn't think Sophie was right about the girl babies in the mill area. I didn't want to believe anyone would murder a baby just because it was a girl, and neither Sophie nor I had enough knowledge about the community or their culture of origin to make these assumptions. But, at the time, I empathized with her desire to protect the children in her care. Even if she was misguided, and she was looking at the situation through a lens of what today would certainly be identified as racial prejudice, I believed that her intentions were good. She had a responsibility to those children, and she would do whatever she could to protect them. She was a little like Mrs. Harbinger, a force of nature that carried away mighty obstacles.

But I expected she was right about the girl who went into the bush and came back without her baby. I'd heard a lot of stories about the pressures women—especially Indigenous women—felt from the religious men around here. Even Cynthia, a woman who had her own house and property, faced pressure.

Later in the week, Cynthia phoned me. Her voice was hard and flat. "There's a social worker here who says he's come to take Charlotte away from me."

"What?" I wasn't sure I'd understood her. *Charlotte? Why?*

"Yeah. He says I was negligent because she got scalded, and he's going to put her into an adoptive home." Cynthia spoke quickly.

"Who's the social worker?" I could guess.

I heard her ask, "What's your name?"

She returned to the phone. "Collin something."

It *would* be Collin. "Put him on," I said.

He came onto the phone, sputtering with belligerence. "This isn't any of your business," he began. "Don't you try to interfere with this. I know what I'm doing. We have a policy order to place as many Indian children as we can in appropriate homes."

"Too bad. You aren't getting this one." I was directive, authoritative, and determined. Sophie had been an inspiration. She was defending the little girls in her district. I'd defend those in mine.

"I told you. Stay out of it." He sounded like a child.

"Listen up, Collin. If you try to take Charlotte, I will personally hire a lawyer and sue your ass. I will testify that Cynthia is a good mother, and I will charge you with harassment. Don't be such an idiot." Because he was acting like a child, I acted like an authoritative parent.

He slammed the receiver down. I waited a moment, took some deep breaths, and phoned back. Cynthia answered.

"He's gone," she said.

"Without Charlotte?" I was almost afraid to ask.

"Without Charlotte." Her voice softened. "Thanks."

"I am so mad, Cynthia. He had no business being there."

"He wouldn't have come if I was white," Cynthia said matter-of-factly.

"That's true, and it's sickening." Collin had admitted he had an agenda—to pick up Indigenous kids.

"Thanks for helping." Cynthia's voice quavered a little.

"The benefit of being white," I said bitterly.

"You're upset?" Her voice was a little stronger.

"Damn right." What would have happened if I hadn't been available on the phone? Collin would have grabbed Charlotte. That child would have believed there was no safe place in the world. My hands shook. What was the welfare department thinking? I hated this. Maybe I wasn't strong enough to be a health nurse in this country. Maybe I should run back to the Coast and find a job where I wouldn't have to fight prejudice, ignorance, and downright meanness. Common sense prevailed. There wasn't a nursing job in the world without challenges.

Cynthia said, "I'm upset, too. Want to meet Charlotte, the baby, and me for coffee?"

That sounded like a great idea. "I could use your company."

I nipped into Rita's office and told her what I'd said to Collin. I knew she'd support me, but it would help if she knew what had happened before the supervisor from Social Welfare phoned to complain, especially about the language I'd used. I didn't know why it was worse to use bad language than to kidnap a child. More hypocrisy. Rita was experienced in the politics of health care. She would tell off the supervisor, but very politely.

I met Cynthia at the Lakeview Café. I was still steaming. Charlotte toddled up to me and patted my knee. I hugged her. The new baby cuddled on Cynthia's chest in a sling, cozy and comfortable. I peeked at her.

"Lovely." I looked up at Cynthia. "And the last?" I waited.

"That's right. She's the last," Cynthia said.

I ran my hands over Charlotte's soft hair, checked her arms, and peered at her chest. "The scars have really healed."

"Yeah, she's better. Still a bit clingy because she was away from me for so long." She stroked Charlotte's arm.

"I'll talk to Paul at Social Welfare. He's reasonable. Maybe he can rein in Collin." I toyed with my coffee. How could I get Collin out of town? Would his replacement be any better?

"Mr. Clayton's okay. At least that's what the rumour is."

Cynthia picked up rumours, probably from her many relatives, but they wouldn't be able to stop the welfare workers from snatching kids.

"I don't know what to do!" I almost wailed.

"You keep trying. That's important."

Cynthia broke a ginger cookie in two and gave half to Charlotte.

I watched Charlotte efficiently eat the cookie and slowly reach over and grab the rest from her mother's plate.

"It makes my bones shrivel."

Cynthia patted my hand. "Mine too."

Unlike Paul, who had a university degree in social work, most social workers were untrained. They were just people who were interested in the job, so they were better at taking orders than evaluating a directive and acting ethically. If there was a directive from Victoria, as Collin had said, others workers might try to snatch Indigenous kids.

"I don't know what to do," I repeated.

"Sometimes you just hang on," Cynthia said. "That's what I do. *You* might be able to influence people, change rules, maybe the policies of social workers. I can't do that. You did good today, Marion. Don't let it drown you."

I nodded. Her support was important to me, and I appreciated it, but I still felt helpless.

I was getting a much clearer idea of the two-tiered social life of Williams Lake—the Indigenous society and the non-Indigenous society. The systems of health care, social welfare, justice, and religion were designed to keep Indigenous people apart and in poverty. It was obvious now, but it was as if most of the professionals I worked with didn't notice.

RITA ARRIVED one morning in February with a stack of records.

"You are now the nurse for Canoe Creek Reserve," she said and plopped the records down on my desk.

"A reserve?" They were usually serviced by federal nurses. "Where is Canoe Creek? And how many people?"

"Near Dog Creek. Across the Fraser River from Gang Ranch— and about sixty people. They are Shuswap. Not Carrier like the people around Williams Lake. You go out that way to Gang Ranch, so I told Indian Health we'd take it, at least temporarily, because their nurse can't manage to cover that district." Most health units had a doctor in charge, but here, at the Cariboo Health Unit, Rita took that position. She had been the temporary acting director for five years. When I first met her, she had been dressed as a rancher, but at work she dressed in a uniform that the community expected from management: a suit, neat shirt, and navy-blue sweater.

"I don't see why the federal nurse can't cover it. It's Patricia Stone who looks after that area. She goes to Alkali Lake. That's only an hour from Canoe Creek."

"She won't go," Rita said.

We stared at each other. Did Patricia fear someone in Canoe Creek? Did she cause a problem there and not want to go back?

"Why not?"

"She stays overnight at a cabin near Alkali Lake," Rita said, "and doesn't want to extend her day by travelling to Canoe Creek."

"She's close. Why can't she make the trip to Canoe Creek?" I insisted.

Rita looked at me and said nothing. Then, I remembered the gossip I'd heard about Patricia.

"Don't tell me. She has a lover there." Part of my mind found it hard to envision fifty-year-old Patricia, plain and a little dumpy, with a lover, but that was the rumour.

"Yes," Rita said. "Mike Carstairs, the Catholic priest for that area."

"Hmm." I supposed Patricia was entitled to her chance at happiness. "I wish them well."

"Yeah, me too. But you get Canoe Creek for now." And she left the records on my desk.

"Okay," I said to her back. It really wasn't a choice. Rita had already made the arrangements with the federal health services.

I didn't do anything about Canoe Creek until an Indigenous woman arrived at my office and asked me for a permission slip for a doctor's appointment. She was in her mid-thirties and very quiet and polite.

"A permission slip? For the doctor? Could you explain that to me?" I hadn't heard of it.

She told me all the people from Canoe Creek who came to town and wanted the federal health services to pay for their bus fare had to show they were seeing a doctor. The public health nurse had to sign the slips stating they *were* seeing a doctor. To do that she had to phone the doctor's office and confirm their appointments. The doctor this woman was seeing didn't take appointments, just had a walk-in clinic, so there was no way the woman could comply with the federal requirements.

I sat back. It took me a moment to absorb the implications. Indian Health Services required all Indigenous people to get a nurse to sign permission slips—as if they were children, and I was their parent.

I snorted. "That's insulting. To you, I mean, and to me as well. Why should I know your business? And why should I care if you come to town for groceries or to go to the doctor? And *I* should be spending my time policing their crazy rules?"

If Indian Health was so worried about fraud, they could ask the doctor to sign the slips. I bet the doctors wouldn't do it.

She looked up at me and shrugged.

I grabbed the phone and dialed the federal health services.

"Hey, look," I said when I finally got through to someone who had some authority. "I'm not going to sign slips for adults to say they're behaving themselves. It's ridiculous."

I listened while I got the explanation that it was the rules, and Indian Health wouldn't pay if the slips weren't signed. I finally hung up.

The woman looked at me and raised her eyebrows. "No go?"

I was so annoyed I didn't bother to be discreet. "Stupid. Obstructive. Wound up in their own red tape."

She giggled.

I stared at her; I didn't think it was funny. "Let's see what else I can do."

She was silent then, still smiling a little.

"Okay. How about this? I pre-sign a bunch of slips and leave them on the counter here. Anyone from Canoe Creek can come in and take one or request it, and the receptionist will simply hand it to you. No one will ask questions. Would that work?" It was all I could think of.

She smiled, broadly this time. "That would work."

"Okay, let's do that. Stupid, insulting . . ." I sputtered.

"You're different," she said. She was serious now. We looked at each other, recognizing the injustice. If I was different, there was something badly wrong with our health systems.

"I refuse to be part of this mess," I said. I refused to let the bureaucrats get in the way of ethical nursing. If that meant I was fighting them, then I would fight them.

I got a call from Cynthia later in the afternoon. "I hear you're starting a revolution in Indian Health." She sounded amused.

"Where did you hear that?" I was surprised. I hadn't told anyone.

"My cousin came in to see you today."

"She's your cousin?" I hadn't noticed any similarities.

"They're everywhere," Cynthia explained.

"Oh, my God." I was still angry. "It's such a patronizing system."

"It's exactly that," Cynthia said. "Anyway, people are talking."

"Oh, well. Let them talk," I said.

She laughed and hung up.

CARL AND I left town for a four-day trip on Wednesday night. I'd managed to get Thursday and Friday off, pleading an important conference in the city. Carl had arranged for his dad and mum to take Keo, feed his cattle, and make sure the pipes didn't freeze. Cattle had to have water. His dad would keep it running.

We flew to Vancouver. Carl rented a car, and we drove to the Hotel Vancouver. This was an old and prestigious hotel in the heart of downtown—high ceilings, wainscoting, French provincial furniture, and velvet curtains that draped to the floor. It was a pretentious and elegant experience; I loved it. While the Cariboo was shivering in snow, dealing with cruel temperatures, Vancouver in February was anticipating the cherry blossoms. It felt warm and exotic. Crocuses poked up from the ground. A few daffodils waved from sheltered spots near the buildings.

Carl drove out to the University of British Columbia where he was attending a conference on wind energy, and I walked to the Communicable Disease Centre where I had a two-day conference on the new polio vaccine. We met in the evenings and managed to take in a hockey game, a concert, and a couple of pub dinners. We came home full of knowledge and relaxed from our time away.

Sally had a new patient for me when I returned. She stopped at my office to report on what had gone on in home care while I was away. I usually admitted the home care patients and set up the care plans.

"She's a bit gaga, I guess," Sally said. "Her daughter wants to keep her and not send her to a residential care home. Dr. Wilson thought we could visit maybe a couple of times a week and support the daughter."

"Sounds fine," I said. Dementia patients can be very difficult or not difficult at all. It's a capricious and unpredictable disease.

"And today she needs injectable antibiotics for a touch of pneumonia." Sally read off the chart and then handed it to me. "You might as well give the shot while you're doing the assessment."

The home was more a shack than a house, settling into acreage at the edge of town with weathered board siding and a corrugated tin roof. There were a couple of rusting cars on blocks near the front door. A rooster, braving the cold, crowed at me by the door.

When the daughter of the patient let me in, the rooster rushed in behind me.

"Uh-oh," I apologized.

"No problem," she said. "He can stay."

I followed her in.

"I'm Georgia," she said. She looked to be in her late forties with grey streaked hair hanging loose. She wore a man's shirt and jeans and huge woolen socks.

"Miss McKinnon," I replied. I rarely introduced myself by my first name. It was the professional way my instructors had taught me.

She smiled. "This is my mother, Mrs. White."

Her mother was ensconced in a double bed in the middle of the living space. She was tiny, probably less than five feet, and thin. She grinned at me with very few teeth. She looked like an elderly pixie. And beside her on the bed, resplendent in its brown and white coat, lay a Nubian goat.

"Hello, Mrs. White." I approached her.

"Hello," she said. "This is Chelsea." She gestured beside her.

I glanced at Georgia. She smiled benevolently at her mother and the goat.

"Chelsea is such a comfort to mum," Georgia said.

I nodded, as if goats as bed companions were normal. I used my stethoscope to check Mrs. White's lungs. They sounded clear. I took her pulse and respirations. All normal. I'd give the antibiotics, though. If Dr. Wilson said there was pneumonia, there probably was. He would have done an X-ray. I glanced at Chelsea. She seemed unperturbed by my presence. I wished my university public health instructor was with me at this moment. I'm sure her experience in public health didn't include goats. I glanced quickly around. Besides the rooster and the goat, there was a dog and several cats. The environment had advantages. It was a lot livelier than the usual residential care home.

"I'm going to need to give your mother a shot," I said to Georgia.

"No problem. Mum doesn't mind."

I put my black bag on the kitchen counter, washed my hands at the sink, and got out the syringe. Georgia handed me the medication she'd purchased, and I withdrew it with a needle on a syringe. When I turned back to the bed, the syringe in my hand, I found Mrs. White still beaming at me and the goat still occupying the bed.

"Uh." I nodded at the goat. "I'd like to give this shot without the goat quite so close." As she was crowded up close to Mrs. White, I wasn't sure I could maneouvre around her. I had visions of the syringe flying out of my hand or even going into the goat by mistake.

"Oh, Chelsea doesn't mind." Georgia said.

Obviously, the fact that I minded was not important here. I put the syringe down inside my black bag and turned back to the bed.

"Chelsea," I addressed the goat. "Can you move off the bed?"

She butted her head on my hand like a cat looking for affection but didn't move.

I studied the goat. The goat studied me.

"Mrs. White, could you roll onto your side, and maybe put your arms around Chelsea? That way, I could give the shot on the other side."

"Come on, Mum," Georgia said. "Give Chelsea a cuddle."

Her mother obediently rolled on her side. I grabbed the syringe, darted to the other side of the bed, pulled down Mrs. White's pyjama bottoms, and gave the shot into her tiny glute muscle. I rubbed the site with alcohol after I'd finished.

"All done," I said brightly.

Mrs. White turned her head and Chelsea turned hers. Two pairs of bright eyes looked at me with mild curiosity.

"Thanks so much, Nurse," Georgia said.

She gave me a cup of coffee, which I thought I'd earned, and we sat at the kitchen table, discussing Mrs. White's diagnosis, her health, and Georgia's care of her.

"If you can send someone to help with her bath twice a week," Georgia said, "that would be wonderful. She wiggles."

I blinked. The image of the pixie, the goat, and the bathwater was difficult to absorb.

"Twice a week," I agreed.

Sally would enjoy this household.

IT WAS a treat to go out to Carl's ranch on the weekend. The sun was shining, the air was cold, but not piercingly cold, only about ten degrees below freezing. Even so, the cattle needed attention. Because the lakes, streams, and the river were frozen now, they couldn't drink unless Carl provided water.

We drove to the frozen pond. Carl pulled out an axe and began chopping at the ice. "I'll break out a section near the shore, so the cattle can walk close and drink." He gestured to the dark water spreading along the edge of the ice.

"What's to stop it from freezing in an hour?"

He pointed to the centre of the pond. "The beaver will swim underwater to this ice-free area and stir up water and mud to keep it clear. They'll also smack the newly forming ice with their tails and keep it open for a day or so."

I stared at a snow-covered hump in the centre of the pond. "That's a beaver lodge?" It looked like a heap of sticks and dead trees.

"Yeah, they live in there, with food they've stored for the winter and work the edges of the pond when they can." He talked about the beaver with affection, as if they were pets or farm animals.

I turned to the west end of the pond. "Is that a beaver dam?"

Carl nodded and put the axe back in the box on the trailer. "It is. I owe my water supply here to the beaver. They created this dam, keep it in repair, and make sure there is always enough water for them—and for me."

The pond wasn't the only water supply for the cattle. Carl had several water troughs throughout the ranch with shut-off valves about six feet below the ground. Some of the stand pipes were wrapped in heat tape, long electric lines down to the valves. If the valves or the lines froze, the water wouldn't flow, the trough wouldn't fill, and the cattle would dehydrate and die. Keeping the valves clear of ice was important. Carl fed the cattle hay every day as well, taking loads out to the meadows where the cattle gathered, which is what we were doing this afternoon.

He pointed out the grouse tracks.

"Where are they?" I looked around, trying to see where the tracks led.

"Probably in the fir trees. You won't see them unless they whirr away. Usually they stay still when anyone is around." He pointed to another set of tracks. "Coyotes."

"Do the coyotes get the grouse?"

"Sometimes," he said.

The ubiquitous whiskey jacks fluttered around the tractor, waiting for Carl to throw seeds. The sun glinted off the ice crystals on the fir branches. It was lovely, but it was February and, Coaster that I was, I wanted to see spring.

I sighed. "No daffodils."

"Sorry," Carl said. "Not for a few months yet."

We saw some deer tracks. Carl told me about his upcoming deer hunting trip. He and his dad were going to go into the mountains on horseback.

"Do you put it in your freezer?" I asked.

"Yes, I put some in my freezer, but I trade some for pork. "

"I noticed you don't keep pigs." Rita and Jim had a couple of pigs, and I saw them on other ranches I visited.

"I can't," he said emphatically.

"Why not?"

He shrugged. "They're like dogs. Too smart, too much personality. I can't stand to butcher any I raise, so I trade my venison for pork. I don't have a friendship with *those* pigs and none with the deer."

I supposed there were plenty of deer in the surrounding hills. "You hunt out of season?"

"It's my land," he said. "I'm not asking permission. I only take bucks."

Obviously, Carl and I both bent the rules when it suited us.

CHAPTER SEVENTEEN

TRANSLATOR TRIALS

I WAS DISAPPOINTED in March, which did not come in "like a lamb." It tumbled in with alternating days of warm weather, melting snow, dirt covering vehicles, mud on my boots, snowstorms, minus ten degrees Fahrenheit, and ice on every surface. I dreamed of daffodils.

One morning, early in the month, Mrs. Harbinger called me at my office.

"I want you to come with me to visit Mrs. Parmar."

I searched my mind for some picture of Mrs. Parmar and came up with nothing. "Why?"

"Her husband is handicapped, her son is in high school, and her daughter's in grade seven here. She's on your class roster."

Presumably that made the Parmars my responsibility. We set a date and a time, and the next Monday I picked up Mrs. Harbinger at the school and drove her toward the sawmill where Mrs. Parmar lived.

"Her husband worked for the mill," Mrs. Harbinger said once she'd settled into the car seat. "He was making good wages and sent for a bride from India. He was in luck and got Kathi, twenty years younger, full of good spirits and kindness. Yes, he was very lucky with Kathi."

I nodded but concentrated on driving. Last night had been cold, and there was ice under the drift of snow on the road. The sun would soon melt it, and then I'd have skidding conditions. I listened though.

"The mill had a party, and the Parmars attended. On the way home, Mr. Parmar slipped on the ice and cracked his head. Mrs. Parmar put him in the car and drove him to the hospital. They told her he was drunk and sent him home."

Uh-oh. I wondered who had been the doctor on call.

"Kathi told them he didn't drink and hadn't been drinking, but they ignored her. He got worse, and two days later she brought him back. They sent him to Kamloops with a brain injury. He'd been bleeding into his brain all that time."

I was silent. I wanted to apologize for the mistakes of the medical staff at the local hospital. I wanted to tell Mrs. Harbinger that such misdiagnoses were rare, but none of that would help.

"He came back damaged," she said. "He has been at home, puttering around, getting progressively worse now for ten years."

"How is Kathi managing?"

"She's cooking at the hotel. The kids are helpful. Andy looks after them like a thirty-year-old."

"Andy?'

"Her son in high school. His name isn't Andy, but that's what he goes by. It's something with a lot of vowels." Many immigrants anglicized their names.

"I must be hard on the kids, too."

"Andy is old before his time, but that's what he has to be. Suki is in grade seven and is involved in sports. Mum and Andy see that she gets to her sports events. She's going to be all right."

I trusted Mrs. Harbinger's assessment of Suki and the rest of the family. But I didn't quite trust her motivations bringing me into the family.

"And you want me to . . .?"

"For now, I just want you to meet them."

I doubted it. She had an agenda. I was sure all would be revealed in time.

Kathi was about thirty-five, stocky, light on her feet, and seemed full of energy. She answered the door and brightened at the sight of Mrs. Harbinger.

"My dear. My dear. Come in. Do come in."

Mrs. Harbinger introduced me. Mrs. Parmar shook my hand. "Call me Kathi."

"I'm Marion." This seemed like a social visit.

She bustled around her kitchen, which was clean the way a hospital kitchen or a café kitchen should be. Her husband, who looked like an old man with a grey beard and sad eyes, sat in a rocking chair, keeping warm beside the Franklin heater.

We divested ourselves of our coats, scarves, and gloves. We left our boots at the door on the mat and, as was the custom in many South Asian and East Asian households, pulled on the slippers provided for guests.

"Tea?" Kathi beamed at us.

"Love some," Mrs. Harbinger said.

I was not fond of tea, but I was committed to being a good guest, so I nodded my thanks. When I did drink tea, I had it plain, no sugar, no milk. She must have put about four teaspoons of sugar in it, because it was as sweet as syrup.

Kathi put a mug on a small table beside her husband. He smiled at her and she smiled back, patted his hand, and bustled back to us at the table.

"My Suki? She is okay at school?"

"Of course," Mrs. Harbinger said. "No worries about Suki. She'll do you proud, that girl."

Kathi's beaming smile upped in wattage. "That's good." She drank her tea.

"Are you working tonight?"

"Yes, yes. I have the late shift. It works well as Andy is home and makes sure everyone is fed. Then he sees that Suki does her homework." She grinned. "And Suki sees that he does his."

We talked about the local hockey team, about the coming town elections. Then Kathi brought out some papers.

"I got this from the lawyer for the mill," she said.

"After all this time?" Mrs. Harbinger asked.

"I am not sure if I should sign it."

Mrs. Harbinger was silent as she read the letter. She turned the letter over and wrote a name on the back.

"You take it to this lawyer." She tapped what she had written. "He may be able to get a final settlement from the mill. Give me two days to get in touch with him, so you won't have to pay."

Kathi nodded.

I wondered how many people—dentists, doctors, grocers, lawyers, social workers, and non-profit benevolent societies—were on her roster. I expected I was on it.

"Kathi," Mrs. Harbinger said, finishing the last of her tea, "would you have time when you are on the evening shift and free during the day to do some translating for the health unit?"

Kathi looked at me and smiled. "That would be wonderful."

"It's a paid program. The Department of Health will pay you." She named quite a good hourly rate. How did she find out about that program? I hadn't known about it. "I know Miss McKinnon goes into homes of new immigrants from India when they have babies and talks to them about our health care system and checks out the babies."

I nodded. That was true.

"And she often has no one in the house who understands English."

I might as well go along with this. It would help Kathi and probably help me as well. "It can be confusing for us all," I said.

"Wonderful." Mrs. Harbinger stood. "Thanks for the tea, Kathi. You're doing a splendid job with those two youngsters of yours. Miss McKinnon will call you about the arrangements." She turned to me. "Do you have her phone number?"

I dutifully took Kathi's phone number. "I'll get the application form from the health unit."

"You don't need to go to that trouble. I have them," Mrs. Harbinger said. "Kathi and I can fill them out and give them to you to send in. You just have to sign that she is needed."

She was efficient and manipulative, and I admired her for it.

"Fine, then," I agreed. "When I get a notification from the hospital that a mum is going home with a baby and needs an interpreter, I'll call you. We'll set up a time at your convenience."

"Oh, very good," Kathi said. "Very good."

I shrugged into my coat and tugged on my boots.

Kathi patted my shoulder as we left.

In the car, we were silent for the first few minutes as I concentrated on getting out of Kathi's driveway. Then Mrs. Harbinger spoke. "She needs support."

"And you provided it. It's okay. I can use an interpreter."

She nodded, and we said little else. When we arrived back at school, she popped her head back in the car after she'd gotten out. "Thanks."

I grinned. "Any time." I was sure there would be another time.

I put the paperwork through within a week, and it was the next week, after the Department of Health had agreed to pay Kathi, that I phoned her and reported that I had three homes to visit and asked if she could accompany me. We agreed on a day the following week when she had time off. I gave her the names and phone numbers of the families and asked her to call and make the arrangements, allowing about an hour for each visit.

She called me back the next day and gave me the addresses. This might work out very well.

The following Tuesday, I picked her up at her house and we headed into the area around the mill. Many immigrant families settled there, partly because other families from India lived nearby and partly because the housing was cheaper than in the main part of Williams Lake. I worried that there would be social polarization, but that didn't seem to be happening. The immigrants mixed with the residents, in the schools and at the library, and played on hockey teams. They didn't mix in their religious gatherings, but aside from that, there didn't seem to be much separation. It might exist and be hidden from me, but it wouldn't be allowed in Mrs. Harbinger's school. Perhaps that set the tone for the rest of the community.

At the first house, I spoke to the mother, a tiny woman of about twenty, with her first child, a little boy. She smiled at me a little shyly and then almost beamed at Kathi.

"Hello," I said. "I am Miss McKinnon, the public health nurse." I didn't need an interpreter to announce my occupation as I was in uniform and I carried that ubiquitous scale.

Kathi burst into a melodious torrent of words, among which I recognized "McKinnon" but not much else. Mrs. Sandhu looked at me with a kind of awe. What in the world was Kathi telling her? That I was a miracle worker?

We went through the ritual of exchanging our boots for slippers before I was able to examine the baby. I told the mother through Kathi how well the baby was doing. I asked about feeding, sleeping, bowel movements, and her feelings about being responsible for this new life. We had our obligatory cup of sugared tea and were off to the next visit. Kathi was obviously enjoying herself.

After the third visit, though, I began to have an inkling of the problems in having an interpreter. I took Kathi for coffee at a café close by. I needed to counteract the three cups of sugared tea with bitter coffee. Once we were seated in a booth, I asked her exactly what she had been telling the women.

"I told them everything you said," she said.

"And?" I prodded.

"And I told them what my mother did and what I did."

"What had you and your mother done?"

Kathi leaned forward. "One of the things we did was to put oil on the eyes and ears of the babies to help them see and hear better."

I was dumbfounded for a moment. "Kathi, that can introduce infection to their eyes and ears. Don't advise that. Did those mothers think that *I* was telling them that?"

Kathi was silent. I didn't want her to think she was a failure, and I did want her to continue to interpret for me. But she couldn't be handing out folk remedies, as if it was advice from the Department of Health. Sometimes, traditional remedies were effective and I supported them, but I had to understand the scientific principles behind the treatment before I could recommend it. My mother used a poultice of brown sugar and soap to treat skin infections. It was effective because brown sugar changed the osmotic pressure and drew out fluid, and soap had antiseptic properties. But I had no idea about the science behind what Kathi was advocating.

"Can we come to an agreement? You tell the women *only* what I say. You can see that if you add to it, they will think I am giving that advice. It isn't fair to me or to them."

She studied me for a moment. "I want to help."

"I know that, and you are. If you want to go back and talk to them as a friend, you can give them all the advice you like, but you have to say that it is your own advice."

"Ah." She considered this. "You still want me to come with you?"

"Absolutely. You are invaluable."

"Especially if I don't play nurse." Her eyes sparkled.

I laughed. "Yes, especially if you don't play nurse."

After that, she was a treat to work with and only occasionally drifted into a discussion, which I was sure was either off topic or an embellishment. At those times, I'd just look at her and wait. She'd say, "Uh-oh," and rattle off an explanation that gurgled through the many vowels of her language. I expected she was giving an apology and explaining I hadn't authorized that part of the conversation. She was a wonderful help and a lively companion. Mrs. Harbinger had been right, as usual.

CHAPTER EIGHTEEN

RESPONDING TO DEMANDS

MY MARCH TRIP to the Likely-Horsefly area coincided with a window of good weather. Aside from the ubiquitous mud, I didn't anticipate problems on the roads.

After my school visit at Big Lake, I pulled into the driveway of a ranch about four miles past the lake. Mrs. Pritchard had phoned and asked me to visit. She said she was looking into a placement for her mother, and she'd explain more when I arrived. She'd called on her telephone party line where anyone on the same line could listen. Callers tended to keep their conversations short.

The ranch was at the side of the Likely Road, which meant I wasn't spending an hour trying to find the correct trail into the back country. The driveway was long but gravelled and climbed a small hill. I parked, lifted my bag from the car, and stood still while two border collies dashed out to bark at me. They circled me with interest but not, I hoped, malicious intent. Mrs. Pritchard called to them. "Spike. Dory. That's enough."

Obediently, they slunk away.

"Thank you for coming." She held her kitchen door open for me.

"I was passing. It's no trouble to stop."

"I'm Susan Pritchard," she said, bustling over to the stove and rescuing the coffee pot from boiling over. She set out the cups, milk, sugar, and a plate of cookies. I left my coat and boots at the door and joined her at the table. From the kitchen window, I could see over the road, to the fields, and far out over the lake. The sunsets would be beautiful.

"Marion," I said. I wasn't comfortable being Miss McKinnon if she was Susan.

She smiled. "I know you're busy, so I'll tell you what the problem is. It's my mother. I need to find her a home."

"Are you looking for a place, a home for the aged, where you mother could live?"

She nodded.

"Where is she now?"

"My mother lives in that cabin over there." She gestured to a neat cabin under a tall pine tree to the left of the house. It also had a wonderful view of the lake. It looked ideal.

"She wants to leave?" Did they quarrel?

"She doesn't want to leave. She wants to stay here because the kids are here. When they come home from school, they always go over to her and have a snack, and she hears about their day. She loves them, and she doesn't want to leave them. I want her to stay, but I can't manage anymore."

I waited.

"You know we run about two hundred head of cattle."

That was quite a number for a small ranch. That meant they worked at it constantly.

"And I am raising five hundred chicks for market." Barns and henhouses were likely behind the house, perhaps beyond the copse of poplar I had glimpsed as I drove in. She was telling me the ranch was a thriving business.

"You're very busy," I said.

"I am wildly busy. And I can't be with my mother all the time. I have to be out in the henhouses and out riding the fence line. At this time of year, we're watching the cows to make sure we don't lose any calves. I can't be with her all the time." Her voice rose until she was almost wailing.

I reached over and stroked her hand. "It's hard."

She sniffed. "Yes, but it's harder for my mother because she doesn't understand that I can't be with her, and it's hard for me because my mother is getting more and more unreliable."

"Dementia?" I guessed.

"Yes. The doctor said it would get worse, but I didn't think it would happen so fast. She's only seventy-two. This shouldn't be happening."

Dementia can take many years to progress, or it can happen quickly. She was right; it was tragic.

I sipped my coffee and waited. There wasn't any cure for dementia, only custodial care. Susan could no longer provide that care. I didn't see how I could help, but I could spend a little more time with her.

"Why don't I go over and meet your mother?"

"Would you? That would be great."

We shrugged into our coats and boots and walked the short distance over to the cabin.

It was small, only one bedroom, but it had a neat kitchen with a fridge, stove, sink, and cupboards. I glimpsed a bathroom beyond a half-open door. The living room had an electric heating bar along the baseboard and was warm. An upholstered rocking chair was positioned to take advantage of the lake view. A small television was mounted on a bookcase. It was clean, snug, and a wonderful place for a family member, but not a place for a woman with dementia.

"This is Miss McKinnon, Mom."

"Marion, this is my mother, Mrs. Watson."

We shook hands. Mrs. Watson remained in her chair.

"Would you like tea?" she said.

I sat on one of the kitchen chairs Susan had pulled up. "No, thank you, Mrs. Watson. I am fine."

She sat in silence and then looked out the window.

"Are you waiting for the children to come home?" I asked. It was not yet ten in the morning but perhaps she had a loose conception of time.

She smiled. "That's right. They get off the bus, right down there."

She pointed to the spot where the Likely road and the ranch driveway met.

I stayed for a few minutes chatting about the beauty of the countryside, and then Susan and I returned to her house.

"What happened?" I asked her when we were again in her kitchen, "to make moving your mum an immediate problem?"

Susan stared at the wall for a moment, then said, "She left the stove on again and a tea towel on the element. Robin dropped in after school and a fire had started up the wall. Mum was sitting in her chair smiling at Robin, totally ignoring the fire. Robin put the fire out. She's ten. Robin's ten. We have extinguishers in the house, and Robin knows how to use them. She even cleaned up the mess before she told me about it."

I was full of admiration for the ten-year-old who dealt so capably with the fire. Ranch life seemed to make children self-reliant, but it must have been frightening, nevertheless.

"That was a close one," I commented.

"Mum hadn't even noticed the fire. Robin said she offered her cookies. My daughter shouldn't have to be afraid for her grandma. None of us should have to be so afraid for her."

"It must make the whole family anxious."

She nodded. "It does. Now Mum's taken to wandering. I'll get up in the night and see her outside in her nightgown. It's cold!" Tears rolled down her cheeks. "It's so cold. She'll wander off and die."

It was a real possibility. Wandering was a caregiver's nightmare. They never knew when their patient would suddenly decide to leave.

"I don't suppose you are getting much sleep."

"No, I'm afraid to go to sleep for fear she'll get lost. We're on twelve hundred acres here, with another thousand leased for grazing. She could go anywhere. I tried to get her to sleep in our house. The kids could double up, not that they want to, but they'd do it and let her sleep here. But she won't come. She says it wouldn't be right. She doesn't realize she's outside at night. She thinks she's in the house."

"You're working a full-time job as a rancher, looking after your family, cooking, cleaning, and trying to look after your mother. What does your husband say?"

"He says it's time to let her go."

At that point, she put her head down on the table and cried. I stroked her hair and let her cry. There wasn't much of an alternative to sending her mother away to a care home. I didn't think there was a home close by either. We didn't have anything in Williams Lake, and Mrs. Watson was not a candidate for Darla's boarding house. She was beyond Darla's ability to care for her. Kamloops was three hours away and Vancouver an eight-hour drive. I did not see any comforting solution to Susan's problem.

She sniffed, got up, and found a handkerchief.

"What does your doctor say?" I asked her when she returned to the table.

"He gave me a list of two homes in Kamloops and one in Vancouver. Do you know of any others?"

"I don't, but there might be private ones. The trouble is the private ones don't want to care for a patient who wanders. Too much responsibility. Your mother will need a locked floor and nursing staff."

"Oh, God!" Susan said. "It's so terrible. She was the most loving mother. It's like she's already died."

Now, I was crying. I took a deep breath. "It is very sad. I am so sorry."

She half-smiled through her tears. "Thanks. I wish you had an answer for me."

"So do I."

We sat in silence. Then Susan took a deep breath and stood. "Thanks for coming by. Here, take a couple of cookies to nibble on your way." She wrapped a couple of oatmeal cookies in waxed paper and handed them to me. "I appreciate your coming."

"I'm sorry I couldn't help."

"It helps to have you listen." The tears were still on her cheeks, but she smiled.

I thought about her as I drove to Likely. There was no home for the aged that took patients as difficult as Mrs. Watson. There was one that provided help with medications, meals, and sheltered living, but not nursing care or a locked floor. Mrs. Watson was not so unaware that she wouldn't realize she was away from her family and isolated when she was moved to a home in Kamloops or Vancouver. That would torture her daughter. But I couldn't see any other option. Williams Lake needed a specialty home that provided the kind of care Mrs. Watson required, a place where old people could have professional care as they regressed through the stages of dementia. One day, perhaps we'd have that, or a cure for dementia.

THE WORK was routine and uneventful in Likely and Horsefly, but I ran into a problem at Black Creek. A delegation of four women waited for me at the school. They sat patiently while I finished my work with the schoolchildren and then invited me into the teacher's living room, which was adjacent to the school. It served as a community centre.

"We got a problem," said Mrs. Deacon.

"Sure do," another woman I didn't know said.

"It's them Trapps."

At first, I thought she was talking about coyote traps or bear traps, but then I realized she meant the family named Trapp.

"What's the matter?" I asked Mrs. Deacon.

"They've got their privy right on the creek, and my cousin, George, gets his water from the creek. That's not right."

"Going to poison the whole neighbourhood," the third woman said. She was thin, about sixty, and had a determined look in her eye. "I ain't lived here for forty years to be poisoned by no Americans."

"They're from the States?

"Right. Moved here last spring. Don't talk to no one. Put their privy on the creek. Stupid."

"I see," I said. "Did anyone talk to them about it?"

"I did," the older woman said. "Told them to move it or I'd get the public health in. They didn't move it. You're the public health."

If the Trapps did have their privy on the creek, they were contravening public health law. They were required to have the privy at least a hundred feet from a source of water. Section 66 of the health act prohibited contamination and Section 60 said the privy could be torn down if it was contaminating the water. All public health nurses had some knowledge of the laws around water supply and waste management.

"I will take a sample of the water," I promised her. "In the meantime, make sure anyone living below them boils the water."

I had to leave my car at the bottom of the driveway to the Trapps' cabin. While there was a cleared path, it was a combination of mud, dirty snow, and a couple of tree stumps that looked as if they could put a hole in the oil pan of my vehicle. I walked.

Mrs. Trapp was a pleasant-looking woman of about fifty with long grey braids and kind eyes.

She nodded when I introduced herself. "We're healthy here." She started to close the door.

"Mrs. Trapp." I was insistent. "I have come to take a sample of your water." I had aluminum containers with me, part of the collection of oddments I kept in the car trunk. "Where's the stream?"

Those eyes now flashed anger, but she pointed to a well-traveled path through a copse of poplar trees. I followed the path and found the privy, much too close to the stream. It was a mere ten feet, not the hundred it should be. That alone would be enough to force them to remove it. It wasn't my job to tell the Trapps this, though; it was the job of the sanitary inspector Dave Brown who worked from the Williams Lake Health Unit. I'd report to him. I wished I'd thought to bring my camera from the car. Oh, well. By the time I could have the film developed, Dave would have dealt with the problem.

I walked past the privy to the stream, knelt on a flat stone at the edge, and took the samples. I wondered if that flat stone had been placed there so the Trapps would have a convenient place to fetch water. I shuddered. How could anyone not get the connection between the privy, the water supply, and disease? I took three samples, tightened the lids on the aluminum containers, and walked back to my car. I didn't see Mrs. Trapp again nor anyone else on the property.

I delivered the samples to Dave. He sent them off to the provincial lab, and in a week the results came back. He stopped in my office to tell me about them.

"Full of pathogens."

"What kind?"

"Principally, E. coli."

Escherichia coli. It could cause severe gastro-intestinal reactions. "Nasty. What are you going to do about it?"

"I'm going out there tomorrow. How many households are drawing water from the stream below them?"

"At least one, maybe two."

"The Trapps are probably doing so as well."

He did visit the Trapps and told me he had explained the situation to them. They would have to move their privy, or he would issue an order and have it taken down without their permission. Dave tried to get cooperation from people to work toward a healthier community but he did have a solid law behind him when he didn't get that cooperation. He could order a bulldozer in there.

The Trapps didn't move fast enough. On my next visit to the community, I stopped to check on the removal of the privy. There was an empty spot with a jumble of sawdust, gravel, and logs where it had been.

I took three more samples and stopped to see Mrs. Trapp.

"You!" she said. "You told that inspector about our privy."

"Yes, Mrs. Trapp." I remained at the door. "You can't have an outhouse so close to a stream. It's the law."

"Canada has crazy laws."

"The same law exists in the US, I'm sure. The outhouse waste puts disease-carrying organisms into the water. People can die; fish and other animals can die or get sick. We can't have that."

"We aren't sick. We put ashes down and lime and kept it clean."

"The samples showed it was contaminated, which means, however hard you have tried, you haven't been effective. In any case, I see you took it down."

She leaned on the door jamb. "*We* didn't take it down. The neighbours took it down. We went to town last week for groceries, and when we came back, it had been wrecked. Just wrecked. It was them Deacons. I know it was."

I looked at her for a moment, absorbing the implications of what she'd said. My first reaction had been to burst out laughing, but I repressed it. Mrs. Trapp did not see this as funny. On sober reflection, I saw how this could escalate. It might be the beginning of a feud. I could see it happening.

"I'm coming in," I said.

She stepped back and motioned toward the small table and chairs near a stove. I sat down but didn't take off my coat.

"Mrs. Trapp, you can be bitter and angry toward your neighbours, but the fact remains your activities were causing them harm. Do you think you could offer them an apology?"

"Me? They're the ones that wrecked our privy."

I definitely didn't want a full-scale feud going on in Black Creek.

I took a breath and tried to be conciliatory. "I understand that you're angry about this."

"I'm right pissed," she said.

I looked at her and started to smile. "That's a good word."

She recognized the aptness of being "right pissed" at the treatment of her outhouse. Her mouth twitched, and she said with less heat, "Well, I was pretty mad." She said she had been mad, but her voice was mild and her eyes lit with humour.

"No doubt," I said and laughed.

She laughed as well. "Want some coffee?"

"Thanks, no. Another time. You know the Health Unit would have taken that privy down."

She shrugged. "I suppose. My man, Abner, is digging a new one. Between here and the barn. More handy, he said."

"That's good." I rose to leave.

"I suppose the neighbours are never gonna forgive me, right?"

It would be lonely here if she was at odds with her neighbours. "Maybe you could take some baking to the school for the upcoming fair and offer to help."

"That might be pushin' it."

It might.

I dropped by to talk to Mrs. Deacon. I gave her six empty water sample jars.

"Take samples next week from the spring downstream from the Trapps and again the following week. Have someone drop them off at the Williams Lake Health Unit or mail them to the lab; the address is on the outside. The results will come back to the health unit. Keep boiling the water until we get a clean result."

"Will do. You want to hear about how we got rid of the privy?"

"I'd love to," I said frankly, "but I'd better not know the details." I couldn't advocate vigilante action even if I approved of it, which I wasn't sure I did. "Maybe the neighbours could build the Trapps a new privy."

"Now there's a thought," Mrs. Deacon said. "We could build it, and then my old man could get Abner Trapp drunk in the bar one night, and the men could haul it up there with a front-end loader. Could be done."

I left the problem with her.

CHAPTER NINETEEN

ARGUING
WITH A GUN

SPRING IN the Cariboo was depressing. The landscape was bleak and the temperature, too cold to allow growth, was warm enough to thaw the ground. The result was mud—omnipresent, pervasive mud. There was mud at the entrance of every building where people scraped their boots, mud in the halls at the schools, mud on the roads, and mud up to the door handles of the cars. A clean car meant a new arrival in town or someone who had foolishly washed their vehicle. In our homes, we took off our boots at the door because mud seemed to be permanently attached. I wasn't used to it. When we had mud on the Coast—thin mud, occasional mud—the rain washed it away quickly. This mud was a danger.

"Do not go off the roads," Rita warned us. "If you get stuck, you'll have to be pulled out. You can't use chains to get traction or rock the car to inch forward the way you can in snow. Don't pull off onto the shoulder. You might be there a long time."

When I went out to the Likely area in April, I drove sedately and carefully, keeping off the side roads. By now, new growth flushed the fields, but the mud persisted in low-lying areas. Snow clung to the edges of the roads and in patches on the hillsides. I yearned for violets, daffodils, and tulips. Tulips, Carl's mother had informed me, bloomed in June. That seemed ludicrous to me, an affront to the natural order. April was tulip time in my childhood.

One morning, I tried to enjoy the almost constant sunlight and the greening of the willow bushes. I'd completed my work in Likely, left early after another of Mary's big breakfasts, and was heading toward Horsefly. Just before I turned onto the Beaver Valley Road, a huge yellow grader approached me coming from Williams Lake. It wasn't travelling fast, and I would turn off before I met it. It was encouraging to see the Department of Highways smoothing out the spring potholes. I waved. He waved back, quite energetically. It must be lonely for him working this far from town. I left him behind and swung east on the Beaver Valley Road, heading for the mill site at the other end of the valley. I was about a mile along the road when a pool of water stopped me.

Half the road had been washed away and a four-foot waterfall cascaded down and gurgled into the field beyond. It looked as though a giant had taken a bite of half the road, leaving the water to flood over the gravel, and drop to the cavern on the lower side. I left the car and walked over to view it, staying well back from the edge. A large section of the road had been carried into the lower ditch. On the high edge of the road there was still some roadbed, and it seemed solid. My car would just fit in the space between the ditch on the higher side and the waterfall as long as no more of the road fell away, and it wasn't too soft. I tested it with my boots. I didn't sink. There was no mud on the narrow strip except a patch of it near the ditch. I got back in the car, strapped on my seat belt, put it in first gear, and carefully drove into the dry strip of roadway. I was almost clear of the washout when I felt the back end of the car slip toward the ditch. I must have caught that mud. I shoved my foot down on the accelerator and gunned it. The car resisted for a moment and then shot onto the solid gravel. I slammed on the brakes.

I heard a thump and looked behind me. The rest of the road had fallen into the hole. I took a deep breath and let it out slowly. That was close. I must have jarred loose the last of the roadbed. There was no way back now. I hoped there wasn't a blockage or washout farther along.

"If you get into an accident," Rita had said when I'd first arrived in Williams Lake, "the Department of Health will pay for it. They don't have insurance on the cars. It's cheaper to pay for the accidents."

My father had been horrified. "What if they decide they won't pay? That leaves you responsible."

He owned an insurance company, and somehow he managed to buy me insurance. If I got into an accident and the government wouldn't pay, my insurance company would. I was sure I was the only government worker in the province with such coverage. I had malpractice insurance as well. No other nurse I knew carried that. My father was sensitive about those things.

There were no more hazards on the road. It was rutted with mud patches, but I got through to the mill site and was on time. When I pulled into the school yard at Beaver Valley, the principal was waiting on the front stairs. This wasn't her habit. Something must be wrong. I hoped it wasn't an emergency: a worker whose hand had been caught by a saw, a fire victim, a logging disaster. Emergency nursing was not my forte. She leaned forward, peering at me.

"What's the matter?" I asked, as I opened the car door.

"You're okay?"

"Sure." Why did she think I wouldn't be?

"The Beaver Valley Road is closed from the Likely end. You weren't supposed to travel along it." She stared at me as if to reassure herself that I was, indeed, all right.

"There wasn't any sign." Usually, the Department of Highways put up a danger sign when a road was closed.

"The grader was just coming up to put the sign there when you turned in. He tried to signal you, but you just kept going. He radioed up to the mill site and the manager phoned me."

No wonder the grader operator had waved so energetically.

"I'm sorry you were worried. I thought he was just being friendly. There's a washout at the far end of the road, but there was enough room for me to get by."

"There isn't enough room now," the principal said. "It's totally washed out."

I didn't tell her I knew that.

"We were praying for you." She accompanied me into the school.

This was a very pious community, predominantly Seventh-day Adventist people.

"I expect I'm someone who needs prayers," I said.

The rest of the trip went easily. No more road hazards.

AT HORSEFLY Lake, Marge served me fresh rainbow trout.

"Easier to get now it's thawed at the edge of the lake," she said.

I noticed subtle signs of spring along the road to Black Creek. Willow bushes with their bases in snow had produced pussy willows on bare branches. A trickle of water snaked along in the ditch beside the road. It was a long way from the extravagant fields of yellow daffodils, hedges of pink japonica, and low-lying purple crocuses that announced spring on the Coast.

I had one side trip to make to visit a new mother down a five-mile trail off the Likely Road near 150 Mile House, the small village at the junction of the Likely Road and the Highway. It was on my way home, and I thought I could manage the visit and be home in time to eat supper with Carl.

The first section of the road was gravelled, but about three miles along, it deteriorated until I was skidding along in mud. Trying to avoid a large pothole, I slid off the road and stopped dead. The car tilted toward the ditch on the passenger side. I pressed the accelerator, which didn't make the car move ahead one inch. I turned off the motor, got out, and assessed the problem. Revving the motor had caused the tires to spin and dig the passenger-side wheels into the mud. They were buried up to the hub caps. I could not drive my way out of that or rock the car to get out of it. Any movement would make it worse.

I left the baby scale but hefted my black bag and purse and headed off on foot for the remaining two miles. I could walk two miles.

Cattle grazed beneath the poplar trees on both sides of the road. I hoped they would ignore me; they were a little frightening. I kept a steady pace and stayed in the middle of the road for about a mile when I came upon a cow standing in my way. I stopped. She contemplated me and swished her tail. Did that mean she was angry? I watched and waited. I had no place to go for safety if she decided to charge. Finally, she ambled down the other side of the road and into the trees.

I resumed walking and, luckily, met no more cattle. I was getting close to the ranch when I glimpsed a very large animal moving through a grove of trees near the road. I stared. It was a huge moose, taller than me at its shoulders but without antlers. It had a baby following it, a miniature, clumsy-looking youngster. I'd never seen a moose before and this pair were beautiful. They kept pace beside me, as if escorting me. Did the mother feel protective of me? Or curious? Somehow, I felt comforted by her presence.

I came upon the ranch house, and, accompanied by the usual barking dogs, I knocked on the back door. I glanced over my shoulder, but the moose had disappeared.

"Mrs. Anderson?" I said when a young red-headed woman answered the door.

"Oh, Nurse." She peered past me. "I didn't hear your car."

I explained where I'd left it.

"The road is pretty bad. We manage okay in the truck, but the last few days have been pretty slippery. The ground is just oozing moisture."

"While I'm here, perhaps I could phone for a tow truck?"

"No phone. But my husband will be home in an hour or so and he'll pull you out. You'll stay for supper, won't you?"

"Thank you. That's kind of you." I wasn't going anywhere until my car was free. It was nice to know I wouldn't be hungry.

"There were cattle on the road."

"They wander over it quite often. They won't bother you. Now, what you have to watch out for are the moose, especially in the spring. They can be aggressive."

I had been hanging up my coat on a hook near the door and halted, the better to listen.

"They can be really aggressive. Especially if they have a little one around. Charge you and stomp the life out of you."

And I had been afraid of the cattle. I had a lot of learning to do. I took off my boots, put my bag on the kitchen table, and sat.

"A moose followed me," I said. "She had a calf with her."

"She didn't charge you?"

I shook my head, imagining the charge of a moose, the fearsome power of those hooves.

"Where was she?"

"She followed me to your yard."

"I'll tell Sam. We'll watch for her. I'll stay close to the house when I'm on foot. Mind you, they'll charge a horse too and even a truck."

I was mute, thinking of how close I'd come to a ton of muscle knocking me down, hooves pounding me into pulp. The sheer horror of it shook me for a few seconds. How naive I was.

"Are you a city girl, Miss McKinnon?"

I shook my head and finally found my voice. "I grew up on a farm, but we didn't have moose around."

"You have to watch out for them," she said.

That was clear.

I did the assessment on a healthy newborn baby. Mrs. Anderson left me to mind the little girl while she nipped down to the creek and caught some trout. If she was going to feed me supper, she had to catch it first.

Her husband did come home in an hour, and, after supper, he fired up his tractor and drove to my car with me standing behind him on the guard rail, mud spinning up from the tires and coating my legs, while I scanned the trees for any sign of moose. It didn't take long to pull the car from the mud. He took my keys, got in my car, and turned it around for me, so I was facing in the direction of home.

"I'll follow you until you get onto the gravel," he said.

I accepted his custodial care and made it back to the main road without slipping off over the edge again.

CARL CALLED me at work one sunny afternoon when I'd just decided that the beginning of May had the promise of summer. The air was warm, the snow had finally gone, and the lilac trees along Borland Street had started to bud, sending sweet perfume over the town. Even the buildings looked somehow brighter.

"What's up?" I asked. He rarely phoned me at work.

"I just got a call from Jobina Sampson. She lives with her husband, Charlie Williams, in a cabin below the railway tracks. Charlie works for me sometimes—in haying season and in the fall roundup. He's a good worker and a nice guy, but he goes on these drinking binges, and then he's a problem."

"Okay," I said, waiting to find out where I came in.

"Usually, when Charlie drinks, Jobina takes the kids and goes to her mother's at the end of the lake and just stays there until Charlie sobers up and is himself again," Carl explained carefully.

"But," I prompted.

"But this time, Charlie wouldn't let her take Joe, the little boy, with her. She took the other two kids to her mother's, but she couldn't get Joe, and she's worried Charlie won't feed him or let him go to school. Then, of course, once he's not in school, the social workers might grab him."

I wished I could change the personnel at the Social Welfare office—except for Paul. I was quiet while I thought about it.

"I'll call Paul. We'll go down there. I'll see that Joe gets back to his mum. Where is Charlie?"

Carl described the cabin. I could picture it at the end of Oliver Street, across the tracks, and then down the hill.

"Where's Jobina?" I asked.

"She's at the Ranch Café in town, using the phone there," he said.

"Okay. Tell her I'll bring Joe to her there."

"Thanks, Marion."

"Is Charlie dangerous when he's drinking?" I was not as intrepid as Sophie.

"Maybe to Jobina, but he's never given me any trouble." That was a dubious recommendation. He might or he might not be dangerous to me.

I called Paul, and he met me on the other side of the railroad tracks. A road ran parallel and then down into a ravine. We could see several cabins beside the creek, looking as if they were slumbering in the sunshine. It was beautiful and quiet. The train came through only twice a day. It would be idyllic most of the time, a pocket of warmth where spring came early. The poplars were already bursting with green leaves and the firs sent out the spicy scent of pitch.

We hadn't walked very far along the road when we met Charlie coming up. He had Joe with him—and a rifle.

We stopped.

"Hello, Charlie," Paul said. "I'm Paul, and this is the public health nurse, Miss McKinnon."

I noticed he didn't reveal he was a social worker. Paul was a little taller than me and about my age. He was thin, his shoulders hunched forward, and he wore glasses. His arms were well-muscled, though, so he might be stronger than he looked.

"Hello, Charlie," I said as if he didn't have a gun and this was a pleasant social visit. "This must be your boy, Joe."

"This is Joe," he said. "He's staying with me. And nobody's taking him."

Joe was a sturdy little boy with thick dark hair. He darted a quick glance at me then stared at the ground.

Paul nodded. "Okay. We'll just sit here a while and talk about it."

Paul moved over to the bank beside the road and squatted on the grass. I did the same. We sat there on our haunches, conversing with Charlie who stood on the road, one hand resting on Joe's shoulder and the other gripping the rifle. The rifle wavered between pointing at Paul and pointing at me. I don't know why Charlie stayed to talk to us when he could have turned around and gone back to his cabin. I expect he thought we'd call the police—and we might have—if he didn't let Joe leave. It seemed bizarre to sit in the warm sunshine with green grass around us and the soft breeze rustling the trees across the road while a man threatened us with a gun. I should have been terrified, but it seemed too nice a day to die. I was rattled and not thinking rationally.

"Are you making out okay down there?" Paul nodded down the road. "Getting enough to eat?"

Little Joe hadn't said a word and stood quietly. Occasionally, he would glance sideways at the rifle. I thought he was well aware of the dangers of that gun. His attitude made me sure it was loaded. I was calmer now and paying attention.

"We're getting by." He let go of Joe and brought the gun up, aiming it at my chest.

That gun looked dangerous, but as a nurse I was expected to remain calm in an emergency. *Do not panic in an emergency. Panic later.* Paul had talked to keep the situation from escalating. I'd do my share of talking.

"That's good," I said. "Do you need anything?"

"Yes," Paul said. "Can we get you anything?" Paul seemed almost relaxed. I concentrated on breathing normally.

The gun wavered and moved over to cover Paul.

"Like what?" Charlie said. He was in his late twenties and hand- some, in spite of those bleary eyes, dishevelled T-shirt, and scuffed boots. He was muscular, too. I didn't think he was impulsive. I hoped not. An impulsive man with a rifle was dangerous.

"Oh, food, medicine, blankets," I said.

The gun came back my way. My thighs ached from sustained squatting, but I dared not stand. I would not panic. I ground my teeth and held my body still.

He stared at me for a few seconds. "Food, maybe. My old lady took off."

"She's okay," I said. "She went to her mother's."

He laughed, a cynical, derisive laugh. "Sure. She always goes to her mother's."

"But she comes back," I said, trying to reassure him that life would get back to normal.

He nodded. "True. True. She always comes back."

He dropped his hand and the gun dropped, pointing now toward the ground.

"She comes back," he said again.

Paul shifted a little on his haunches. "Why don't we let Miss McKinnon take Joe here to his mother, and you and I will go back to the cabin and see what food you need."

Charlie looked at Paul, then studied me. I tried to look reliable, but probably just looked young. Charlie spoke seriously to Paul, as if I wasn't there.

"She will look after Joe? He's only six."

"She will," Paul promised. He shifted his weight and stood.

"No taking him to those welfare police or those priests?" Charlie stepped back, the gun still pointed to the ground.

"Absolutely not," I said. "I promise I'll take him to Jobina." I moved slowly and stood.

He stared at me for a long time. "Okay," he finally said.

Charlie nodded to Joe. Joe walked toward me. I held out my hand.

"And Charlie," Paul said. "Why don't you let me carry the rifle, and we'll walk back to the cabin?"

"Okay," Charlie said and passed the rifle over. It's possible Charlie was looking for a way out of the mess he'd created. It was hard to guess what he was thinking.

Paul, the brave man, walked down the hill to the cabin. Joe and I walked silently up the hill, across the railway tracks, and onto Oliver Street, and the half-block to the Ranch Café. Joe kept his head down.

A woman was standing outside the entrance to the café. She was short, a little plump, with long, dark hair.

"Is that your mother?" I asked Joe. I didn't want to hand him over to the wrong person.

He looked up, nodded, dropped my hand, and ran to her. She gathered him into her arms and hugged him fiercely. I left them to their reunion for a few moments then approached her.

"I'm Miss McKinnon, the health nurse. The social worker, Paul, is with Charlie. He's going to see he has food and maybe help him get over this binge."

"Thank you." She hugged Joe and then straightened and looked at me. She had beautiful dark eyes and smooth skin. "You're Carl's woman?"

I hesitated for a moment and then said. "Yes."

"He's a good man." She nodded at me, her arm still around Joe. Joe was sticking like a limpet to his mother's side.

"Yes, he is." It was true. Carl was a good man.

"My Charlie is a good man—most of the time," she said, and she smiled.

We stared at each other for a few moments, then I smiled at our shared experience with good men.

It was lovely to see her reunited with Joe, but I was worried about Paul. I was talking to Jobina while listening for the sound of a shot.

I went back to the railroad, crossed over, and waited. I saw Paul coming up the road with the rifle in his hand. I felt a wave of relief.

"You're okay? He's okay?" I asked.

"Yeah. There isn't much liquor left in the place. I expect he's coming down from the binge. I said I'd keep the rifle until he was sober. He wouldn't let me take it until I said I'd give it to Carl." Paul walked beside me. He seemed unruffled. I wondered how often he had to face a gun.

"That was weird," I said.

"Yeah." He looked at the rifle and started to pass it to me.

I backed away. "I'm not walking through the streets of Williams Lake with a rifle."

He was quiet for a moment then said. "Follow me to my place. Janet will give you coffee. I can put the rifle in your car, and you can take it to Carl. I'll have to go grocery shopping and get back to Charlie. Maybe I could cook him something—bacon and eggs, something." He sounded a little vague, as if wondering if he could manage to produce a meal. I wish there were more Pauls in the welfare system.

I agreed. It seemed the best idea. "I'll phone Carl from your place."

At Paul's house, Janet gave me coffee and sympathy. When I thought about the soft grass, the breeze, the little boy and the rifle, my knees shook and my legs felt weak. I tried *not* to think about it.

THE NEXT time I saw Charlie was at Carl's ranch. Carl had hired two men to help move the cattle up into the higher meadows where the grass had "greened up." One of them was Charlie. Charlie rode a beautiful grey horse he had trucked to the ranch in his trailer. He doffed his stetson to me when I met him at the corral. I nodded and smiled. He looked sober and about ten years younger than the last time I'd seen him. Ollie, Carl's dad, had ridden over and planned to help with the mini cattle drive, so there were several men on horseback in the yard.

There was still a lot of mud around the ranch and in the woods. Carl said horses were more practical in the mud than trucks for moving cattle. They didn't leave a mess on the trails and they could manoeuvre quickly. Probably everyone just loved getting out on the horses. It was a chance to prove horses weren't simply pets but a necessary part of ranching.

I sat on the corral fence and watched Carl on Pammie move the cattle toward a far gate with Keo running at his side. Carl was at the back of the herd and his dad on a black horse behind him. Charlie took the right-hand side of the field and another man on a roan mare took the left. They separated the pregnant cows from the steers as Carl wanted the cows on the best grass and not too far away. Calving season started in a few weeks, and he would be out checking on them frequently. They moved the cows first and then came back an hour later and moved the steers and heifers up the road, toward the farther pastures. I watched them ride along the road as far as I could see up into the hills. Carl's mum, Betty Jean, stood beside me.

"I never tire of it," she said.

"Do you ever join them?" I asked her.

"On my ranch, I do. But here I let Carl and Ollie have some 'together' time, and I get the meal ready."

"It's a good thing you came over. I'd no idea Carl was supposed to provide a feast at noon." I hadn't thought about what the men would eat or the fact that Carl would have to provide it.

"He'll have most of it ready—because I made sure he did." She shot a sideways look at me.

I laughed. "You'll have to teach me."

"Don't take over all the household chores, or like any man, Carl will let you. It's a matter of habits," she said. "If you like splitting wood, then just do it and don't expect him to do it all. But if you don't like it, you can leave it for him. He'll assume you can't do it. Same goes for cooking. If you hate baking bread, just buy it. If you hate canning, never do it. Just trade something with the women around here who love to can. Start off the way you mean to go on."

The way she was talking implied I would be with Carl permanently. I wasn't ready for that kind of conversation. I scraped my boots at the kitchen door, left them on the boot rack, toed into my slippers, and followed her into Carl's kitchen.

There were two huge picnic baskets on the table and a monster soup pot on the stove.

She nodded at the soup pot. "Ollie carried it in. I don't lift weights."

I slanted a glance at her and raised my eyebrows. She was shorter than me and thin, but she looked strong.

"Unless Ollie isn't there, and then I sling bales and lift machinery," she amended. "I told Carl to buy four different cakes at the bakery. I didn't care what kind as long as two of them were chocolate. If you and I don't eat any, that's one cake for each man. Should do them." She peered into a box on the counter. "Apples and bananas. I told him to get those. I brought over my coffee urn."

"And the coffee," I said, spying the can on the counter.

"I was sure he'd forget to buy coffee. We have about an hour before they come back for lunch. Let's have our own coffee." She headed for the cupboard and the mugs.

We sat at Carl's table by the window and looked out over the corrals. We'd be able to see the men as they returned.

"I hope," Betty Jean said, "you don't object to me taking over in this kitchen for today."

I looked at her. She was trim, athletic, and about fifty with short streaked blonde hair. She reminded me of a whiskey jack— inquisitive, alert and intelligent.

"It isn't my kitchen," I said.

"Well, you might feel it was."

I thought about that. "A little, but not enough to object to your managing the lunch. I wouldn't know how to feed those men. I mean, I would have probably fussed too much. I can see you minimized the effort. You had the soup ready ahead of time, the sandwiches made, and a lot of things bought at the store. I might have tried to cook everything from scratch, which would have been a disaster."

"A waste of effort, too. These men are hungry and will eat almost anything." She sipped her coffee and looked out over the yard toward the hills. She seemed relaxed. I was a little on edge.

"So I appreciate you showing me how." I was grateful.

She smiled. "You can come over when Carl helps Ollie move our cattle next week. Same thing happens there. You might get out with the men. I plan to."

"I'd like that," I said carefully.

"We'll need a gentle horse for you."

I smiled. I was beginning to know her a little better. "And you want me to bring?"

"Sandwiches," she said promptly. "Bologna and cheese. Don't fancy them up with mayonnaise or parsley or anything else. Cheddar cheese, big hunks. Store-bought bread."

She was making it easy to fit into Carl's family. I felt ambivalent about that. On the one hand, I wanted to be liked by Carl's family; that would make our relationship a little easier. On the other hand, I didn't want them to expect marriage; that was too much pressure.

CHAPTER TWENTY

LEARNING
EXPERIENCES

ALICE, THE NEW nurse, had settled into her district smoothly. She had been a public health nurse for ten years and knew what she could demand from the bosses in Victoria. She understood the programs, didn't need much direction, and was willing to help other nurses. She was easy to work with, confident, and experienced like Sophie. But Alice had tightly permed hair compared to Sophie's wild bush. Her speech was precise compared to Sophie's impetuous blurts. I didn't see her socially, but Sophie told me she had started dating a friend of Rita and Jim's, an Italian builder.

"It blows your mind," Sophie said. "That passionate, chain-smoking Italian with our proper Alice."

I shrugged. Other people's choices were unfathomable. My own weren't always clear.

ONE FRIDAY in May, Alice phoned me from Riske Creek, a few miles into the Chilcotin.

"I stopped to see a Mrs. Matilda Black out here," she said, "and she's gone to town. Her sister-in-law thinks she's staying at Sinn Chiu's Rooming House. Could you check to see if she's there? She needs a TB test."

"Sure." The child health clinic had just finished, and I had a few hours free before Carl picked me up for a dance at the Soda Creek Hall. It would be the first time I could dress up and go to a dance without putting on boots. The snow and mud had retreated into the earth for at least the next four months. I was looking forward to going out in my fancy, feminine shoes.

I carried Audrey Cook's misread test and subsequent death on my shoulders, so I was determined to find Mrs. Black. Every TB test was important.

Sinn Chiu's Rooming House was on First Street, not far from the railway tracks. It was a long, low building with a central hall and about six rooms on either side. Sophie told me it cost two dollars a night to stay there. I'd met Sinn Chiu several times. He was a short Chinese man, somewhere between fifty and seventy years old. His English was understandable, if I concentrated on it, and he was always gracious to me, making me feel welcome and helping me locate people.

He asked me to stand in the hall because he had lent his office to a mother who wanted a quiet place to nurse her baby. When people came to town from the outlying areas, they often had no place they could retire in private. Sinn Chiu let them use his rooming house. I expect it was a kind of social club for many. It was quiet in the hall, and I relaxed as I waited. Late afternoon sun slanted in through the front doorway. The days were getting longer and the air drier. The sunshine was hazy as it carried a lot of dust. It was Friday, and I was going to be off work soon. I shook myself back to the present and asked about Mrs. Black.

Sinn Chiu knew who I meant and brought me down the hall. He knocked on a door. Mrs. Black opened it and Sinn Chiu left us. I gave the test. I talked to Mrs. Black. She understood the importance of reading it and calling Alice with the results. That didn't take long. I packed up my bag and headed down the hall. I was mentally reviewing my wardrobe for that night's date when Sinn Chiu stopped me. He stood at his office door, empty now of nursing mothers, and beckoned to me, indicating a chair.

I stuffed down my impatience to be gone and sat. Sinn Chiu had, after all, saved me hours of searching for Mrs. Black; I could give him some time. It was an interesting room. A picture of a temple and some stone carvings occupied a high shelf. Beaded deerskin moccasins hung from a hook on the wall. Several photos sat on his desk.

"Your children?" I indicated the picture of two boys.

"My wife and two sons are in China." He smiled. He was missing a lower front tooth, but I'd glimpsed a flash of gold farther back.

"Do you get to see them very often?" I studied the two boys. They were bright-eyed and healthy looking.

"Maybe three or five years."

"That's a long time between visits." Poor kids, and poor Sinn Chiu who didn't get to watch them grow up.

"They're good boys. Big now." He gazed at the photo.

"I'm sure they are," I said politely. What kind of dire circumstances in China made living apart a good idea? Did Canadian laws prohibit their immigrating?

"I work hard here," he said.

"I know." I looked around. At two dollars a night, how could he earn enough money to support himself, a family in China, and trips home every three to five years? I don't believe he was dealing in contraband liquor. I'd heard no rumours of vice about him. He just worked hard, spent nothing, and sent it all home.

As if reading my mind, he said, "I always work hard. I cook at the Gang Ranch. Did you know? Long time ago."

I shook my head. He seemed to want to talk about his past. It was getting late. Carl would be coming. *What was I going to wear?* I let my mind wander over my wardrobe and my shoes. Tonight I wanted to wear my green high heels with embroidery on the toes. I nodded to encourage Sinn Chiu and said, "Is that right?" and "My, my!" in what I thought were appropriate pauses, but his melodious voice rising and falling with his story almost lulled me into a daydream. Suddenly, his voice came through to me very clearly.

"And then we threw the body in the river."

I stared at him.

He nodded to emphasize his announcement.

"You did?"

"That's right." He smiled.

I tried to recall what he'd been saying. Something about Gang Ranch. Something about the cliffs by the Fraser River. I had condescendingly nodded and encouraged him while not listening. I couldn't admit to such rude behaviour now. If I asked him to repeat the story, he would know that I hadn't been listening. I stewed in frustration for a moment but couldn't see a way to get that story from him without admitting I had been ignoring him all the time he'd been talking.

I said my goodbyes, well aware that I would never know that story. *What body? Why?* Strange things happened in the Cariboo a long way from police stations. *Did they find a body? Did he witness a murder?* My mind ranged over the possibilities. I promised myself I would never pretend to understand someone when I didn't. I never again wanted to miss such a tale and be left frustrated with burning curiosity.

I NOW had systems on how to ensure I did all the TB tests that were needed and had Ellie check that I had done them. I had a reminder system for postnatal visits, so I could see all babies within six weeks. But I was still not able to make the changes I wanted in some areas. The police still picked up Indigenous men, as if those men had no rights, and threw them into jail—and I couldn't stop them. The priests still exerted power, mostly over Indigenous women. I suspected abuse where I couldn't prove it or do anything about it. The more problems I discovered in the community, the less I seemed to be able to accomplish. I was learning to have a list of goals and pick the ones that I could actually address.

Adam Estie was a medical student and was spending two weeks in our health unit as part of his third-year studies. Rita orientated him to the principles and practices of public health. Field nurses like me took him on home visits. He was a serious, humourless, dedicated young man. I had him for only one day.

When he got in the passenger seat of my car, I passed him two files.

"We're going to go do two postnatal visits today." I nodded at the files. "You can read the material on them. They should be routine. I'm not expecting any problems. There might be something to look for in the first visit as the hospital maternity nurse said she thought the mother was a bit awkward."

"Awkward? What does that mean?" He looked up at me from his perusal of the records, pushed his glasses up and waited.

"Hard to say. It might mean that she didn't know how to feed a baby. It might mean that she was just tired in the hospital. We'll find out."

The house was on the outskirts of town in a sunny spot against the hill on Paxton Road. Mrs. Jewel MacRea and her family lived in what appeared to be near poverty. Bits of machinery littered the dead grass on the front lawn. There was no car in the driveway. A blind dangled from a broken cord on the window. I'd try to see if they had enough food.

Mrs. MacRea was happy to see me. She looked tired, but nothing dimmed her beauty. She was blonde, blue-eyed, had luxurious hair, and slightly protruding teeth, which somehow made her look younger than her twenty years. I let Adam carry the scale but had told him to just observe the visit this time.

The smell hit me the minute I was inside. *Rotten eggs. Gas!*

Mrs. MacRea made a space on her kitchen table for the scale and went to fetch the baby from her bassinet. Mr. MacRea, a young man of about twenty-four, sat at the table. Not smoking, thank God.

"Where's the gas shut-off?" I asked with commendable calm. Adam was still standing by the door.

Mr. MacRea rose and took me to a small room at the back of the house. He pointed. I turned the switch until it was at ninety degrees to the line.

"It's going to get cold," he said.

"Better he be alive and cold, than dead and unable to feel any-thing. You've got a gas leak."

The young man looked worried, but I wondered how he'd lived to his mid-twenties, since he didn't seem to have much common sense. It's possible the ward nurse realized that there weren't a lot of spare brains in this house.

"I'll send over an electric heater. Do you have an electric stove?" I asked.

He nodded.

"Put the oven on and leave the door open."

"Okay. I can do that." He nodded and seemed happy to have instructions to follow.

"Good."

"I know we have to do something about that leak. I called the landlord, but he's not doing anything." He stared at me, a puppy looking for guidance.

"Give me the landlord's number." I was determined to help him deal with this. "I'll call him."

"Would you? Thanks. It's a bit of a worry. Jewel won't let me smoke inside." He shrugged.

"Very good idea," I said. Probably the only reason they were all alive.

Jewel MacRea returned with the baby. I examined the little girl, head to toe, doing several reflex checks, and found normal reactions.

I weighed her and made the entry in my record and in Mrs. MacRea's little blue record book. I entered the baby's name on my records. "Jennifer? Pretty name." I didn't tell her it was the sixth baby Jennifer this month.

She looked at record of the weight and then at the baby.

"She's not gaining." She frowned.

"What are you feeding and how often?" I asked.

She told me, and I reassured her that she was doing fine, and I'd return the next day to see if the baby had gained any weight.

I'd introduced Adam, but everyone ignored him, and he said nothing.

He had plenty to say when we were back in the car. "That baby needs more nourishment. You didn't spend nearly enough time trying to get the mother to feed it more. It should be on breast milk. She's just giving it formula. There's a lot more you could have done." He gave me instructions dogmatically, as if I needed his direction. I was about his age but felt years older.

I shut off the car in the health unit parking lot and turned to him.

"This is public health, Adam. First, we get the gas leak fixed, and then, if they're all alive tomorrow, we concentrate on the baby." *Prioritize, you idiot,* I thought but didn't say.

I stomped off to my office to deal with the landlord.

Rita stuck her nose in my office. "Are you through with Adam?"

I put my hand over the phone. I was on hold. "I wish," I said fervently. "But no. He can come out with me. I have another home visit. I'll let him do the exam."

"Fine. He seems to think he was dismissed." She raised her eyebrows.

I snorted.

He walked into my office, just as I got the landlord on the phone. I waved him to a chair and concentrated on the phone call.

"Miss McKinnon calling. I'm the public health nurse, and I have just been to the MacRea house. You are the landlord of that property?" I started out firmly but hoped to get cooperation.

He agreed that he was.

"There is a gas leak that is severe and dangerous. I am going to call the fire department, and send someone out there. Can you meet them and be prepared to fix that leak immediately? I will be out again tomorrow to check. There's a new baby in that house, so you will have to take an electric heater. They need to be warm while the gas is being repaired." I outlined the problem clearly. He didn't have a lot of options.

He squawked that he'd get around to it in a couple of days.

"No, that won't do," I upped the degree of firmness. "It must be done immediately. Get out there now. My next call is the fire department, and if they don't find you there, my next call will be to the police department. Leaving that family in danger is intentional criminal neglect."

He squawked more but agreed he'd repair the leak—today.

"I'm sure the fire marshal will have something to say to you about how you do that." I applied more pressure. I didn't want substandard repairs.

He sighed and said that he'd better bring a gas repairman with him.

I'd make sure he did. "Yes, good idea. Within a half-hour. Good-bye." Promises were more reliable when there was a threat looming.

I disconnected, looked at the inside cover of the phone book, and phoned the fire department.

"Marshall, is that you? It's Marion McKinnon." Marshall was the fire marshal. He was a friend of Carl's. "Look there's a family out on Paxton Road who are living in a gas leak. Yes, it smells. They know, but the landlord isn't fixing it. There's a new baby." That's all Marshall needed to hear in order to act. "Right away? Thanks." I gave him the address and hung up the phone.

Adam stared at me. "The landlord and the fire marshal . . . they just do what you say? Because you say it?"

I looked at him for a second. "They want to help. I'm just giving them the opportunity."

He looked puzzled, as if the world had shifted slightly.

"Now," I said to Adam. "We'll visit another family. You can do the infant exam this time. You saw me do it, so you know what's usual."

"I know how to examine a baby." His voice was pompous.

"Good." I wasn't going to manage a personality reconstruction of Adam Estie—as much as I'd like to.

This couple was also young, in their early twenties, but the mother, Mrs. Cawston, was a farm girl and had plenty of experience with mammal babies like lambs and calves. As well, she'd told me on the phone, she had a little sister whom she'd looked after when she lived with her family. Her confidence showed in the way she handled the baby. She was breastfeeding. Adam would have no quarrel with her about nutrition.

I introduced Adam as a medical student and asked their permission for him to examine their daughter. The mother and the father stared at Adam for a moment or two and then agreed.

Adam did a capable job. He recorded the weight, the length, and the circumference of the head and the torso, as I would have done. He did the startle reflex, but he didn't warn the parents he was going to do that, and they were concerned. They looked at me.

"That's a normal reaction," I reassured them. "And what he did was a test for normal function."

"Okay." They relaxed a little but still watched Adam like a pair of hawks.

He said nothing and handed the baby back to Mrs. Cawston.

She looked at me. "Would you do the exam yourself?" she asked.

I didn't look at Adam. I know he was insulted, as his exam had been thorough, but he hadn't explained anything to the parents.

"Sure," I said and proceeded to do everything over again—but I talked as I worked.

"What is the baby's name?"

"Stephanie? Oh, lovely." Another Stephanie. That made three this month. We had a tally going at the health unit. "She's lovely. Good colour on her skin. She's nursing well?"

The mother told me all about her breast feeding and the baby's bowel movements and what differences she had seen in her. I noted how the baby responded to the mother's voice by turning her head when she heard it. I asked the father to come closer and talk to the baby, and I saw how the baby searched past my face to stare at her father. Bonding seemed to be occurring normally.

I told the parents about a parenting group they might want to join in a few months and about the child health clinics in their area.

I also left my phone number and encouraged them to call me if they had any questions.

"There are always questions," I said.

They smiled and waved good bye.

Adam was silent. I was sure he was upset at having his examination questioned by the parents. Maybe this was the optimum teaching moment. I pulled into a café and said, "We'll have coffee and talk about it."

We found a booth near the back of the café and ordered coffee and a Danish each. Adam waited until the waitress was at the other end of the café before he burst out with, "I did everything you did! What was wrong?"

"Well, you did all the tests," I said carefully.

"So, what was wrong?" he demanded.

Maybe he was one of those people who had to have all the social clues pointed out to them.

"The parents didn't trust you." That was the basic problem.

"Why not? *I'm* a medical student." And *you're* just a nurse was what he was implying.

"Probably because you didn't seem to relate to their baby. You didn't convey the notion their baby was special and wonderful."

"Relate to their baby? Special?" He looked at me with disbelief. "Like what was I supposed to do, kiss it?"

"You could have asked her name and addressed her by it," I said mildly. Adam was not going to take this well, and I wasn't sure he was going to learn anything, but I'd try.

He was still, considering my suggestion. "I could do that, I suppose." He shrugged. "All that touchy-feely stuff. It's not efficient."

I took a sip of coffee and said quietly. "Adam, what do you know about failure to thrive?"

His eyes moved up and to the right. I could see him searching for the definition. I'm sure he had a medical encyclopedia engraved on his neocortex. "Failure to thrive: a condition in which an infant or a child inexplicably does not retain nourishment." He sounded like a text book, and he was correct.

I nodded. "And what causes that?"

"They aren't sure," he said defensively.

"But recent studies suggest failure to thrive equates to lack of love."

"I've read that," he admitted.

"So, when you were examining the baby, did you assess whether she was loved or not?"

"I didn't consciously. Did you?" He was aggressive with that question.

"Yes, I did. If you remember, I asked the father to talk to the baby, and I noticed she looked past me and focused on him. That means he's spending enough time with her to bond with her. She followed her mother's voice. She turned to it when her mother spoke. That indicates bonding. Mum's breastfeeding and spending a lot of skin-to-skin time with her baby. Then there were all those presents stacked on the counter. The parents are getting support. Did you pick up on any of that?" I was trying to tell him how to assess love. You'd think he'd have *some* experience with it.

He shook his head.

"If a baby comes into your office, and it is failing to thrive, are you simply going to do blood tests, or are you going to try and find out if it's loved?" Maybe if he saw a practical application, he'd admit its importance.

He was silent. "There are some things I don't notice, I guess."

"You can learn. We all have to learn." I paid for the coffee and drove him back to the health unit. I'd done my best with him. It might help.

I had a learning experience of my own looming. Betty Jean had asked me to speak to her Women's Institute group. She was the president and responsible for bringing in speakers. The group consisted of ranchers—a formidable group of women. They ran ranching businesses, homes, and families. I simply did one job.

"What would I talk about?" I'd asked when she suggested it.

"Talk about child development. They are always interested in child development." Betty Jean seemed to think anyone could give a talk.

"But they all have children, and I don't." They would all have ideas of their own.

"Just admit that up front, and maybe give them some of the latest theories and ask their opinions on that. You do assess kids to see if they are developing normally, don't you?" She peered at me over her reading glasses. She had asked me to drop in after work, so we were having coffee in her kitchen. She had some mending on her table that she'd shoved aside, but she still wore her half-glasses.

"Sure. All the time."

"Tell them how you do that." She seemed to think it would be simple.

I got out my textbooks and put together a twenty-minute presentation on childhood development and then set up questions about theories around children's behaviour, so the women could discuss them.

Monday afternoon found me with Betty Jean at the Soda Creek Hall. There were tables and chairs set out and ten women were waiting. They had a business meeting first.

"We all know," Betty Jean said, speaking as the president, "the Andersons lost their house in a fire last week."

"So sad," a woman beside me said. "And them not married a month."

"Dreadful," another said. "She's not working, and his job doesn't pay a lot."

"I move," an older woman said, "that our Women's Institute give them five hundred dollars to help them rebuild."

Five hundred dollars was more than a month's salary for me. The motion passed unanimously.

"And now," Betty Jean said. "How are we going to raise that money?"

I was astounded. I'd assumed they had five hundred dollars in their WI treasury, but they didn't. They just decided how much the young couple should have, and now they were going to figure out how to raise it. I'd never met such a bold bunch. By the time the business part of the meeting closed, they had mapped out their path to achieve their goal: bake sales, a meat draw, bingo, and several other events. It would take energy and time and they seemed happy to do it.

Then it was my turn. I stood and admitted my lack of practical, personal experience with children then gave them the theory of behaviourism. I talked about operative learning and stimulus response. I touched on Skinner's work and then the work of others with animals. I related it to the way in which animals were taught to expect to be fed at certain times and how horses were taught to obey riders. I asked them if they thought reward and praise got better behaviour or more lasting behaviour change from children than punishment. I asked them if they thought the role of parents was to be a teacher or a controller. Those two questions kept them in lively discussion for an hour. They were opinionated, articulate, and knowledgeable, and I didn't try to disagree or even direct the conversation. Betty Jean kept the meeting rolling along until the end when the coffee and goodies were passed around. I was relieved when it was over.

"You know, Miss McKinnon," a woman sitting beside me said. "That man Skinner talked about how behaviour changes when you learn something. That's really interesting in animals." She was about forty-five, blonde, thin, with beautiful rosy and luminous skin. Betty Jean had called her Helen. "We took in a lamb last spring. You know how it is." She nodded at the group. "The idiot mother would only feed one of her twins, so we took the poor wee thing into the house and fed it."

Carl had told me about sheep rearing. It was difficult because coyotes and foxes were active predators and even dogs could kill the lambs. As well, the obstetric problems of sheep were many because they were bred for multiple births. To complicate the birthing, some ewes seemed to have little maternal instinct.

"You know how much time that takes, bottle feeding every two hours, but we persisted, and the wee thing grew," Helen said.

"How did you keep it warm?" one of the women asked.

"Now, that was a lucky thing," Helen said. "We had two pups, and they snuggled up to that lamb right away. So we had no worries about it getting chilled."

"Hard to put that one back in the flock," was the comment from another woman.

"Impossible," Helen agreed. "He grew up to be a fine young wether."

"But still in the house," Betty Jean guessed.

Helen nodded. "I managed to get him to sleep in the lean-to with the dogs, but, yes, he sometimes comes into the house. He's a dear thing."

"Do you still have it?" Betty Jean asked for us all.

"Well, you know how it is. We'll probably build him a retirement home."

The women laughed.

"But that isn't the strange thing. The strange thing is the way living with us and with the dogs changed the lamb's behaviour." She turned to me.

"In what way?" I asked.

"Well, you know sheep just get terrified if they see a coyote." She looked for agreement from the women.

Betty Jean spoke for them. "That they do."

"Yesterday, I looked out the bedroom window, and I said to Roy, 'Come and look. There's coyote in the lane, racing away, and he's being chased by the dogs *and* the lamb!' The three of them were racing after the coyote, the dogs barking, and the lamb bleating. They stopped at the end of the lane, the coyote ran off, and all three came trotting back." She turned to me. "What do you think? Is that behaviour operant learning? The lamb learning to act like a dog?"

"I wouldn't want to push that too far," Betty Jean said. "The coyote could still eat it."

Helen had taken what I'd said about Skinner's operant learning and applied it to her experience. Like many of the ranchers I'd met,

she was intelligent and interested in new ways of thinking. She and
the women around her enjoyed learning. It was like being with a
group of students. I realized I felt comfortable with them.

CHAPTER TWENTY-ONE

MEDICS IN THE CHILCOTIN

JUNE IN the Cariboo was an extravagant rush of growth, as if the whole plateau was infused with fertility. Nature was profuse, pushing everything she had been withholding since March into this month. Flowers I had been used to seeing emerge gradually over the months of spring on the Coast—daffodils, tulips, roses, peonies—suddenly burst out all together. Along the streets of Williams Lake, the lilac bushes, heady with scent, looked like smoky brush strokes in a Monet painting. The tulips and daffodils bloomed scarlet and brilliant yellow in the gardens, giving a Van Gogh accent. The birds had returned: robins, finches, flickers and the hermit thrush with a song of entrancing bell-like resonance. I'd never heard anything like those pure tones floating in the evening air. The ducks were back in rafts on the lake—pintails, teals, mallards and grebes—quacking, squawking, whirring in flight. There was no such thing as the quiet countryside—every bush was alive. The hills surrounding the town flushed green as the trees and grasses responded to the warmth of the sun. The temperature moved higher every day. The heat and dust told us summer was rushing in behind the quick spring.

Most of the nurses had finished their school work. We had some referrals to check to ensure parents had taken their children to the dentist or the optometrist, as we had suggested, but we were scaling back. We had a staff meeting to decide who was taking holidays when and who would cover the absences. We each had six weeks of holidays, much better than the hospital nurses who got three weeks. I planned to vacation the later half of July and all of August. Alice took her holidays in June, so Rita asked me to cover her area and travel out to the Chilcotin to Puntzi Mountain to check on a couple of new babies and hold a child health clinic at the school.

Puntzi Mountain, about one hundred miles from Williams Lake, was an American radar station. It seemed odd to me that the United States of America had a base in Canada, but so it was. American airmen (no women) operated the radar site, ready to defend the US against incoming missiles from the Soviet Union. Farther north in the Arctic, there had been the DEW line—the Distant Early Warning Line—to warn the US if Soviet missiles were flying over Canada, but recently it had been disbanded. I wondered how effective this small radar station in the Chilcotin would be in reporting an invasion by the Soviets. It seemed a little puny when measured against the might of Russia. There was an American village on the base where the families of the airmen lived. They had their own medics and military health care system, but there was a settlement of Canadians around the base who either worked for the US military or at the nearby mill.

"You'll have to stay overnight at the base," Rita said. "I'll phone and tell them you're coming. Alice always stays there. They're used to nurses, and you can eat there as well."

The drive out this lovely June morning was a different proposition from my trip to the Chilcotin last December. No snow. No ice. Just oncoming summer. Yellow and white daisies looked like confetti scattered on the fields. Here on this grassland plateau, the lush green land and cobalt blue sky expanded to a far-distant horizon. Ribbons of pink and dusty green wild roses grew in the ditches alongside the road. I rolled down the window and let the scent waft through the car. Heavenly.

I'm not sure where the Puntzi "Mountain" is at. Perhaps it was a rise of ground that was imperceptible to a Coaster like myself who defined mountains as something over three-thousand feet. I saw the lake and the Air Force base, the community, and the school, but I swear the mountain was a figment of someone's imagination.

Alice had left me a note asking me to immunize a grade five student who had been away when she held her clinic in March. I found the student, checked the consent, and gave the immunization. I also visited two new babies. At the last house, the mother had coffee and cookies ready for me. I stayed to talk.

"How long have you lived out here?" I asked her. She was young, perhaps twenty-one, blue-eyed with pale skin. Her cabin was small but had two bedrooms and looked comfortable.

"A year," she said. "It's pretty lonely. Jake has a job at the mill, but I asked him to transfer to Williams Lake. The company owns the big mill there, and my sisters live there."

It occurred to me that Jake might not want to live near her sisters.

"Are there other families close by here?"

"There are. We get together for coffee and let the kids play, and we all support the school, but there isn't much else to do." ·

I thought about the expanse of wilderness around her, populated by communities of Indigenous people who seemed to socialize quite a lot.

"Do you go to any of the events at Redstone Reserve or the Alexis Creek Reserve?" I knew they had dances and movie nights.

She looked shocked. "Oh. No. Those are for Indians."

Well, lady, I thought to myself. *If you won't socialize with the local people, you are going to be lonely.* She saw herself as remote from others, as if there was no one in this country but herself and her friends, expats from Williams Lake, when she was surrounded by layers of society she wouldn't even explore.

The social divisions continued. I drove onto the American base. The guard at the gate recognized the Health Department emblem on my car and saluted. *What did he mean by that? Was I important? Had he mistaken me for someone else?* I didn't know what to do.

Salute back? I hadn't a clue how to execute a salute. And he was an American. Was it unpatriotic to salute an American? I settled for a nod and felt like the queen recognizing her subject.

"Just go up to the BOQ," he said.

"The BOQ?" I repeated.

"The Bachelor Officers' Quarters." He pointed.

I could see a parking lot. I drove up, unloaded my black bag and suitcase, and walked into the BOQ.

The airman on duty called me "ma'am" and showed me to my room. It was comfortable the way a college dorm is comfortable with no frills, but it had a bed, dresser, and my own bathroom. That was a treat. I assumed the others in the building were men, so I appreciated my own bathroom.

"It's usually a visiting major's room," the airman told me, "but we give it to the nurse."

He looked to be about eighteen, slight, not quite developed into his full growth.

"I trust no major will arrive?" I smiled, trying to put him at ease.

"Not likely way up here," he said.

I heard a little regret in his voice. "Where are you from?"

"Georgia."

"Oh, my. Winter must be hard on you."

"Cold," he agreed. "On the other hand"—he sent me a quick smile—"no snakes."

I was still smiling about that when I wandered over to the cafeteria.

Rita told me my meals would be gratis. Everyone would know who I was and not to worry about paying. I picked up a tray and slotted in behind a group of men. They nodded to me but didn't chat. I got my meal, some kind of pasta which looked good. I had just taken a forkful of food and then a sip of coffee when a uniformed officer, all badges and stripes, swooped down, picked up my tray, and said, "Follow me."

I sat there for a moment, took a drink of my coffee, which I still had in my hand, and watched him cross the room with my tray.

He turned to look behind him, discovered I wasn't following, and looked up to where I was sitting. He returned.

"Would you please follow me, Nurse? You are an officer, and you need to be in the officers' mess." He delivered the order politely, but it *was* an order.

I considered that for a moment. It was ridiculous. I wasn't an officer in anyone's air force, but I assumed nurses were automatically officers in this one. I imagined their protocols and rules mattered to them, and, temporarily, I was in a different country. Perhaps I had to obey their rules. Something annoyed me greatly though. Maybe it was the officer's peremptory commands, or the fact that the Americans were laying claim to this patch of the Chilcotin. I got up slowly, still holding my coffee, and started after him. He whipped around and headed for the door. I turned back to the room where every man (and it was only men in the room) stared at me. I raised my coffee mug and waved it at them. I caught several grins, but they were careful not to wave back.

The officers' mess looked exactly like the airmen's mess. There must be a difference in someone's mind, but I couldn't see it. Authority's rules were satisfied. At least my dinner hadn't cooled, and I finished it there.

When my empty tray had been removed by a hovering waiter, a couple of men came over and asked if they could sit down. I nodded.

They were medics, highly trained medical assistants, but they were asked to perform as nurses. While they were probably more efficient than most at emergency care, they seemed uneducated in public health from the questions they asked about chronic care and communicable diseases. They were casual and polite, one dark with glasses, a short haircut, and Maclean on the badge on his chest, the other fair with hair so short he seemed bald and Kunz on his chest. I answered their questions about tuberculosis and told them to refer anyone with a communicable disease to the provincial health department for treatment and also for contact and monitoring work. I asked them to go ahead and treat venereal diseases as they had been doing but to give us contact information, so we could follow up in the community. I'd send them some forms.

"Makes sense," Maclean said. "Cut down on infection in the whole area."

I wanted to point out that was the basic goal of public health but decided I had their cooperation, and I didn't want to sound condescending. I realized I *felt* condescending. I was probably still reacting to the strange culture of this military compound. I'd better adjust my attitude. These two were influential in the health care here.

They told me they worked with a community of wives of airmen and officers who lived within the camp.

"The women must be incredibly lonely," I said. I thought of the women in the surrounding area who refused to mingle with people who were not their own race and so didn't participate in local events. How much worse for the women here? "They must feel trapped."

"Yeah, we hand out Valium like it's vitamins," Kunz said.

"Uh," I stared at him. "You just give the Valium? No counselling? No group therapy? Just Valium?" It was benzodiazepine and acted on the central nervous system. It was supposed to be given under a doctor's supervision. It had more side effects than many people thought, and it was definitely overprescribed.

"Keeps them calm," Kunz said with smug satisfaction.

I held onto my temper. "Let's talk about this," I said. "Have any of the women shown signs of increased depression, euphoria, appearing drunk, or have experienced seizures?" I rattled off all the side effects I could remember.

"It can cause those things?" They looked a little shocked.

"It can. It has to be monitored carefully. Could you start some kind of group therapy sessions and cut back on the Valium?" I suggested mildly.

They sat back.

"I'm not good with that touchy-feely stuff," Maclean said.

"Me neither," his buddy agreed. "We'd need a psychologist for that."

They needed a psychologist for a coffee session but didn't need a psychologist, psychiatrist, or even a doctor to distribute Valium. How could I persuade them to be more careful with that drug?

"Maybe all you need to do is invite them to meet, provide coffee and cookies, and leave them alone for an hour. They might work out their own problems. You could offer a subject like 'what helps deal with depression' and then leave them alone." I tried to remember I was teaching, not blaming.

"It's quicker to give out the Valium," Kunz insisted.

"Check out the side effects," I said. It was quicker, and many physicians were doing the same thing, but it seemed to me they were treating the women as if they were cattle that needed to be kept docile, and I resented that. I strived for a professional attitude, to teach, not criticize. It was a struggle. It horrified me that a couple of guys with only rudimentary pharmaceutical training were "keeping the women calm" by drugging them. I'd leave a note for Alice. Maybe she could involve the wives in the local Women's Institute. Those WI women would get them working for the school and community. They probably needed something useful to do. It would be worth a try and might help some.

THE NEXT day, the weather for my return journey was again warm and sunny. I stopped the car at one point and stared at a field of huge yellow daisies. Sunflowers, they called them here, and they did capture the sun as bright splashes of gold in the wide fields. They even covered the sides of Sheep Creek Hill, the approach to the Fraser River. In June it was a careful drive but not the wild, frightening, dangerous slide it had been in December.

The rest of the week in Williams Lake was uneventful. We had a speaker from Victoria on the new polio vaccine. We were to give it on a spoon, as it was a live virus. The other vaccines were attenuated—they couldn't live or multiply or infect anyone. This live polio vaccine could. It was going to take careful handling, and I wondered about its ability to spread in the air.

I got a call from Mrs. MacDougal. She had a baby of about four weeks and wanted me to look at a rash. She didn't have a car, so I offered to make a home visit. She wasn't far from the health unit, and I had time.

I parked my car in the driveway and hauled my black bag from the seat beside me. I trudged to the bottom of a flight of stairs. I assumed the bedrooms were on the ground floor because it looked as if the kitchen and living area were up those stairs. I was almost at the top when a cacophony shattered the air. The wild baying of a wolf? The snarls and shouts of a rabid dog? I jerked, slipped, grabbed the railing, dropped my bag, and stared at the writhing, angry wolf-type dog straining at the rope that held it to a steel loop near the door. I froze.

Mrs. MacDougal opened the door, clutching an infant to her chest. "Shame on you, Fergus. Stop that at once."

Fergus stopped barking, dropped his tail, and sat back on his haunches.

"Funny," Mrs. MacDougal said. "He did that to the minister when he came by. Fergus is usually pretty good."

My heart was still racing at about 120 beats a minute, and I panted, trying to get my breath. Mrs. MacDougal held the door open for me. I picked up my bag and crept toward her, keeping one eye on Fergus. He was keeping one eye on me as well and growled as I got closer.

"Fergus!" Mrs. MacDougal bellowed at him. She was a tiny woman, and Fergus was a big dog, but there was no question who was in charge. Fergus hung his head and turned away, ambling back toward the wall of the house where he flopped down, still watching me.

I breathed a little easier when the door between Fergus and me was shut.

Mrs. MacDougal lay the baby on the kitchen table. She took off the little one's diaper, so I could see the rash. I examined it carefully.

"It's caused by the diapers, Mrs. MacDougal," I said. "Williams Lake has hard water with lots of minerals in it. It's difficult to get the diapers soft enough for the baby's skin. Try using this ointment." I wrote down the name of an ointment other mothers had found useful. "It's waterproof, so it keeps the moisture and the rough diaper away from the skin. It smells of cod liver oil, though, because it has some in it."

"I can deal with the smell, if I can just clear up this rash." She stroked her baby's arms as she spoke.

"You can leave her without diapers as much as you can. That will help."

"What about those new fabric softeners?" She continued to stroke her baby, running her fingers over her head and along her arms and then carefully with one finger stroking her cheeks. The baby's eyes closed.

"You can try those. They might irritate your daughter's skin, but they might help. There's also a new paper diaper called Pampers, which might be worth a try."

The baby was doing well. I hadn't brought in my scale, much to Mrs. MacDougal's disappointment, but I could see the baby was filling out, looking plump and rosy as a normal baby should.

"She's lovely," I said as Mrs. MacDougal picked up her daughter and cuddled her.

"Yes, she is, and she's probably the only child I will have." She dropped a kiss on her baby's head.

"You think one child is enough for you?" One child was unusual, except in the rare households where both parents were professionals.

"No, it's not that. I'd like to have three children, but Dr. Craisson says I can only have one. I'm Rh-negative, and he says the first baby is fine, but my body has built up antibodies, and the next baby will die. I don't think I could stand that. I'm not having any more."

Dr. Craisson again. He was right about his prognosis *if* this baby was Rh-positive. The Rh factor was a protein in red blood cells. Some people had that factor, and they were Rh-positive; some people did not, such as Mrs. MacDougal, and they were Rh-negative. An Rh-positive baby stimulated antibody production in the mother. Those antibodies lay in wait in the mother's body, and in the next pregnancy, they could attack the Rh factor killing it in the baby's blood and so kill the child. The best the medical world could do was to help prevent pregnancy or, when babies were at risk, transfuse them with units of O-negative blood. But many babies died before they could get that help.

"Did Dr. Craisson tell you if your baby... what's her name?"

"Jennifer."

Of course, another Jennifer.

"Did he tell you if Jennifer is Rh-positive?" That was important.

"No, he didn't." She looked puzzled.

I explained. "If Jennifer is Rh-negative, you can have another baby because you have not been sensitized to Rh-positive blood, and so you haven't produced any antibodies."

She stopped patting her baby and stared at me. "If Jennifer is negative and I'm negative, then we can have another baby?"

I nodded.

"Oh." She gazed at her daughter. "I'm not in a hurry, mind you, but that's really lovely to think about. I'll ask him what she is."

I smiled, and then I had another thought. I was dealing with Dr. Craisson after all, not the most competent doctor I'd ever met. I might as well ask the obvious question.

"Is your husband Rh-positive?"

She shook her head. "No, he's Rh-negative, too."

Now it was my turn to stare at her. "If your husband is Rh-negative and you are Rh-negative, there is no way you can have an Rh-positive baby. So there is no way you can produce antibodies to the Rh factor." That was basic science.

She slowly transferred the baby to her other shoulder. "I can have all the babies I want?"

I nodded.

Jennifer was asleep now. Mrs. MacDougal laid her in the bassinet, her little bare bum up in the air. We smiled at her and at each other. Suddenly, Mrs. MacDougal seemed transfixed. Her face glowed, her eyes lit, and she started to cry.

"Sorry. Sorry." She sat down on the chair with a thump. "I'm just taking it in. I can have more babies."

"Take your time." I mentally smacked Dr. Craisson on the side of his head.

Mrs. MacDougal dried her eyes with a tea towel. "Thanks, Nurse. You've given me lots to think about. I guess I'll tell Dr. Craisson to stop worrying about me."

It always amazed me that, given evidence of incompetence, patients went back to the same doctor. They had a choice. We had universal health care. They could go to any doctor they wanted with no charge, but they returned, inevitably, to the one they knew.

"You might just tell him you forgot to let him know your husband was Rh-negative," I suggested.

She grinned. "Rather than remind him he didn't ask?"

I smiled back. "Yeah."

"I'll be nice," she said. I hoped she didn't tell Dr. Craisson she got her information from me. He hated to admit to a mistake.

Doctors and nurses were the gateway to information for patients. There were no medical libraries available to the public. It was a huge responsibility, driving me to constantly learn. Doctors were not accustomed to having their opinions challenged, and patients were usually unable to do so, as they didn't have enough information. Some doctors were willing to take the time to explore alternatives with patients, but others issued diagnoses like decrees from on high.

Nurses walked a delicate line between correcting false information while avoiding criticizing the doctor. It wasn't just good manners that prevented us from telling the patient the doctor was wrong; it was professional ethics. We could lose our licence if we criticized them. But we could lose it if we didn't give the patient correct information. A nice, delicate situation. Sometimes, of course, we were wrong and had to be careful we weren't giving information beyond our scope of practice. I often felt, especially with Dr. Craisson, as if I was skipping the ropes of ethics and was going to get tripped up at some point. Most doctors were cooperative. They helped nurses learn, and nurses helped the doctors learn. But there were always the Dr. Craissons out there.

CHAPTER TWENTY-TWO

DECISION
TIME

THIS WOULD BE my last trip into my eastern district until September. My patients in the back country came to town in the long summer days when the roads were better, and they didn't need as many home visits. Because we didn't have enough nurses to cover our vast district over the holidays, we would concentrate on clinics and visits close to town for the next two months.

The road was clear of logging trucks and I was on time for my clinic at Big Lake. The teacher informed me she'd taken a job in Victoria in the fall and would be leaving. I wasn't surprised. No doubt her supervisor had forced that move with the encouragement of the parents. Her teaching methods were old-fashioned and so controlling, it was a wonder she'd lasted the year. A teacher was rarely fired, just moved to another unsuspecting school. In a larger school, the principal might be able to teach her how to coax children to learn and not make them obey out of fear. I really hadn't liked her but had tried not to let that show. I had felt sorry for her, but that hadn't stopped me from having a word with her supervisor. I'd asked him to pay attention to her, and perhaps he had. The kids here didn't need to learn in fear.

The day was sunny, the sky the deep blue typical of the Cariboo. The gravel road in front of me was free of trucks, but there were other hazards. I rounded a bend and almost drove into a slow-moving white cloud, blocking the road and covering the surrounding ditches and shoulders. I hit the brakes. My bag flew off the seat.

The scale behind me clanged against the back of my seat and clattered to the floor. I stared.

Hundreds of sheep spread like a carpet in front of me, dots of white with splashes of black as far as I could see, rolling forward down the road, spilling over the verge. A woman in jeans, a plaid shirt, leather vest, and hat walked behind them. Two sheep dogs, black and white border collies, darted about on either side. There must have been at least a hundred and fifty sheep moving as if connected with kinesthetic energy, surging and ebbing but always moving forward. I pulled over to the side of the road, shut off the motor, and got out.

"Hi," I said to the woman. "Where are you going?"

"Hi." She was friendly but kept walking. Her eyes darted from one dog to the other. "We're going into the mountains for the summer. I've a contract with McKenzie's Forest Products to keep the weeds away from the new seedlings. I'm Lettie."

"I'm Marion, public health nurse." She was taking the sheep to the mountains where McKenzie Forest Products had reforested the logging sites. Her job would be to graze the sheep among the young fir seedlings allowing them a better chance at growth.

She nodded.

"The sheep don't eat the conifers?" I asked.

She shook her head.

The strong waxy smell of lanolin hung heavy in the air, a little spicy but almost pleasant. Most of the sheep were adults, but there were a few large lambs.

"Lambs too?" I asked

"Just the ones I'm going to keep. I sold the rest last week at the sale."

The Williams Lake livestock sale held down at the Cattleman's Barn near the railway was usually well attended and lively. I wanted to know all about her sheep and what she was doing, but although she was polite, she wasn't talkative.

"You'll stay up in the mountains all summer?" I walked beside her.

She nodded.

"You're not going to attend the Stampede at the end of the month?" I asked.

"No." She shook her head. "Too many people. I'll stay up in the mountains all summer." She seemed shy. "My husband will come for some of the time, and he'll bring me supplies, but I love it up there."

I smiled at her. "I expect these sheep make a lot of work."

She smiled in response. "Yes, although I'll have Max, my Great Pyrenees with me. My husband will bring him up later. Max is no use on the trek there, but he's a great help in keeping the bear and the cougars away."

A Great Pyrenees was as big as a small horse. He would impress the cougars.

"You'll have a gun?" I pictured her up in the mountains alone with bear and cougars, protecting her flock.

"Of course." She stopped to whistle at a dog who changed direction and ran after a wayward sheep. "And my husband will bring my violin." She grinned at me. She seemed to relax and become a little more talkative. "The cougars don't like it."

I pictured her sitting on the edge of a mountain, playing her violin to the coyotes and cougars. I walked with her for about a quarter of a mile.

When I looked back, I could see two cars behind mine, the drivers waiting patiently to get by the sheep.

She pointed to a meadow up ahead. "I'll take the flock in there for about half an hour. You'll be able to pass." She turned away and whistled to her dogs. The crowd of white began to move toward the meadow.

"Thanks. Good luck," I said to her back. I walked quickly to my car. By the time I got there, the road was clear of sheep. Heading again for Likely, I passed her at the meadow. I waved. She was sitting on a rock, drinking from a thermos and munching on a sandwich. The dogs were patrolling the edges of the flock. I wished I was an artist and could paint that picture.

It was a treat to drive without any fear of getting stuck in the mud. Summer, which was coming fast, meant dry roads—and dust. But I preferred the dust to the mud. I noticed with approval that the Department of Highways had oiled the road in front of Mr. Scalin's house. He was a pensioner and lived alone near Likely. He suffered from asthma, and the dust from the road made it worse. I'd phoned the manager at the Department of Highways to request the petroleum oil. It looked as though the manager had sent out the oil truck. I'd have to thank him.

The next night, Marjorie at Horsefly Lake was very busy, and I got a much smaller room than usual.

"Sorry. Tourist season," she said. "We're up to our ears."

I could see that. The tourists wandered around the lodge dressed in camouflage pants and shirts and wide-brimmed cloth hats with fishing flies hooked on the bands. I wondered if they thought the fish could see them, and I wondered aloud how many of them could actually fly fish.

"Most of them," Marjorie said. "They're avid, these guys. Come every year."

I ate in the kitchen this time, as all the tables in the dining area were taken by tourists.

"You don't mind?" Margorie said a little worriedly.

"No, not a bit." I found the hustle and bustle of the kitchen stimulating, and at the same time relaxing because I wasn't responsible for any of the work.

The drive home the next day gave me a lot of time to think. I'd been in this district almost a year. When I first came to Williams Lake, I'd planned to spend two years working here and then move further north. With more nursing experience, I'd look for more and more independence. In the far north, nurses often acted alone in remote communities where they had a broad scope of practice and an official blessing to make some diagnoses and prescription decisions. After about three years experience, I planned to go south to the University of British Columbia or the University of

Victoria and get my master's degree. But that was before I met Carl, and before I made friends with Dorrie, Sam, Janet, and Paul—and Carl's parents. It was getting complicated.

Dorrie and Sam were getting married this summer.

"Might as well," Dorrie said. "Sam and I click, and he's up for adventures. Married to Sam, I'll have to stay here, which I hadn't planned to do, but we can get away for winter vacations to explore other countries and for short jaunts to football and hockey games on weekends. I think I'll like it."

We'd been fitting a dull brown cover on the sofa Betty Jean had donated to our apartment. It successfully hid the garish orange flowers of the original upholstery.

"Are you going to keep teaching?" I asked her. Teachers were hard to recruit to this town, and the staff would want Dorrie to stay. Most women didn't work outside their homes after marriage, although some, like Mrs. Harbinger and Janet Clayton, did. I couldn't imagine Dorrie retiring.

"Oh sure. I'd go nuts staying home. I really don't want my own children, at least not for many years, so yes, I want to teach." Having children inevitably meant staying home with them.

"I hope you'll be happy with Sam," I said. "I don't see why you won't be. If something isn't going your way, you'll be sure to tell him."

She laughed. "True. And you will be my bridesmaid?" She tucked in the last stray piece of material and admired our camouflage job on the sofa.

"I will," I promised.

I would travel to the Coast in August to attend the wedding. Carl would attend as well, as one of the ushers. It would be the perfect time to introduce Carl to my parents. I really couldn't put it off any longer, but it wouldn't be easy. My parents had their own plans for me, and I knew that included some man from their own social circle. I couldn't see myself saying, *This is Carl, the man I've been having a love affair with for months.* That wasn't something they'd want to know. It made me uncomfortable to think about it.

Before all that happened, though, I was going to experience my first Cariboo rodeo. We had rodeos on the Coast, but they seemed to be a copy of the real thing, a kind of artificial celebration of American movies. Here, a rodeo was a community event that attracted cowboys from local ranches.

In the last week of June, vehicles started to arrive from the Chilcotin. Ranchers and ranch hands arrived not only in trucks and trailers but also in buckboards hauled by horses. The first time I saw one of those on the main street of Williams Lake, I stopped dead and stared. A dark sturdy horse was harnessed in shiny leather with red and white tassels on the bridle. A man and a woman sat on the wagon seat which, as far as I could tell, had been cut from a car. That made sense. It would have springs and be more comfortable than a wooden seat. Several children bounced in the back, eagerly pointing out sights to each other.

"Where are they going?" I asked a passerby.

"Down to the Stampede grounds. The area around the arena slopes up, and people camp there for a week or so. It's a kind of a makeshift campground, and they get a good view of the Stampede."

The Stampede grounds were at the end of Williams Lake and in a huge natural amphitheatre. There was a grandstand with tiers of benches on one side, a race track, and a corral in the centre—a large oval-shaped area surrounded by five high fence rails and some horse pens on the far side. Farther out in the centre of the race track was a set of corrals, which confined the livestock used in the rodeo: calves, horses, bulls, and steers. It was an impressive collection of buildings and fences. On the other side was the tiered, rising ground where the travellers camped.

Carl planned to show me everything there was to see during the two days of the Stampede, and I was looking forward to it.

"You have to dress the part, though," he said. "Jeans, plaid shirt, cowboy hat, and boots."

I refused to pay for a new pair of boots. "I'll wear my runners," I said. "I'd feel ridiculous wearing cowboy boots anyway when I'm not a ranch hand."

"Neither is Sam, and he's going to wear his." Carl tried to persuade me.

"Well, I'm not paying good money for something I'll use once a year." There was much of my frugal father in me.

"If you had all the money in the world, would you buy a pair?" he asked.

"Oh, probably, but I'm not going to." If I had all the money in the world, I'd buy a horse.

During the week running up to the Stampede, I realized Carl was right, and everyone wore cowboy regalia, including boots, as the town geared up for the event. Although it attracted many tourists, it seemed the Stampede was not so much a tourist attraction as a celebration of the life of the people in the area. It was brought home to me with startling clarity when I was walking from the health unit to the social welfare office one morning and saw a horse tied to a parking meter with its bridle reins. I stopped and stared at the dappled white horse with lovely grey and black markings on its face. It could have pulled away, but it was well trained and stood there, saddled and waiting.

A man who had been walking in front of me stopped and stared at the horse as well. He looked from the horse to the meter and back to the horse. Then he reached into his pocket, pulled out some change, put a nickel into the parking meter, patted the meter, and walked on. The horse flicked one ear.

More and more cars, trailers, and buckboards arrived in town and set up out at the Stampede grounds. At night, campfires flickered around the site as people got together to talk and visit in the warm evening air. The temperature was rising along with the excitement. People moved a little faster and a little more impatiently.

In the midst of all the anticipation, my work continued. We had several meetings with Social Welfare, Indian Health, and the health unit workers from nearby towns to plan work for the next year. I had just returned from one meeting where I'd represented the health unit.

"Dress in business attire, not your uniform," Rita had said, when she instructed me on what she wanted me to achieve at the meeting. She was scheduled to attend a meeting of doctors at the hospital to explain the coming polio vaccine and was frustrated because she couldn't be in two places at once. She gave me instructions. "Just get rid of Canoe Creek from our case load. It isn't our responsibility, and we can't really service it very well."

I agreed with her. I hated working under the federal rules and quite often refused to do that. I was going to get into hot water with them sometime soon. I'd talked to the chief of Canoe Creek to make sure she agreed that the federal programs would serve her community better than those of the provincial health and, with her blessing, was ready for the meeting.

I managed to graciously hand Canoe Creek back to the federal health services and was returning from the meeting when I decided to stop in to check on a new mother. Estelle was in her late thirties with her first baby and was unsure of mothering. I'd worked hard with her to establish breastfeeding, and she had managed pretty well but needed encouragement. I decided to see how she was doing. She was an Indigenous woman from farther north near Quesnel. She was single, but she had family support as she was living with her sister.

I knocked and was admitted by Paula, Estelle's sister, a stocky, solid woman and quite a contrast to her lean sister. Estelle had seemed devoted to her baby, and I hoped everything was going well.

The living room was an olive-green colour, a popular choice, but I found it dark. A large table served the kitchen and living room. It held the remains of breakfast with toast crusts on the Formica top, a peanut butter–encrusted knife amidst the toast crumbs, and coffee cups still half-full. A late breakfast, then, or they hadn't cleaned up. The radio crooned from the kitchen, and I was informed by Patsy Cline that she was "Crazy" for loving. Something made me uncomfortable, but I was reassured to see Paula looking with affection at the baby. Whatever was bothering me wasn't anything to do with the baby. I didn't have my scale, but I could tell the little one was flourishing. I sniffed. No gas leak. I took a quick look around. Nothing threatening that I could see.

I spoke to Paula. "Baby doing okay?"

She nodded.

"What's it to you?" Estelle said, and I suddenly realized she was very drunk indeed. This was what was wrong. I should have noticed her condition earlier.

"The baby looks good," I said and rose to leave. My mouth felt dry.

Estelle stood up suddenly. Hostility flashed from her eyes. Paula darted in front of me, facing Estelle and blocking her.

"Out. Out," Paula hissed at me over her shoulder. "You have to leave." She turned and herded me to the door, still using her body to block a furious Estelle.

Estelle was screaming at me. I couldn't make out what she was saying, but I didn't think it the time to ask for clarity and allowed Paula to push me out the door.

"My bag?" I said.

"Stay there." She shut the door. I waited. Estelle had been intent on hitting me. Her arm had been raised, and her sister had saved me from a fist in the face. Estelle had never shown me animosity. What had set her off? I was breathing rapidly, but Estelle's attack had happened too fast for me to develop full-blown fear. Paula returned and handed me my bag.

"She thought you were the social worker," Paula said apologetically.

I looked down at my high heels, nylons, skirt, blouse, and suit jacket. No uniform. No baby scale. No wonder she thought I was the social worker.

The baby had looked fine to me. I expected the baby would have a home with Paula if Estelle continued to drink. I definitely wasn't going to call the social worker.

Whenever I thought I was learning a lot, getting more experienced, and becoming more competent, I made a mistake. This time, I'd misread the situation. Was I still so naive I didn't recognized hostility when it was coming at me in waves? I should have gotten myself out of there and not depended on Paula to assess the situation and keep me safe. Part of me thought the baby's upbringing might be a little precarious—Estelle drinking and violent—and part of me revelled in Estelle's determination to protect her child. She may have been drunk, but no social worker was going to snatch her baby.

CARL PICKED me up on the first day of the Stampede about ten in the morning.

"We need to get a good spot to see the parade," he explained.

I looked in his truck. "No Keo?"

"Too hot for him. He's home in the shade."

He parked the truck near the town hall, put a hand on my arm, and stopped me before I could dismount from the high seat.

"I bought you a present." He looked a little wary as if the present might not be acceptable.

He handed me a big box, and I opened it carefully. Inside were shiny cowboy boots. They smelled of leather and oil and almost glowed in their rich red glory.

"Oh, my." I was impressed.

"You said you'd wear them if you had them. You will, won't you?" He sounded worried.

"I will." I leaned over and kissed him. "No woman could resist red cowboy boots."

He beamed. I changed into them, hoping they'd fit. They did.

"How did you get the perfect size?" I turned my ankle, admiring the tiny white flowers carved into the red leather.

"I stole a pair of your shoes and took them into the tack store."

Kind and smart, too. He was pretty irresistible.

I stomped around town in my cowboy boots, and, at first, felt a little self-conscious, but gradually I realized almost everyone was wearing cowboy boots, and I began to feel like a part of the community.

I met Cynthia waiting for the parade as well. Her kids were crowded on the curb, staking out their territory for viewing and, I expected, scooping up any candy that might be thrown from the floats. She was holding the baby.

I looked around for her husband. "Where's Ron?"

"He's pulling his entry for the bull riding," Cynthia said. "All the names of the bulls are put into a hat, and then the riders draw out a name. That's the one they have to ride."

"Daddy's going to ride Yakatoo, I just bet," one of the older kids said.

"Yakatoo?" I looked at Cynthia.

"He's a famous bull." Cynthia said. "No one has ever ridden him. I hope Ron doesn't draw him."

"You must have a fit when he's riding." Bull riding was dangerous. For one thing, the bull was powerful and swung in circles, trying to dislodge the rider, and, for another, when the rider hit the ground, the bull tried to gore him.

She lowered her voice. "I try not to let it show because the kids think it's exciting, and Ron looks forward to it so much, but, yeah, it scares the bejesus out of me."

Later that afternoon when Carl and I were watching the bull riding from the grandstand, Ron did ride Yakatoo. He didn't last the eight seconds, but he did walk safely away, protected by the clown whose job it was to keep vicious bulls away from the riders. That was all Cynthia wanted.

Some of the events seemed cruel, such as the calf roping.

"Those calves must be terrified," I complained.

Carl looked at me and then back at the cowboy who had roped the calf and was running to wrestle it to the ground, tie its feet together, and then stand back—all in seconds.

"It's the skill of the cowboy we're supposed to be looking at. The record here is nine seconds." He was used to these events. I wasn't.

"Hmm," I said.

I didn't like the experience of the calves, but I could admire the skill of the riders and their horses. The announcer gave their town or area when he announced their name, and pockets of the crowd cheered support. The competitors came from Anahim Lake, Alkali Lake, Miocene, Gang Ranch, Redstone, Alexis Creek, Deep Creek, and Soda Creek. Carl seemed to know quite a few of them. I expect he saw them at cattle sales and cattlemen's meetings, and, probably, some of them were friends from high school.

Sam and Dorrie met us for dinner at the Ranch Café. It was noisy, and so was the dance hall at the Lakeview—loud but fun. Our dates refused to let us dance with anyone but them.

"Much, much too rough tonight," Carl said.

We didn't stay late as it would get too wild. We dropped off Dorrie and Sam and headed home about ten. Keo was delighted to see us and pranced around until we gave in and took him for a walk. At this time of year, summer twilight lingered. Although the sun had set, it was not yet night. The barn, hay shed, tool shed, and tractor hut were dark silhouettes with long shadows reaching into the dim light of the yard. Keo sniffed and scuttled around. There was always the possibility of an unwary rat or vole. He didn't kill them, but he liked to chase them.

"No luck tonight, Keo," I called to him as he darted around, ever hopeful.

"Any luck for me?" Carl said and pulled me close.

"Probably," I said.

He kissed me, and I thoroughly enjoyed it.

"Any luck for me, permanently?" he asked.

I stood still. This was a proposal. I wasn't ready for it. Fleeting visions of northern nursing, my master's degree, an exciting world of new adventures flashed through my mind. I knew he felt me stiffen.

"How about," he said whispering in my ear, "we have an engagement. Maybe a long engagement, so you can make some decisions."

I leaned back in his arms and thought about it.

"You mean you eventually want to marry me, but you aren't in a rush?" I needed to be clear about this.

"Oh, I'm in a rush, all right, but you aren't. What do you think?" His arm stayed close around me, not tight but comfortable.

"I think I'd better get out of these boots before I have a blister. And . . ." I paused. "I think I will take you up on that."

I felt as if this year I had walked into a new world where colours, shapes, and sounds were sharper, more brilliant, and more compelling. I had planned to stay in Williams Lake only another year or two and then go north. I had to face the fact that Carl couldn't leave the ranch. If I left, I'd have to go alone. Would I, as an engaged woman, want to go north away from my love? Or would I be married by then? And how would that affect my future?

That problem was at least a year away. At this moment, being engaged to Carl felt right. I wasn't sure how I was going to reconcile this engagement with all the plans I had and all the things I wanted to do. I would rather use reason than emotions to make this decision, but I'd search out the reasons later. I'd go with the emotions right now.

RITA CALLED me into her office for my year-end evaluation. I wasn't worried that I would be fired or not get my yearly increase in wages. There were too few nurses willing to work this far north for there to be any serious competition for my position. But I did want to know what I did well and where I could improve. At least one part of me wanted to know that. The other part of me didn't want to hear any criticism at all.

"To start," Rita said as she put some papers in front of me, "your overall performance is very good."

My mother would have insisted I strive for "excellent" She wasn't here. I would accept "very good" and be happy.

"I gave you excellent ratings on reliability, acumen on knowing when to refer patients, completing assignments, and taking initiative."

I nodded. *So far, so good.*

"I rated you a little lower in cooperation with agencies."

I lifted my head and looked at her.

She shrugged. "I appreciate that Indian Health is a pain to deal with, but you need to learn how to be more subtle about your goals with them."

"Crafty, you mean?"

"I do."

I might learn that.

She asked me to sign the form and make any comments if I thought she hadn't been fair. I signed and handed her back the paper. She set them to one side and folded her hands together. It looked as if she was going to pronounce something important. I sat up straighter.

"You are, I believe, going to be headhunted for a management position. You have a science degree when most of us working in the health units do not. Head office in Victoria will likely be looking to move you as head nurse somewhere in the province. You need to be ready to respond to that."

"Now? They are going to offer me that now?" I was astounded. I was a new nurse, a beginning nurse, one who had a lot to learn.

Rita nodded. "I protested. I need you here for at least another year. It takes a year to get to know your territory and your people. They agreed. I've held them off for a year."

Management. A job like Rita's? In the office and around the town most of the time. Attending meetings. Cooperating with and manipulating other agencies. No thanks.

"I don't want that. At least, not now."

"What do you want?"

"My master's degree, at some point."

"That's hard to get from here."

"I don't want to leave here," I said. And there lay the conundrum.

She was quiet and then said, "You might register for some correspondence courses. Look up what courses your master's program requires and find out if you can take a course or two by correspondence. Maybe you could cut your away time from two years to one."

I didn't know what I was going to do in the future. But I did know that I was going to work at this public health nursing job for another year here in Williams Lake before I made any decisions.

I headed out the door into brilliant sunshine. The dust was thick in the air. The mill must be sawing wood as bits of sawdust landed on my arm. I walked down the street to the grocery store. I'd pick up some supplies and then head out to Carl's. I saw Jobina picking over the new apples in the fruit section.

"Hi," I said. "Is that Joe?" I smiled at the little boy beside her.

"Yes. Say 'hi' to the nurse, Joe."

"Hi," he said softly.

"He's grown a lot in a short while." Perhaps he was just standing a little taller.

"He's going to be as big as his daddy."

I met Paul and Janet as I was leaving the store.

"Back from your holiday?"

"It was lovely," Janet said. "But it's nice to be back. School's starting soon."

I loaded my groceries into my car. Cynthia waved from across the parking lot. She had the little one in a sling on her chest and a line of kids behind her. I waved at them until they disappeared into the store.

I wasn't going anywhere. I belonged here.

ACKNOWLEDGEMENTS

I WOULD LIKE TO acknowledge the enthusiasm of my friends and family who thought this story worth telling. My thanks to Jennifer Barclay, agent and editor extraordinaire, who gave me her time and professional advice. Dr. Evan Adams gave invaluable advice about Indigenous terminology, and I thank him for that and for his warm support over the years.

I would like to acknowledge the many, many nurses who took their skills, knowledge, and courage to the people of remote communities—and those who still do. They were committed to continual education, trying new methods, and improving health care. They still are. After obtaining a PhD, it was my privilege for a period of eleven years to teach nursing at university, where I could see that the young nurses of today are still intrepid, incisive thinkers, compelled by their strong sense of responsibility to improving the health of their communities, and willing to work hard to do so. In different ways, these young nurses are carrying on the tradition of my compatriots of the '60s. We all wanted to make a difference.

MARION MCKINNON CROOK is a nurse, an educator, and the author of more than fifteen books. She began writing short stories in the 1960s while working as a public health nurse in the Cariboo. In addition to her nursing degree, McKinnon Crook holds a master's in liberal studies, and a PhD in education. Now a full-time writer, she lives on BC's Sunshine Coast with her dog and cat, who hate each other. For more information, visit marioncrookauthor.com.